ARDEN PERFORMANCE EDITIONS

W9-ADQ-560

HAMLET

ARDEN PERFORMANCE EDITIONS

Series Editors: Michael Dobson, Abigail Rokison-Woodall and
Simon Russell Beale

Published titles
A Midsummer Night's Dream edited by
Abigail Rokison-Woodall
Hamlet edited by Abigail Rokison-Woodall
Romeo and Juliet edited by Paul Menzer

Further titles in preparation
Macbeth edited by Katherine Brokaw
Much Ado About Nothing edited by Anna Kamarilli
Othello edited by Paul Prescott
Twelfth Night edited by Gretchen Minton

ARDEN PERFORMANCE EDITIONS

HAMLET

Edited by
ABIGAIL ROKISON-WOODALL

THE ARDEN SHAKESPEARE
LONDON • NEW YORK • OXFORD • NEW DELHI • SYDNEY

THE ARDEN SHAKESPEARE
Bloomsbury Publishing Plc
50 Bedford Square, London, WC1B 3DP, UK
1385 Broadway, New York, NY 10018, USA
29 Earlsfort Terrace, Dublin 2, Ireland

BLOOMSBURY, THE ARDEN SHAKESPEARE and the Arden Shakespeare logo are
trademarks of Bloomsbury Publishing Plc

First published 2017
Reprinted 2018, 2020, 2022 (twice)

Editorial matter and selection © Abigail Rokison-Woodall, 2017

Text is taken from *Hamlet*, Arden Shakespeare Third Series,
edited by Ann Thompson and Neil Taylor, © 2006

Abigail Rokison-Woodall has asserted her right under the Copyright, Designs
and Patents Act, 1988, to be identified as author of this work.

Cover design: © Paul Knight/Trevillion images

A catalogue record for this book is available from the British Library.

Names: Shakespeare, William, 1564–1616, author. | Rokison-Woodall,
Abigail, 1975– editor.
Title: Hamlet / edited by Abigail Rokison-Woodall.
Description: London ; New York : Bloomsbury Arden Shakespeare, 2017. |
Series: Arden performance editions
Identifiers: LCCN 2017012858| ISBN 9781474253888 (pbk.) |
ISBN 9781474253918 (epdf)
Subjects: LCSH: Hamlet (Legendary character)—Drama. | Kings and rulers—
Succession—Drama. | Murder victims' families—Drama. | Fathers—Death—
Drama. | Revenge—Drama. | Princes—Drama. | Denmark—Drama. |
Tragedies. | Shakespeare, William, 1564–1616. Hamlet.
Classification: LCC PR2807.A2 R58 2017 | DDC 822.3/3—dc23
LC record available at https://lccn.loc.gov/2017012858

ISBN: PB: 978-1-4742-5388-8
ePDF: 978-1-4742-5391-8
eBook: 978-1-4742-5390-1

Series: Arden Performance Editions

Typeset by RefineCatch Ltd, Bungay, Suffolk
Printed and bound in Great Britain

To find out more about our authors and books visit www.bloomsbury.com
and sign up for our newsletters

CONTENTS

PREFACE

The impulse for the Arden Performance Editions came from a shared interest in creating an edition of Shakespeare that would best serve actors in a rehearsal room and also students in the classroom seeking to bring the text from page to stage. We wanted to provide a reliable text of each play, drawn from the scrupulously-prepared Arden Third Series editions and thus informed by the latest textual and historical scholarship, but newly thought-through, reannotated and redesigned with the practical needs of theatre-makers in mind.

This was partly about convenience – in terms of weight, print size, placement of notes, and concision of glossing. It was also about empowering actors and readers by making easily visible the sorts of editorial choices about lineation, punctuation and textual variants that can be less easy to discern in more lavishly-edited scholarly editions. We wanted to provide a clear sense of the available choices in terms of viable textual variants (where differing versions of a play survive from Shakespeare's own time), without getting embroiled in generations-old academic debates about whose emendations to which Elizabethan printer make the most sense. We also wanted it to be easy for our actor-readers to identify cases of ambiguous lineation, where different later editors have chosen to divide Shakespeare's verse-lines at different places: these editorial choices can prove misleading to an actor looking for certain 'clues' to delivery in the structure of the verse.

The punctuation of these editions was a matter of debate. We began by thinking that we might remove some of the bulky punctuation included in most modern editions, stripping it back to something more akin to that of some of the editions published in Shakespeare's lifetime – sparse punctuation that is often perceived as more 'actor-friendly'. However, it soon became clear that this was going to be difficult to implement across the board. Whilst we could have punctuated *Hamlet* based on the relatively sparse punctuation of the second quarto (1604), the same could not have been said of *The Tempest*, where the only extant early printed text is the heavily punctuated First Folio (1623). Here any choice of a minimal 'Elizabethan-style' revision to the punctuation would have been merely arbitrary, and would in many places have made Shakespeare's meaning less easy to discern rather than more so. In practice we have settled for the punctuation of the Arden Third Series editions, which is principally designed to convey sense to a reader. Actors who find this too cumbersome are encouraged to take the commas and semi-colons supplied throughout these editions lightly. In the preparation of copy for Elizabethan printers and in the setting of that copy in the presses, it was usually scribes and compositors rather than playwrights who made decisions about where such punctuation marks appeared. In the theatre, such choices are still up to actors. We hope that these editions will make them clearer.

We hope these editions illuminate and explain Shakespeare's texts without imposing any specific ideas about how to inhabit, perform, read or enjoy them. Our aim throughout has been to set our actor-readers' imaginations free.

Thanks to:
Margaret Bartley who had faith in the idea and has worked tirelessly to see it realized.

The Bloomsbury Arden team for their support and expertise.

The Arden Third Series volume editors whose expertise has provided us with authoritative, modernized editions.

Ralph Alan Cohen, The American Shakespeare Center, our Series Advisor.

Michael Dobson, Abigail Rokison-Woodall,
Simon Russell Beale

SERIES INTRODUCTION

Actors working with modern editions often run up against editorial decisions which may affect their interpretations. Editorial principles for lineation and punctuation are not always made explicit, and are frequently consigned to the discursive notes at the beginning or end of the text. The principles for the selection of particular textual variants vary between editions, and the possible choices available to the actor are not always immediately apparent.

This edition seeks to open the text to actors, making clear those instances where there is a genuine choice in terms of textual variants, and leaving the lineation of the text as open as possible.

PUNCTUATION

- The punctuation of this edition is that of the Arden 3 text, since this is designed to convey the sense most clearly.

- No extant text of Shakespeare represents the author's own punctuation.

- Even the punctuation of early quarto editions thought to have been printed from an authorial manuscript is likely, for the most part, to have originated with the scribes and compositors who were responsible for the transcription and printing of these copies.

- In some cases the punctuation in the Folio is as heavy, or heavier, than that of many modern edited texts.

- With this in mind it seems arbitrary to pick a particular early modern text from which to take the punctuation – this creates as many problems as it solves.

- Actors are not obliged to follow the punctuation of the text in delivery. They may find that it is sometimes better to phrase according to the metre.

- In cases where the punctuation of an early quarto or Folio seems particularly useful or interesting in providing an indication of a character's mood or thought patterns, we provide a facing-page note.

LINEATION

- The lineation of the edition is, again, based on that of Arden 3.

- However, in cases where the lineation is ambiguous, a facing-page note to this effect is added.

- Where the metrical connection between lines seems unambiguous – so-called shared lines – this edition follow George Steevens and editors since 1793 in indenting the second part of the line in order to make the connection visually explicit.

- In cases where three part-lines succeed one another, each pair appearing to have an equal metrical claim to linkage, this edition does not follow the common editorial practice of representing such lines as one shared and one short line. Instead we make the ambiguous metrical connection apparent by indenting both the second and third portions of the line, thus:

MARCELLUS
    Holla Barnardo!
BARNARDO   Say, what, is Horatio there?
HORATIO   A piece of him

            (*Ham.* 1.1.17)

- In cases where one of the lines might be regarded as an overlapping or interjecting line outside the metrical structure of the scene, we add a note on the facing page, as in this example from *Hamlet*:

HAMLET
    . . . A cut-purse of the Empire and the rule,
    That from a shelf the precious Diadem stole
    And put it in his pocket.
GERTRUDE   No more.
HAMLET   A King of shreds and patches,
                     (*Ham.* 3.4.97–100)

Hamlet's lines could be considered to be continuous with Gertrude's line overlapping. This form of overlap would have been easily indicated to the Renaissance actor working from a cue part by giving the actor playing Hamlet a continuous speech, and the actor playing Gertrude the cue-line 'in his pocket'.

- Where more than three short lines succeed one another and the metrical connection is ambiguous, all lines are aligned to the left hand margin and a note is added.

- This form of lineation is partly motivated by historical evidence suggesting that early modern actors, because of the nature of the scripts they worked with, would not have been able to see the metrical connections between their lines and those of other speakers, and are therefore unlikely to have distinguished between full-line and short-line cues in their delivery.

METRE

- Whilst the dominant metre of Shakespeare's verse is iambic pentameter (five feet per line), Shakespeare increasingly varies this metre, introducing other feet. A note on the metre with more details of metrical variants is provided in the section 'A Note on Metre'.

Long and short lines

- Although most lines have ten (or eleven) syllables, some lines have more or less than this.

- In some instances it is possible to make a line scan as a line of pentameter by eliding a word, for example 'even' being pronounced as one syllable (sometimes represented in editions as e'en).

- In other cases the metre suggests the expansion of a word, for example the pronunciation of 'intermission' as five syllables (**in**-ter-**miss**-i-**on**).

- Facing-page notes are given to alert the actor to such metrical indications.

- The notes indicate the equivalent number of syllables suggested by the metre; for example:

even (equiv. 1 syl.)

in-ter-**miss**-i-**on** (equiv. 5 syl.)

- Bold type in these notes indicates stressed syllables.

- In some cases what appears to be a long line can be scanned by substituting an anapest for an iambic foot. In such cases a facing-page note is provided. The section 'A Note on Metre' explains the use of the anapest.

- Finally, some lines cannot be easily scanned as pentameters. In such cases we provide a facing-page note indicating that a line is either short or long. There is no expectation that the actor will change his or her delivery.

- In a few cases a line of nine syllables is clearly missing the first stressed syllable. This is called a 'headless foot' and its presence is noted in a facing-page note.

- In some cases the verse form suggests that a word might be pronounced differently from its usual sound in both present-day and early modern everyday speech.

- In the case of words ending in 'ed', the metre sometimes suggests that the ending should be pronounced as an extra syllable. In such cases the 'ed' ending is given a grave accent – èd – viz. examinèd.

- In cases where the metre does not suggest the pronunciation of the word-ending as a separate syllable, the word is printed – 'd' – viz. examin'd.

- The aim throughout is to inform and assist rather than to dictate, and the pronunciation of words is, of course, a matter of individual choice.

PRONUNCIATION

- In cases of unusual words or names, this edition provides a guide to pronunciation in a facing-page note (preceded by 'Pron.').

- Pronunciation of character names is given in the *Dramatis Personae* (and not thereafter in the text).

- In cases where a word is used several times, varying in scansion according to the metre, a note is given in the Introduction (and not for each use in the text).

TEXTUAL VARIANTS

- Some of Shakespeare's plays were printed in two or more different early editions.

- Thirty-six of Shakespeare's plays were published in the First Folio of 1623. Prior to the publication of the Folio, eighteen of these plays had appeared individually in quarto form.

- *Pericles* and *The Two Noble Kinsmen* – not included in the First Folio – were also printed in quarto form.
- Some of the quarto texts differ little from their Folio counterparts. In other cases the differences are substantial.
- In most cases there are some variations in terms of individual words.
- Some of these are merely representative of an error of transcription or printing.
- However, in other cases differences between the early texts present the actor with a genuine choice. In such instances we make clear the textual variants in a facing-page note.

Q – indicates a quarto variant

F – indicates a Folio variant

Q1 – First quarto, Q2 – Second quarto, etc.

F1 – First Folio, F2 – Second Folio, etc.

Qq – all authoritative quartos

- In a few cases the quarto and Folio texts contain obvious errors – the result of misreadings, damaged copy or error. In many cases these were emended by eighteenth-century editors. Where this is the case a facing-page note makes the editorial emendation apparent:

Rowe – Nicholas Rowe, 1709

Pope – Alexander Pope, 1725

Theobald – Lewis Theobald, 1733

Hanmer – Thomas Hanmer, 1744

Warburton – William Warburton, 1747

Johnson – Samuel Johnson, 1765

Capell – Edward Capell, 1768

Steevens – George Steevens, 1773

Malone – Edmond Malone, 1790

- Each individual edition provides a clear summary of the variant texts and notes any major textual differences.

SCENE LOCATIONS

- About two-thirds of scenes in Shakespeare plays written for the Globe are unlocated. No indication is given of their precise locale even in the dialogue, and in no early text does an announcement on the page at the beginning of a scene specify where it is taking place.

- When location is important to a scene, Shakespeare usually has characters (or a chorus) vocalize it – for example, 'Well, this is the forest of Arden' (*As You Like It*, 1.4.12), 'The orchard walls are high and hard to climb' (*Romeo and Juliet*, 2.2.63), 'Unto Southampton do we shift our scene' (*Henry V*, 2.0.42).

- As a result, we have resisted the temptation to provide arbitrary locations for scenes.

- The setting of a scene is clearly a matter for each individual production to define (or to leave as ambiguous).

- In texts where scenes have clearly defined locations, these are discussed in the introduction to that edition.

SCENE DIVISIONS

- The early printed quartos contain no act or scene divisions and there is no indication that a play like *Hamlet* was conceived by Shakespeare as being in five acts.

- Act and scene divisions originate with the First Folio. However, in *Hamlet* these are not consistent, appearing sporadically through the first two acts, and then stopping altogether.

- It was with the Quarto of 1676 that act and scene breaks were first introduced into the play, and these have been followed by most editors ever since.

- However, this Quarto introduced a puzzling act and scene division between 3.4 and 4.1, the action of which seems to occur consecutively within the Queen's closet.

- We follow this act and scene division only for the sake of cross-referencing with the many editions and works of criticism which have reluctantly followed this mistake since.

STAGE DIRECTIONS (SD)

- This edition follows the stage directions given in the Arden 3 text.

- The early printed texts of Shakespeare's plays contain relatively few stage directions.

- Where stage directions do not appear in the early texts but have been added by subsequent editors, they are presented in brackets – i.e. [*Exit PHILOSTRATE*].

- There are a few cases in the Folio or quarto texts where a character is instructed to enter in a stage direction, but does not speak. In such cases we provide a facing-page note. The decision as to whether a character who does not speak is to be included in the scene is a matter for each production to determine.

- There are a number of instances in the Folio text of what have been termed 'anticipated entrances' – where a character is instructed to enter on stage before they are required to speak. These entrances may simply indicate the time taken for an actor to get from the back to the front of the Globe stage. However, in some cases they suggest an interesting possibility that a character is seen by the onstage characters before they speak or overhears the onstage action. In such cases we provide a facing-page note indicating the position of the entrance in the Folio (or occasionally Quarto) text.

YOU AND THOU

- In early modern England the pronouns 'you' and 'thou' each served a distinctive function, much like the French equivalents 'vous' and 'tu'.

- Having earlier been the standard form of address, 'thou' became a 'special' pronoun, used affectionately to indicate closeness between speakers, used derogatively in order to patronize or vituperate, and used when addressing allegorical figures, gods or the dead.

- As well as being the plural, 'you' was the more respectful form of address.

- Individual editions contain a brief note on the most significant uses of personal pronouns in the play.

RHETORIC

- Rhetoric – the art of verbal persuasion, studied and codified since classical times – exerted a powerful influence on Elizabethan writing, and rhetorical devices abound in the work of Shakespeare and his contemporaries.

- Some of the most common rhetorical devices are alliteration, assonance, various patterns of repetition, and especially antithesis, which Shakespeare uses frequently to balance lines and to counterbalance clauses, setting light against dark, love against hate, and so on.

RHYME

- Shakespeare uses rhyme in various ways in his plays, the most common being for songs and for rhyming couplets – sometimes isolated, sometimes formed into speeches.

- In Shakespeare's early plays, one of the most common uses of the rhyming couplet is to end a scene.

- In his later plays these final couplets are less common. Sometimes a scene finishes on a couplet followed by a short line which gives a different momentum to an exeunt.

- Couplets are also used to end speeches, adding a flourish to their conclusion.

- A further use of rhyme comes in the form of aphorisms, where characters seem to be coining or citing pithy generalizations.

- One difficulty for the modern actor is that changes in pronunciation from the early modern period to the present day mean that lines that once rhymed do so no longer.

- In such cases we provide a facing-page note. An actor is free to ignore the rhyme and pronounce the words as they are commonly spoken or to employ a deliberately antiquated delivery in order to point up the rhyme.

VERSE AND PROSE

- Most of Shakespeare's plays are written in a mixture of verse and prose.

- *Henry VI Parts 1* and *3* (c. 1591), *Richard II* (c. 1595) and *King John* (c. 1596) are written entirely in verse.

- *The Merry Wives of Windsor* has the highest proportion of prose – 90 per cent.
- The characters who most often speak prose are:
  - servants, clowns, sailors and workingmen;
  - upper-class characters coming into contact with working-class characters;
  - foreign characters;
  - drunken characters;
  - characters experiencing madness and psychological imbalance;
  - characters in disguise.
- Prose is commonly used for lesser subject matter than verse and for comic dialogue.
- The majority of letters and proclamations are in prose.
- A move from verse to prose within a scene often marks a significant change in tone. There is an increasing tendency in the process of Shakespeare's career to modulate from one medium to another within a scene.

  Where a scene moves from verse to prose or vice-versa, this is indicated in a facing-page note.

- During Shakespeare's career his use of prose becomes more varied, and prose is more often spoken by characters from the upper classes.
- It is sometimes difficult to distinguish between verse and prose. This may be deliberate. In such cases we provide a facing-page note.
- Each individual edition provides a summary of the key uses of verse and prose in the play.

SOURCES

- Many of Shakespeare's plays are based on pre-existing sources – ancient texts such as Plutarch's *Parallel Lives*, classical poems, historical chronicles, earlier plays and stories.

- Shakespeare regularly made alterations to his source material, either in order to make it more theatrical, to make it more shocking (as in the case of the tragic ending which only Shakespeare gives to the well-known legend of King Lear), or to make it more politically and socially relevant.

- It can be misleading for an actor to explore the source material for a text as a means of discovering more about a character, particularly in the case of historical figures: an attempt to play Shakespeare's Richard III as though the play were a documentary about the historical Richard III, for example, is likely to produce contradictory and undramatic results.

- Nevertheless, it can be interesting to note the changes made, and to know some of what Shakespeare was deliberately leaving out or transforming.

- As a point of interest, each edition provides a list of key sources for the play.

- Where there is a clear and significant source for a particular reference, we provide a facing-page note in the text, marked 'Source'.

Proverbial sayings

- Shakespeare's characters often use proverbs.

- Some characters make conscious use of common sayings – sometimes to the point of cliché.

- Others deliberately manipulate well-known aphorisms.

- Since it seems useful for actors to be aware of when a character is consciously using proverbial language, key proverbial sayings are marked 'Prov.'.

Biblical allusions

- Characters in Shakespeare's plays frequently quote from or refer to the Bible.
- Such references would have been more familiar to early modern actors and audiences.
- Again, it seems useful for actors to be aware of when their character is invoking the Bible.
- Biblical allusions are marked 'Bib.'.

LIST OF ABBREVIATIONS

SI – Series Introduction
Myth – Key figures of classical mythology
Bib. – biblical
equiv. – equivalent to
Pron. – pronunciation
Prov. – proverbial
Punct. – punctuation
SD – stage direction
SP – speech prefix
syl. – syllable/syllables

Michael Dobson, Abigail Rokison-Woodall,
Simon Russell Beale, *Series Editors*

A NOTE ON METRE

Shakespeare's basic metre is iambic pentameter. Iambic pentameter is made up of five feet (a foot being a unit of verse made up of stressed and unstressed syllables) comprising an unstressed syllable followed by a stressed syllable, annotated thus: u /. A regular line of iambic pentameter is scanned as follows:

> u /   u / u /   u /   u /
>
> HERMIA
> I would my father look'd but with my eyes.
>
> (*A Midsummer Night's Dream*, 1.1.56)

Although iambic pentameter forms the basis of Shakespeare's metre, his metrical line admits a number of variations, particularly as his career progresses.

The essential difficulty with the introduction of iambic pentameter to the English language was that English language has inherent stresses. We pronounce 'inherent' as 'in **her** ent' not '**in** her **ent**', for example. When iambic pentameter was first introduced into the English language, many poets could see little alternative but to use it in a regular fashion. George Gascoigne, in his 'Certayne Notes of Instruction concerning the making of verse of rhyme in English' (1575), one of the first English publications on metre, instructs the poet that 'euen in this playne foote of two syllables [he or she should] wreste no woorde from his natural and vsuall sounde' (George Gascoigne, 'Certayne Notes of Instruction concerning the making of verse or rhyme in English' in *The posies of George Gascoigne Esquire* (London, 1575, 50)).

He gives the following example:

I understand your meanying by your eye
Your meaning I understand by your eye

commenting that,

> in these two verses there seemeth no difference at all, since the
> one hath the very selfe same woordes that the other hath, and
> yet the latter verse is neyther true nor pleasant, and the first
> verse may passe the musters.
>
> (Gascoigne, 50–1)

And yet Shakespeare and his contemporaries could not always compose sentences in alternate stresses (this would have become tedious), and thus they began to introduce variants, three of the most common being:

1. The trochee – a foot composed of a stressed syllable followed by an unstressed syllable (/ u). An example might be the first foot of this line:

   /   u   u /   u   /   u /   u /

   Friendship is constant in all other things

   (Much Ado, 2.1.160)

2. The Spondee – a foot composed of two stressed syllables (/ /). An example might be the first foot of this line:

   /   /   u / u /   u   /   u   /

   Hence! home, you idle creatures, get you home:

   (Julius Caesar, 1.1.1)

3. The Anapest – a foot composed of two unstressed syllables followed by a stressed syllable (u u /). An example might be the first foot of this line:

   u   u /   u   /   u   /   u /   u   /

   Be it so she will not here, before your Grace,

   (A Midsummer Night's Dream, 1.1.39)

Many lines in Shakespearean drama that might otherwise be considered irregular can be scanned by substituting one of these metrical feet for an iamb. In many cases the scansion is subjective. Whilst one person may wish to speak the following line:

HORATIO
What, has this thing appear'd again tonight?

(*Ham.* 1.1.19)

scanning 'What, has' as an iamb (with the stress on 'has'), another might wish to scan it as a trochee (with the stress on 'What') and another as a spondee (with the stress on 'What' and 'has').

In the case of trochees and spondees, the substitution of one of these feet for an iamb does not affect the overall syllable count of a line, and thus we do not regularly give an indication of where we feel such feet might be present.

There are a few instances in Shakespeare's work of full lines of trochaic rather than iambic metre. Most frequently these are present in Shakespeare's 'magic' metre – when he is writing dialogue for the fairies in *A Midsummer Night's Dream* or for the witches in *Macbeth*. However, they sometimes occur elsewhere in the plays, and their presence is noted, for example, in *Romeo and Juliet*:

Romeo, humours, madman, passion, lover,

(2.1.7)

However, the anapest incorporates an extra syllable into a line, making it appear irregularly long if one does not acknowledge the possibility of this foot. In cases where a line can be made to scan as five feet by the inclusion of an anapest, we note this in a facing-page note.

A more extreme example, similar to an anapest, is the quartus paeon, a foot which comprises three unstressed syllables followed by a stressed syllable (u u u /). In most cases the presence or otherwise of a quartus paeon is ambiguous, and a line might equally be scanned as a deliberate hexameter (six feet), as in the following example.

This line can be scanned with the third foot (quish-er as by) as a quartus paeon:

```
u   / u   / u  u  u / u  /   u  /
```
Had he been vanquisher, as by the same co-mart

(Hamlet, 1.1.90)

or as a deliberate hexameter:

```
u   / u   / u / u / u   /   u  /
```
Had he been vanquisher, as by the same co-mart

(Hamlet, 1.1.90)

Some critics suggest that hexameters are rare and that it is preferable to attempt regularization where possible (E. A. Abbott, *A Shakeseparean Grammar,* 397). Others freely admit the presence of hexameters (George T. Wright, *Shakespeare's Metrical Art,* Chapter 9).

There are sometimes a number of possible ways of scanning a particular line. In the following example, either the second (-lling shall not lack) or third (Let us go in) foot might be scanned as a quartus paeon, or the line can be regarded as a hexameter (with a feminine ending).

God willing shall not lack. Let us go in together

(Hamlet, 1.5.192)

In other cases, scanning a line as a hexameter seems the only logical choice:

He heareth not, he stirreth not, he moveth not;

(Romeo and Juliet, 2.1.15)

SHORT LINES

Headless lines

A common variation on the regular iambic pentameter line is that of the 'headless' line. A fairly common metrical device in Shakespeare's work, the headless line is a line that is missing the first unstressed syllable:

(u)/ u / u /   /   u u /
Melted as the snow, seems to me now

        (*A Midsummer Night's Dream*, 4.1.166)

    (u) / u /
HORATIO Where, my lord?

        u / u / u / u
HAMLET   In my mind's eye, Horatio.

           (*Hamlet*, 1.2.185)

Missing beats at the caesura

A further variation on the short verse line is the line in which a beat appears to be missing at the caesura. The caesura is the strong mid-line break in a line of verse, often marked by the end of a phrase or sentence.

If the missing beat is an unstressed beat, this is termed a 'broken-backed line'; for example:

u   /   u / (u) / u   /   u   /
To hide the slain?   O, from this time forth

           (*Hamlet*, 4.4.66)

Other lines may be missing a stressed syllable at the mid-line caesura:

```
u   /  u   /   u (/)  u  /    u  /
```
As he would draw it. Long stay'd he so;

(Hamlet, 2.1.87)

FEMININE ENDINGS/TRIPLE ENDINGS

The regular iambic pentameter line consists of five feet, each made up of an unstressed syllable followed by a stressed syllable. One of the most common variations on this line is the presence of what is commonly termed a feminine (or unstressed) ending. A feminine ending consists of an extra unstressed syllable at the end of the ten syllable line, for example:

```
u  / u  / u /   /  u u  /    u
```
To be, or not to be – that is the question;

(Hamlet, 3.1.54)

Occasionally a line ends with two additional unstressed syllables – termed a triple ending:

```
u  / u    /   u /   u /   u /  u u
```
And tediousness the limbs and outward flourishes.

(Hamlet, 2.2.91)

In this case, 'flourishes' may be seen as equivalent to two syllables.

INTRODUCTION

THE VARIANT TEXTS

Hamlet was written in around 1601. There are three key early printed texts of the play:

- First quarto (Q1) – published in 1603.
- Second quarto (Q2) – published in 1604. The title page of this edition claimed that it presented the play 'newly imprinted and enlarged to almost as much again as it was, according to true and perfect coppie'. It is, indeed, almost twice the length of Q1.
- First Folio (F) – published in 1623.

The word 'quarto' refers to the format the text – a quarto is made up of large sheets of paper that have been folded twice, each printed page being a quarter of a full sheet. A quarto is usually around 8.5 inches in height.

Not all of Shakespeare's plays were printed in quarto form. That *Hamlet* was is an indicator of its popularity. Indeed, *Hamlet* was reprinted in quarto form in 1611 (producing the third quarto (Q3)) and 1622 (as what is now known as the fourth quarto (Q4)).

The word 'Folio' refers to a book of around 15 inches in height, made up of full sheets of paper which have been folded in half. The First Folio is thus about twice the size of the early printed quartos. The folio format was, in general, only used for prestigious books – works by leading theologians, philosophers and historians.

The chart below gives some idea of the origins of the variant texts and their relationship to Shakespeare's (lost) manuscript. However, the reality is far more complex, since it appears that the Folio must have been printed in consultation with a copy of Q2, Q3 or Q4.

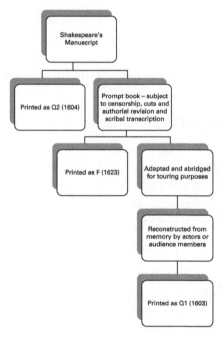

- It is widely agreed that Q2 represents a version of the play deriving from Shakespeare's manuscript (or a copy thereof).

- F is generally thought to derive from playhouse copy – a version of the text which had been adjusted for performance – that is, subjected to alterations such as cuts, expansions and censorship. Shakespeare may have been responsible for some of these changes, but others may have been made by actors, by censors, or by the scribes or compositors responsible for transcribing the text and seeing it into print.

- Although Q1 was the first text to be printed, it is likely to represent the play at a later stage than either Q2 or F. The text of Q1 is substantially corrupt, with some passages making little sense, some sections of the verse mangled and some character names corrupted or altered. It has been widely considered to represent some sort of reconstruction of the text (partly or entirely from memory). Some suggest that Q1 represents a memorial reconstruction and theatrical abridgement of the play, made for use on tour by one of the actors in the company, possibly the actor who played Marcellus, Voltemand and one of the players.[1] This notion is supported by the high level of textual corruption in sections of the play in which this actor would not have appeared, contrasting with close parallels between the lines of dialogue spoken by Marcellus, Voltemand and Lucianus in Q1 and the same lines in the longer texts. Others argue that Q1 is a pirated version of the text, copied down by one or more people at a performance of the play.[2] Although Q1 is rarely performed in the professional (or amateur) theatre, due to its corrupt nature, there are some elements that are of interest to actors and directors as well as to theatre historians and academics. Whilst some of the differences between Q1 and F/Q2 may be the result of adaptation during the reconstruction of the text, they may also represent features of the play as it was regularly performed on the Elizabethan stage. These features include alterations in the order of scenes; cuts; and elements of staging, as recalled through the expanded stage directions present in Q1. Some of these features are discussed in more detail below.

1 Kathleen O. Irace, 'Origins and Agents of Q1 *Hamlet*', in *The Hamlet First Published*, ed. Thomas Clayton (London: Associated University Press, 1992).
2 See Tiffany Stern, 'Sermons, Plays and Note-Takers: Hamlet Q1 as a "Noted" Text', *Shakespeare Survey* 66 (2013): 1–23.

THIS TEXT

The text used in this edition is based on the Arden 3 Q2 text, edited by Ann Thompson and Neil Taylor.[3] However, this text also includes passages present only in the Folio (F), on the basis that it is easier for actors and directors to cut out such passages than to add them into a text. Any passages which are particular to either F or Q2 are marked with brackets, making them easy to identify.

Whilst the Arden 3 text includes F variants only in cases where Q2 is widely considered to be erroneous or misleading, this edition also uses F variants where these are commonly used in performance – for example, 'Neither a borrower nor a lender be' (F) rather than 'Neither a borrower nor a lender boy' (Q2) (1.3.75).

This text also uses the common F variant of 'he' where Q2 uses ''a', since we consider this to be more actor- and audience-friendly. Actors and directors are, of course, free to substitute the Q2 reading, as they are with all variants throughout the text.

It should be noted that the notes on metre refer to the text as printed on the left-hand page. Textual variants can, and regularly do, affect the metre. We have, however, resisted the urge always to opt for the most metrically regular variant, since this assumes metrical regularity as the norm, which is not always the case with Shakespeare's writing.

MAJOR TEXTUAL DIFFERENCES

Q2, the authorial text, contains around 230 lines not present in F. The most substantial Q2-only passages are as follows:

---

3   Ann Thompson and Neil Taylor, eds, *Hamlet* (London: Bloomsbury Arden, 2006).

1.1.105–22

1.4.15–36

4.4.10–67

4.7.66–80 and 115–24

5.2.105–33 and 187–98

These may represent deliberate theatrical cuts made to the promptbook – the copy for F – and may thus give some idea of how the play was edited for the Elizabethan stage.

This is one reason why a number of theatrical productions choose to cut these lines. Those in the last scene – some of the banter between Hamlet and Osric, and the passages with the Gentleman who merely seems to repeat what Osric has already said – seem an unnecessary (albeit in the case of Osric, comic) hold-up when we are waiting for the play's climax.

The most significant absence from F is in 4.4 – Hamlet's conversation about Fortinbras with the Norwegian Captain, and his soliloquy, 'How all occasions do inform against me', in which Hamlet expresses his admiration for Fortinbras's actions. This section was often cut in productions from the seventeenth to the end of the nineteenth century. Those who want to see *Hamlet* as a political play have tended to retain these lines.

The Folio contains around 70 lines not present in Q2, the most substantial being 2.2.236–65 and 2.2.332–57. The first of these passages contains some quite famous lines, including 'Denmark's a prison', 'there's nothing either good or bad but thinking makes it so', and 'I could be bounded in a nutshell and count myself a king of infinite space'. Many editions and productions that use a predominantly Q2-based text nonetheless choose to include these lines.

The second of these Folio-only passages is the Player's account of the boy players – the 'little eyases' – whose success has led to the actors needing to travel. One suggestion for this being in F and not Q2 is that it may have been in the original text and in the prompt book, but cut from the printing of Q2 on the basis that by 1604 the 'war of the theatres' between London's child-only and adult acting companies no longer seemed topical, or because by this time the children's company, the Children of the Chapel, had come under the patronage of Queen Anne (consort of James I) and such criticism might not have been wise. Although the lines might have been cut from performances after 1604, they clearly remained in the prompt book that served as copy for F.

THE FIRST QUARTO (Q1)

The placement of 'To be or not to be'

Most editions of the play and most productions that you will see are based on a mixture of Q2 and F. However, there is one notable feature of Q1 that is sometimes used in productions that otherwise use one of the more authoritative texts, namely its placement of 'To be or not to be'.

In Q2 and F, 'To be or not to be' comes in Act 3, Scene 1. This gives Hamlet's character the following trajectory:

He starts depressed at his father's death and mother's remarriage. He learns that Horatio has seen the ghost of his father. He meets the ghost of his father who tells him that he was murdered by his brother (Hamlet's uncle). Hamlet realizes that he needs to test the word of the ghost who might be a 'goblin damn'd' (1.4.38); the players arrive and he formulates a plan: 'The play's the thing / Wherein I'll catch the conscience of the King' (2.2.598–99); and then the next time that we see him he is seemingly suicidal: 'To be, or not to be' (3.1.54).

In Q1 the speech comes earlier, so that the actor would instead get this trajectory:

He starts depressed at his father's death and mother's remarriage; learns that Horatio has seen the ghost of his father; meets the ghost of his father and is told that his uncle murdered him; realizes that he needs to test the word of the ghost; feels suicidal and speaks 'To be or not to be', after which the players' arrival allows Hamlet to formulate a plan to test the ghost's word. As many actors have commented, this gives Hamlet a smoother through-line – more of a revenge hero trajectory.

This difference in the placement of this speech might be due to a slip of memory by the reconstructor/adapter; it might be a deliberate change made by that reconstructor/adapter; or it might represent a change made early in the production history of *Hamlet*. However, a number of modern productions have chosen to use the Q1 placement of 'To be or not to be' in otherwise Q2- or F-based texts. These have included Ron Daniels' production with Mark Rylance (RSC, 1989); Matthew Warchus' production with Alex Jennings (RSC, 1997); Trevor Nunn's production with Ben Whishaw (Old Vic, 2004); Michael Boyd's production with Toby Stephens (RSC, 2004); Gregory Doran's production with David Tennant (RSC, 2008); and Franco Zeffirelli's film version with Mel Gibson (1990).

The lack of a firm location for the speech has also led some directors to move it elsewhere in the play. Peter Brook, directing Adrian Lester, famously moved it to Act 4, leaving some people wondering whether he had cut the most famous speech in the play; and recently Lyndsey Turner, directing Benedict Cumberbatch, moved it to the very beginning of the play during the previews of her 2015 production, subsequently moving it back to 3.1.

The scene between Horatio and the Queen

Another major structural difference between Q1 and the other texts is the presence in Q1 of a scene between Horatio and the Queen – Scene 14 – for which there is no immediate equivalent in either of the other texts. The scene essentially replaces 4.6; the section of 4.7 where the King receives Hamlet's letter; and the start of 5.2 where Hamlet recounts the details of his voyage to Horatio in the longer texts. The scene was included by Michael Boyd in his RSC production of 2004.

Hamlet's age

A further feature of Q1 that has received substantial attention, and made its way into some modern productions, is the information that it gives about Hamlet's age. In Q2 and F the exchange between Hamlet and the Gravedigger in 5.1 suggests that Hamlet is around thirty years old.

First, we have the exchange about how long the gravedigger has been in his post. He says that he has been a gravedigger since the day 'that our last King Hamlet overcame Fortinbras' (5.1.142), which was 'that very day that young Hamlet was born' (5.1.145). A bit later he expands: 'I have been sexton here, man and boy, thirty years (5.1.158–9). Second, we have an exchange about the dead jester, Yorick, whose skull 'hath lain i'th' earth three and twenty years' (5.1.169–70). Hamlet recalls that Yorick 'hath borne me on his back a thousand times' (5.1.181–2). If Yorick has been dead twenty-three years and Hamlet rode on his back (presumably as a young boy), then he is around thirty.

In Q1, however, the timings are different. In Scene 16 the Gravedigger tells Hamlet that the skull has lain in the ground 'a dozen year', implying that Hamlet is around eighteen.

Whilst many directors choose to cast actors nearer to the age of thirty (or even forty) than eighteen, others have felt strongly that Hamlet is a young student. After all, Hamlet is referred to as 'young' or a 'youth' a number of times in the play. He is also a student at Wittenberg University, which would have been unusual for someone in their thirties. Trevor Nunn had this element of Q1 in mind when he chose to cast the 24-year-old Ben Whishaw as Hamlet at the Old Vic in 2004.

Q1 stage directions

Another special feature of Q1 is its expanded stage directions. Whether Q1 was written down from memory by an actor, or copied down in the theatre by a pirate, it is possible that elements of the staging may have been recorded alongside the dialogue (they may equally have come from the imagination of the reconstructor/adapter). Some of these stage directions have proved of interest to contemporary theatre directors, who have included them in their productions of the longer texts.

In the closet scene (3.4) we get the following stage direction for the Ghost's entrance in Q2 and F:

Enter Ghost (3.4.99)

In Q1 the stage direction reads:

Enter the ghost in his night gowne (Q1, Scene 11)

This stage direction is significant, since on his previous appearance in Act 1, on the battlements, the Ghost was clad in armour. The possible change of costume may serve to define Old Hamlet as a husband and father as well as a soldier and to mark a contrast between the public, military world of the court and the private, intimate world of the closet. Since it was usual for stage ghosts to appear as they were when they died, the Ghost's change from armour to night-gown may also indicate a more in-depth characterization than was typical of revenge-hungry ghosts in drama of the period.[4]

---

4   G. Blakemore Evans, *Elizabethan–Jacobean Drama* (London: A&C Black, 1987), 274.

Another particularly famous stage direction from Q1 comes in Scene 13 (the equivalent of 4.5 in Q2 and F). It is the stage direction for Ophelia's entrance, which in Q2 reads simply '*Enter Ophelia*' (4.5.16), whilst in F it reads '*Enter Ophelia distracted*'. In Q1 the stage direction reads '*Enter Ofelia playing on a Lute, and her haire downe singing*' (Q1, Scene 13). For a female character to appear with her hair down was an indication that she was 'distraught with madness, shame, extreme grief, or the effects of recent violence'.[5] This staging would have acted, for members of an Elizabethan audience, as a visual signifier of Ophelia's mental state. Some modern productions of the conflated texts, including John Barton's 1980 RSC production, have followed this stage direction.

One of the most commonly used stage directions from Q1 comes in Act 5, Scene 1. In F, a stage direction indicates that Laertes '*Leaps in the grave*' (5.1.242) to catch Ophelia in his arms. Hamlet and Laertes then fight; however, it is not made explicit whether Hamlet has descended into the grave or Laertes emerged from it.

In Q1 the direction for Leartes (Laertes) is followed by a marginal indication that '*Hamlet leapes in after Leartes*' (Q1, Scene 16). That this might represent common staging of the scene seems confirmed by an anonymous funeral elegy for Richard Burbage, the original Hamlet, which comments 'oft have I seen him leap into the grave'.[6]

CENSORSHIP OF F

A common variant between the Q2 and F texts is the substitution of 'heaven' for 'God'. This is almost certainly due to

---

5 Alan Dessen, *Elizabethan Stage Conventions and Modern Interpreters* (Cambridge: Cambridge University Press, 1984), 36.
6 Ibid., 21.

censorship of the play that occurred after the publication of Q2. In 1606, Parliament passed a censorship law – 'An Act to Restrain Abuses of Players' – which threatened to fine actors who 'profanely speak or use the holy name of God or Christ Jesus, or of the Holy Ghost or of the Trinity'. The substitution does not have a noticeable effect on the metre since 'heaven' can be pronounced as the equivalent of a single syllable. Censorship was also undoubtedly responsible for the removal of oaths, such as "Swounds' (God's wounds) and 'By the mass', from the Folio text.

PUNCTUATION

As stated in the Series Introduction, the punctuation of this text is largely that of Arden 3. This punctuation is modernized, and designed to best help the reader to understand the sense.

Whilst the punctuation of the early printed texts is often considered to be less heavy and more rhetorical than that of modern texts, this is not always the case. The punctuation of F is considerably heavier than that of Q2, having been subject to intervention at a number of stages of its production – authorial revision of foul papers, the creation of a scribal transcript, and the printing of the text. The punctuation of Q2 *Hamlet* is sparse, and seems quite rhetorical in style – indicative of phrasing rather than grammar. This can be liberating for an actor. However, it can also make the text quite difficult to understand, since whole speeches may be punctuated as a single sentence.

This edition only notes instances of Q2 or F punctuation where a variant provides the actor with a genuine choice, for example at 1.2.232, where Arden 3 follows Q2 in printing Hamlet's line 'What look'd he – frowningly?', whilst F punctuates 'What, looked he frowningly?', suggesting a quite different phrasing.

We also note a few instances where the Q2/F punctuation may seem indicative of a particular dramatic phrasing, for example at 5.1.19–20, where most modern texts give the Gravedigger's lines as 'Argal, he that is not guilty of his own death shortens not his own life', but both Q2 and F punctuate 'Argal, he that is not guilty of his own death, shortens not his own life', suggesting a slight pause before the punch line, which may be helpful for the actor's delivery.

It should also be noted that in the early modern period question marks could be indicative of either a question or an exclamation, and thus it is not always possible to distinguish between interrogation and exclamation. For example at 3.1.86–7, the Arden 3 text prints 'Soft you now, / The fair Ophelia!' as an exclamation, where Q2 has a comma, and F a question mark: 'Soft you now,? The fair Ophelia?'. Again, we note the variant in a facing-page note.

ANTICIPATED ENTRANCES

The Folio text contains a number of what are commonly referred to as 'anticipated entrances' – stage directions for the entrance of a character or characters a number of lines before they are required to speak or are referred to by others. These were generally considered by editors to be the result of actors needing time to get from the doors at the back of the Globe stage to the acting area at the front, and were thus often moved by editors to just before the character in question speaks or is noticed. However, in a few instances an earlier entrance for a character may be dramatically effective – allowing an audience to see them before they are noticed by the characters onstage; allowing them to overhear dialogue; or allowing them to be noted (though not remarked upon or spoken to) by an onstage character. It is for this reason that we note such instances.

VERSE AND PROSE IN THE PLAY

Hamlet is written in a mixture of verse and prose. It adheres in many respects to the common conventions for the use of prose:

- Characters such as the sailor (4.6) and the gravediggers (otherwise designated as clowns) speak in prose.
- Gertrude, the Queen, speaks exclusively in verse, even when conversing with those speaking prose.
- The comic dialogue of Osric (in conversation with Horatio and Hamlet in 5.2) is in prose.
- Some of the more informal dialogue between Hamlet and Horatio/Hamlet and Rosencrantz and Guildenstern/ Hamlet and the Players is in prose.
- When Ophelia goes mad she speaks in prose.
- The letters read aloud in the play – Hamlet's letter to Ophelia (2.2), Hamlet's letter to Horatio (4.6) and Hamlet's letter to the King (4.7) – are in prose (with the exception of Hamlet's love poem to Ophelia contained within the letter in 2.2).
- Scenes often move from verse into prose or vice versa. That a move from verse to prose within a scene often marks a significant change in tone is exemplified by 5.1. In addition to the comic gravediggers speaking in prose, Hamlet and Horatio also conduct their informal conversation at the start of the scene in prose. However, the moment that the funeral procession enters, Hamlet switches from prose to verse and the other characters that enter thereafter all speak in verse.

However, the play also epitomizes Shakespeare's increasing flexibility with the media of verse and prose.

- Whilst the King speaks mostly in verse, as one might expect, he moves into prose when conversing with others speaking in that medium – for example in his dialogue with the 'antic' Hamlet in 3.2 and 4.3.

- Laertes similarly speaks mostly in verse, using prose for two lines only in 4.5, when he converses with the mad Ophelia (who is speaking prose) (lines 169 and 173–4).

- Polonius speaks in a mixture of verse and prose (using prose particularly when in conversation with a prose-speaking Hamlet).

There are also a couple of instances early in the play where Polonius shifts mid-speech from verse to prose and then moves back to speaking in verse. The first comes in 2.1:

POLONIUS
    And then, sir, does he this, he does –
    What was I about to say? [By the mass], I was about to
        say something! Where did I leave?
REYNALDO
    At 'closes in the consequence'.
    [At friend, or so, and gentleman.]
POLONIUS
    At 'closes in the consequence', ay, marry.

(lines 48–53)

Polonius has been speaking in verse, but when he loses his train of thought he moves into prose for lines 49–50, resuming in verse at line 53. This sudden shift can sometimes give the impression that it is the actor rather than the character who has forgotten the lines (and is sometimes played deliberately as such). The second instance occurs in 2.2:

    Hath given me this. Now gather and surmise.
    [*Reads.*] To the celestial and my soul's idol, the most
        beautified Ophelia – that's an ill phrase, a vile phrase,
        'beautified' is a vile phrase, but you shall hear – *thus in*
        her excellent white bosom, these, etc.

QUEEN
> Came this from Hamlet to her?

POLONIUS
> Good madam, stay awhile: I will be faithful.

>> (lines 108–14)

Polonius is speaking in verse. He then begins to read Hamlet's letter, which is in prose. When he breaks off to comment on the letter, his comments (again, much like the example in 2.1) are in prose.

The play also demonstrates a particularly nuanced use of verse and prose within the role of Hamlet.

- Like the other characters in the play, Hamlet begins the play speaking verse.

- However, once he announces his intention to assume an 'antic disposition' (1.5.178), he frequently speaks in prose – most notably to those whom he is trying to convince of his madness.

- This often results in those to whom he is speaking also moving into prose – for example Ophelia in 3.1, who begins conversing with him in verse, whilst Hamlet speaks in prose, but soon moves into prose.

- Although Hamlet speaks in prose to characters such as Polonius, Rosencrantz and Guildenstern, Ophelia and the King after this point, when he is left alone on stage to soliloquize/converse with the audience, he shifts back into verse. This is sometimes taken as evidence that Hamlet's madness is only assumed.

- Hamlet also speaks in verse both to Horatio (in whom he has confided) in 3.2 (lines 51–86) and to his mother in the closet scene, prior to telling her that he is only 'mad in craft' (184).

There are some points in the play where it is uncertain as to whether the lines are in verse or prose. This ambiguous status of the lines seems deliberate at points where the formality of a scene breaks down, for example in 1.5.112–25, where the characters' lines seem to tumble over one another. It is possible to link some of these lines into consecutive lines of pentameter, but the connections are ambiguous:

> I have sworn't.
> *Enter HORATIO and MARCELLUS.*

HORATIO
My lord, my lord!

MARCELLUS
Lord Hamlet!

HORATIO
Heavens secure him!   115

HAMLET
So be it.

MARCELLUS
Illo, ho, ho, my lord!

HAMLET
Hillo, ho, ho, boy, come and come!

MARCELLUS
How is't, my noble lord?

HORATIO
What news, my lord?   120

HAMLET
O, wonderful.

HORATIO
Good my lord, tell it.

HAMLET
No, you will reveal it.

HORATIO
Not I, my lord, by heaven.

MARCELLUS
Nor I, my lord.   125

AMBIGUOUS METRICAL CONNECTIONS

The example above is one of the more extreme examples of ambiguous metrical connections of short verse lines in the play. However, like others among Shakespeare's middle plays, *Hamlet* contains a relatively high proportion of short lines whose metrical connection to one another remains ambiguous. As noted in the Series Introduction, when these take the form of three consecutive short lines, we make the ambiguous metrical connection visible to the actor by indenting both the second and third portions of the line.

However, there are quite a few examples in *Hamlet* of a series of more than three consecutive single short lines with an ambiguous connection. These occur most frequently in passages of interrogation or panic:

HAMLET
  Indeed, indeed sirs, but this troubles me.
  Hold you the watch tonight?
HORATIO, MARCELLUS, BARNARDO
  We do, my lord.
HAMLET
  Arm'd, say you?
HORATIO, MARCELLUS, BARNARDO
  Arm'd, my lord.
HAMLET
  From top to toe?
HORATIO, MARCELLUS, BARNARDO
  My lord, from head to foot.
HAMLET
  Then saw you not his face.

                                    (1.2.223–30)

In such instances (as indicated in the Series Introduction) all lines are aligned to the left-hand margin.[7]

FEMININE ENDINGS

Feminine endings are extremely common in *Hamlet*. In many cases they simply add variety and allow the inclusion of particular words. However, in other cases their presence may be seen to reflect the content of the lines. It has been well documented that 'To be or not to be' begins with four consecutive lines with feminine endings, the extra light syllable at the end of the line giving an upward inflection and a questioning tone to the lines.

IRREGULAR LINES

Again, like other plays of the middle and later periods of Shakespeare's writing career, *Hamlet* contains a number of irregular lines of verse. Many of these can be regularized (as indicated in the notes) if some words are scanned as anapests or quartus paeons (see 'A Note on Metre'). However, this may feel forced in some cases. Others which are short by one syllable may be regarded as headless or broken-backed (see 'A Note on Metre').

Equally there are some lines which must simply be regarded as irregular – either shorter or longer than five metrical feet, for example:

Hyperion to a satyr, so loving to my mother

(1.2.140)

---

7 For a more lengthy discussion, see Abigail Rokison, *Shakespearean Verse Speaking: Text and Performance* (Cambridge: Cambridge University Press, 2010).

In the following twelve-syllable line, the first two syllables (Mark you) appear to be extra-metrical:

Mark you, your party in converse (him you would sound)

(2.1.41)

They might equally be printed on a separate line of text, as are other apparently extra-metrical interjections:

We'll make a solemn wager on your cunnings –
I ha't!
When in your motion you are hot and dry

(4.7.156–8)

Indeed, it must be noted that compositorial or editorial lineation is sometimes responsible for the creation of short or long lines. In the following example, for instance, 'Alack' could be lineated to form a shared pentameter with Hamlet's previous line, rendering both lines of regular length:

What thou hast said to me.
HAMLET
I must to England – you know that.
QUEEN
Alack, I had forgot; 'tis so concluded on.

(3.4.195–7)

Some short lines are the direct result of editorial relineation of a passage, and it should be noted that different editions may lineate in different ways.

This presence knows, and you must needs have heard,
How I am punished with a sore distraction.
What I have done

That might your nature, honour and exception
Roughly awake, I here proclaim was madness.

(5.2.218–22)

Whilst the lineation of this edition (and others) generates a
short line at 220, in the Folio the lines are printed thus:

This presence knowes,
And you must needs haue heard how I am punisht
With sore distraction? What I haue done
That might your nature honour, and exception
Roughly awake, I heere proclaime was madnesse:

And in Q2 thus:

But pardon't as you are a gentleman, this presence knowes,
And you must needs haue heard, how I am punnisht
With a sore distraction, what I haue done
That might your nature, honor, and exception
Roughly awake, I heare proclame was madnesse,

OTHER METRES

The basic metre of *Hamlet* is iambic pentameter. However,
songs and rhymes within the play are written in other metres.

Hamlet's rhyme sent to Ophelia (read aloud in 2.2.) is in
iambic trimeter – three iambic feet in each verse line. Hamlet
speaks a brief rhyme in 2.2 (401–2), which is in iambic tetrameter – four iambic feet in each verse line. Hamlet's rhymes in
his dialogue with Horatio in 3.2 (266–9 and 276–9) after the
play are in common metre – alternating lines of eight and six
syllables – and the Prologue to the play within the play is in
iambic tetrameter – four iambic feet in each verse line.

The metres of the songs are slightly more difficult to define,
and these have been variously set.

Ophelia's songs in 4.5 are in mixed metres. The first – 'How should I your true love know' – alternating lines of catalectic trochaic tetrameter (four trochees, with a missing final syllable) and catalectic trochaic trimeter (three trochees with a missing final syllable). The second – 'Tomorrow is St Valentine's Day' – is in common metre: alternating lines of eight and six syllables. The third – 'They bore him bare-faced on the bier' – begins in iambic tetrameter with a final line of five syllables. The metre of the final song, 'And will he not come again', is difficult to define.

The Gravedigger's songs in 5.1 are in common metre – alternating lines of eight and six.

YOU AND THOU

As in other plays, the use of 'you' and 'thou' helps to define character relationships at various points in the play. No more so, argues Penelope Freedman,[8] than in 1.2 when Claudius uses the distant 'you' form to address Hamlet, having just used the intimate 'thou' form to Laertes, and where Gertrude repeatedly uses 'thou' to her son, only to be met with 'yous' and the artificially formal 'Madam' in return.

Hamlet and the Ghost

The Ghost of Hamlet's father uses 'thou' to his son. Hamlet also uses 'thou' to the ghost, but this is common practice when addressing someone who is dead in Elizabethan drama.

Polonius, Laertes and Ophelia

The family of Polonius are less intimate in their use of pronouns. Laertes uses 'you' to Ophelia throughout his farewell

8 Penelope Freedman, *Power and Passion in Shakespeare's Pronouns* (Aldershot: Ashgate, 2007), 137.

speech in 1.3, as she does in return, and Polonius does the same. However, he uses 'thou' to Laertes when giving him instructions on his departure, possibly as a means of infantilizing him. Polonius continues to address Ophelia as 'you', except in 2.1 when she comes to him in distress.

Hamlet and Ophelia

In the 'nunnery scene' (3.1), Hamlet's use of personal pronouns to Ophelia is telling. Although Hamlet starts by addressing her as 'thou' – 'Nymph, in thy orisons . . .' – he then shifts to the more distant 'you' until 'Get thee to a nunnery', a shift which could either indicate greater vehemence or greater care and affection, a genuine concern for Ophelia. Particularly significant is the fact that the shift back to 'you' comes in the line 'Where's your father?' – a shift often deemed indicative of the fact that this is the moment at which Hamlet realizes that they are being observed. In their next exchange in 3.2 – a public exchange – he uses 'you' to her.

Hamlet and Gertrude

Although in 1.2 Gertrude uses 'thou' exclusively to Hamlet, whilst he uses 'you', in the closet scene there is greater variety in their terms of address. Whilst Hamlet uses 'you' throughout, Gertrude begins by using 'thou', but in frustration moves to 'you' – 'Have you forgot me?'. Thereafter her movements from 'thou' to 'you' and back may be considered significant in indicating the temperature of her relationship with Hamlet.

Gertrude and Claudius

Gertrude and Claudius mostly use 'you' to one another, but this is partly because most of their encounters take place in public.

HENDIADYS

Of all the rhetorical devices that Shakespeare uses, none is more intimately connected with *Hamlet* than hendiadys. Hendiadys can be defined as two words, connected by 'and', amounting to a single, often quite complex, idea. A relatively simple example is that of 'law and heraldry' (1.1.84), which translates as 'heraldic law'; others include 'leave and favour' (1.2.51), which can be translated as 'favourable leave', and 'voice and yielding' (1.3.23), which might translate as 'vocal consent'.

Hendiadys is used, according to George T. Wright, more than twice as often in *Hamlet* as in any other Shakespeare play. Since this figure can sometimes be quite difficult to decipher, we have noted instances and have aimed to supply single definitions.

KEY SOURCES

- Shakespeare's most obvious source for *Hamlet* is a story by Saxo Grammaticus, written in the twelfth century and printed in 1514 in *Historia Danica*. It tells of Amleth who seeks to avenge the murder of his father by his uncle Feng. The story was translated into French by François de Belleforest in his *Histoires Tragiques* (1572), probably Shakespeare's direct source.

- We know that an earlier play based on this story existed, since it is mentioned by Thomas Nashe in 1589: 'English Seneca read by candlelight yields many good sentences . . . and if you entreat him fair in a frosty morning, he will afford you whole *Hamlets*, I should say handfuls, of tragical speeches' (Introduction to Robert Greene's *Menaphon*). This play is widely considered to have been written by Thomas Kyd, but is no longer extant. It is known as the *Ur-Hamlet*.

- More details of these sources can be found in the Arden 3 *Hamlet*, edited by Ann Thompson and Neil Taylor.

KEY FIGURES OF CLASSICAL MYTHOLOGY

Aeneas (A-**knee**-us) (2.2.442) – Greek/Roman myth. One of the Trojan leaders in the Trojan War. Fell in love with Dido, Queen of Carthage.

Cyclops (**Sigh**-clopps) (2.2.485) – Greek myth. One eyed giants who made the armour of the gods.

Damon (3.2.276) – Greek myth. Damon offered himself as a hostage for his best friend, Pythias.

Dido (**Die**-do) (2.2.442) – Greek/Roman myth. Queen of Carthage. Fell in love with Aeneas.

Hecate (**Heh**-kate) (3.2.253) – Greek myth. Goddess of sorcery and witchcraft.

Hecuba (2.2.497) – Greek myth. Wife of King Priam of Troy, who was killed during the Trojan War.

Hercules – (**Her**-queue-**lees**) (1.2.153 and 5.1.284) – Roman myth. Greek hero. Son of Zeus. Famous for carrying out twelve Labours and for his strength and courage.

Hymen (3.2.154) – Greek myth. God of marriage.

Hyperion (High-**peer**-ion) (1.2.140 and 3.4.54) – Greek myth. God of the sun.

Jove (3.2.278 and 3.4.54) – Roman myth. Otherwise known as Jupiter. King of the gods and god of sky and thunder.

Mars (2.2.486 and 3.4.55) – Roman myth. God of war.

Mercury (3.4.56) – Roman myth. Winged messenger of the gods. Also god of eloquence, trading and thieving and conductor of departed souls to Hades and the afterlife.

Neptune (3.2.151) – Roman myth. God of the sea and fresh water.

Niobe (**Ny**-o-**bee**) (1.2.149) – Greek myth. Niobe's children were killed by Apollo and Artemis. She wept for them until she turned into a column of stone.

Phoebus (Phoebus Apollo) (1.1.151 and 3.2.150) – Greek myth. God of the light.

Priam (**Pry**-am) (2.2.443) – Greek myth. King of Troy at the time of the Trojan War. Husband of Hecuba. Killed by Pyrrhus.

Pyrrhus (**Pi**-rus) (2.2.446) – Greek myth. Son of Apollo. Killed King Priam during the Trojan War.

satyr (**sat**-ear) (1.2.140) – Greek/Roman myth. Half man and half goat or horse.

Tellus (3.2.151) – Roman myth. Goddess of the earth.

Vulcan (3.2.81) – Roman myth. God of fire and blacksmiths.

SUGGESTED FURTHER READING

For further detailed information about the play, we refer the reader to the Arden Third Series editions, which contain material on the text(s), sources, critical history and performance history:

Thompson, Ann and Taylor, Neil, eds. *Hamlet*. London: Bloomsbury Arden Shakespeare, 2006 (revised 2016).
Thompson, Ann and Taylor, Neil, eds. *Hamlet: The Texts of 1603 and 1623*. London: Bloomsbury Arden Shakespeare, 2006.

FURTHER READING

Bevington, David. *Murder Most Foul: Hamlet Through the Ages*. Oxford: Oxford University Press, 2011.
Dawson, Antony B. *Hamlet: Shakespeare in Performance*. Manchester: Manchester University Press, 1997.
Freedman, Penelope. *Power and Passion in Shakespeare's Pronouns: Interrogating 'you' and 'thou'*. Aldershot: Ashgate, 2007.
Hapgood, Robert. *Hamlet: Shakespeare in Production*. Cambridge: Cambridge University Press, 1999.
Irace, Kathleen O. 'Origins and Agents of Q1 *Hamlet*', in *The Hamlet First Published*, edited by Thomas Clayton. London: Associated University Press, 1992.
Rokison, Abigail. *Shakespearean Verse Speaking: Text and Theatre Practice*. Cambridge: Cambridge University Press, 2010.
Wright, George T. *Shakespeare's Metrical Art*. London: University of California Press, 1988.

DRAMATIS PERSONAE

HAMLET, Prince of Denmark

GHOST, of Hamlet's father, previous King of Denmark [Old Hamlet]

KING OF DENMARK (Claudius – although he is never referred to as such in the play), brother of the late King

QUEEN GERTRUDE, Hamlet's mother, married to King Claudius

POLONIUS, the Lord Chamberlain – Pron. Per-**low**-knee-**us**

LAERTES, son to Polonius – Pron. Lay-**er**-tees

OPHELIA, daughter to Polonius – Pron. O-**fee**-lia (equiv. 3 syl.) throughout; except at 4.5.154 where metre suggests O-**fee**-li-**a** (equiv. 4 syl.)

REYNALDO – servant to Polonius – Pron. Re-**nal**-do

HORATIO, friend to Hamlet – Pron. Ho-**ray**-shio (equiv. 3 syl.)

ROSENCRANTZ, school friend of Hamlet

GUILDENSTERN, school friend of Hamlet – Pron. **Gil**-den-**stern**

VOLTIMAND, Danish ambassador to Norway – Pron. **Vol**-ti-**mand**

Cornelius, Danish ambassador to Norway – Pron. Cor-**knee**-lius (equiv. 3 syl.)

BARNARDO – a sentinel

MARCELLUS – a sentinel – Pron. Mar-**sell**-us

FRANCISCO – a sentinel – Pron. Fran-**sis**-co

OSRIC, a courtier

Players – playing Prologue, Player King, Player Queen, Lucianus

Gravedigger (Clown 1)

Man (Clown 2)

A Priest

Lords, Gentlemen, Messengers, Followers of Laertes, Sailors

Fortinbras, Prince of Norway – Pron. **For**-tin-**brass**

A Captain, in the Norwegian army

English Ambassadors

HAMLET

1.1   *Enter* BARNARDO *and* FRANCISCO, *two sentinels.*

BARNARDO
Who's there?

FRANCISCO
Nay, answer me. Stand and unfold yourself.

BARNARDO
Long live the King.

FRANCISCO   Barnardo?

BARNARDO   He.

FRANCISCO
You come most carefully upon your hour.

BARNARDO
'Tis now struck twelve. Get thee to bed, Francisco.   5

FRANCISCO
For this relief much thanks. 'Tis bitter cold
And I am sick at heart.

BARNARDO
Have you had quiet guard?

FRANCISCO
Not a mouse stirring.

BARNARDO
Well, goodnight.   10
If you do meet Horatio and Marcellus,
The rivals of my watch, bid them make haste.

Metre – line is short by 8 syl.

unfold yourself – *tell me who you are*

Metre – shared line is short by 2 syl. (but has five heavy beats)

You ... hour – *You are very punctual* (or only just on time)

relief – *(from duty)*

Metre – ll. 7–10 have an ambiguous metrical connection (see SI).

Not ... stirring – Prov.

rivals – *partners*

Enter HORATIO and MARCELLUS.

FRANCISCO
I think I hear them. Stand ho, who is there?

HORATIO
Friends to this ground.

MARCELLUS   And liegemen to the Dane.

FRANCISCO   Give you goodnight.

MARCELLUS
O farewell, honest soldier; who hath reliev'd you?   15

FRANCISCO
Barnardo hath my place. Give you goodnight.   *Exit.*

MARCELLUS
Holla, Barnardo!

BARNARDO   Say, what, is Horatio there?

HORATIO   A piece of him.

BARNARDO
Welcome Horatio, welcome good Marcellus.

HORATIO
What, has this thing appear'd again tonight?

BARNARDO
I have seen nothing.   20

Q2 – Stand ho F – Stand; Q2 – who is F – who's

Metre – Ambiguous metrical connection (see Series Introduction)

liegemen . . . Dane – *sworn servants of the King of Denmark*

Give you – *May God give you*

hath re-**liev'd** (anapest – see 'A Note on Metre'); Q1/F – soldier Q2 – soldiers

Qq – hath F – ha's

Holla – *Hello*   Metre – Ambiguous metrical connection
                                   (see Series Introduction)

Q2 – SP – Horatio Q1/F –SP – Marcellus

Metre – line is short by 5 syl.

MARCELLUS
  Horatio says 'tis but our fantasy
  And will not let belief take hold of him
  Touching this dreaded sight twice seen of us.
  Therefore I have entreated him along
  With us to watch the minutes of this night   25
  That, if again this apparition come,
  He may approve our eyes and speak to it.

HORATIO
  Tush, tush, 'twill not appear.

BARNARDO   Sit down awhile,
  And let us once again assail your ears
  That are so fortified against our story   30
  What we have two nights seen.

HORATIO   Well, sit we down,
  And let us hear Barnardo speak of this.

BARNARDO
  Last night of all,
  When yond same star that's westward from the pole
  Had made his course t'illume that part of heaven   35
  Where now it burns, Marcellus and myself,
  The bell then beating one –

                    Enter GHOST.

MARCELLUS
  Peace, break thee off, look where it comes again.

BARNARDO
  In the same figure like the King that's dead.

fantasy – *imagination*
will . . . him – *will not allow himself to believe*
Touching – *concerning*; twice . . . us – *which we have seen twice*
entreated – *begged*; along – *to come along*
watch . . . night – *keep watch through the night*

approve our eyes – *confirm what we saw*

assail – *attack*
fortified against – *determined not to believe*
Qq – have two nights F – two nights have

Last . . . all – *Last night*   Metre – line is short by 6 syl.
yond same – *that same distant*; pole – *pole-star/northern star*
t'iilume – *to light up*

Metre – line is short by 4 syl.

same figure – *identical shape*

MARCELLUS
Thou art a scholar – speak to it, Horatio.   40

BARNARDO
Looks it not like the King? Mark it, Horatio.

HORATIO
Most like. It harrows me with fear and wonder.

BARNARDO
It would be spoke to.

MARCELLUS   Speak to it, Horatio.

HORATIO
What art thou that usurp'st this time of night
Together with that fair and warlike form   45
In which the majesty of buried Denmark
Did sometimes march? By heaven, I charge thee speak.

MARCELLUS
It is offended.

BARNARDO   See, it stalks away.

HORATIO
Stay, speak, speak, I charge thee speak.

MARCELLUS
'Tis gone and will not answer.   50

BARNARDO
How now, Horatio, you tremble and look pale.
Is not this something more than fantasy?
What think you on't?

Q1/F – it not Q2 – 'a not

harrows – *distresses*

Q2 – Speak to Q1/F – Question

usurp'st – *appropriates*
Together with – *along with*
majesty . . . Denmark – *dead king*
sometimes – *formerly*; charge – *order*

stalks – *moves in a stiff/stately way*

Line is short by 3 syl. (but has five heavy beats)

Metre – line is short by 3 syl.

–tio you **trem** (anapest – see 'A Note on Metre')

on't – *of it*

Metre – line is short by 6 syl.

HORATIO

    Before my God, I might not this believe
    Without the sensible and true avouch   55
    Of mine own eyes.

MARCELLUS   Is it not like the King?

HORATIO

    As thou art to thyself.
    Such was the very armour he had on
    When he the ambitious Norway combated.
    So frown'd he once, when in an angry parle   60
    He smote the sledded Polacks on the ice.
    'Tis strange.

MARCELLUS

    Thus twice before, and jump at this dead hour,
    With martial stalk hath he gone by our watch.

HORATIO

    In what particular thought to work, I know not,   65
    But in the gross and scope of mine opinion
    This bodes some strange eruption to our state.

MARCELLUS

    Good now, sit down, and tell me he that knows
    Why this same strict and most observant watch
    So nightly toils the subject of the land,   70
    And with such daily cost of brazen cannon
    And foreign mart for implements of war,
    Why such impress of shipwrights, whose sore task
    Does not divide the Sunday from the week.
    What might be toward that this sweaty haste   75

Before – *I swear before*
sensible and true avouch – *true testimony of the senses* (hendiadys – see Introduction)
Metre – Ambiguous metrical connection (see Series Introduction)

Norway – *King of Norway*   the am-**bi** (anapest); Qq – he the F – he th'
parle – *parley/argument*
sledded Polacks – *Poles, on sledges or leaded pole-axe* (weapon)
Metre – line is short by 8 syl.

jump – *precisely*; dead – *still*   Qq – jump F – just
martial stalk – *military walk*

In . . . work – *for what purpose/what conclusion to draw*   par-**tic**-ular (equiv. 3 syl.)
gross and scope – *full breadth* (hendiadys – see Introduction)   Q2 – mine Q1/F – my
bodes – *foretells*; eruption – *disruption*

Good – *Good friends*
watch – *vigilance*
toils – *entraps*; the subject – *the people*
brazen – *brass*   Q2 – with Q1/F – why; Qq – cost F – cast
foreign mart – *expenditure abroad*
impress – *forced labour*
Does . . . week – *(they work seven days a week)*
toward – *anticipated*   toward – Pron. – metre suggests emphasis on
1st syl. – **to**-ward

11

Doth make the night joint labourer with the day?
Who is't that can inform me?

HORATIO   That can I.
    At least the whisper goes so. Our last King,
Whose image even but now appear'd to us,
Was as you know by Fortinbras of Norway –   80
Thereto prick'd on by a most emulate pride –
Dar'd to the combat, in which our valiant Hamlet
(For so this side of our known world esteem'd him)
Did slay this Fortinbras, who by a seal'd compact
Well ratified by law and heraldry   85
Did forfeit with his life all these his lands
Which he stood seiz'd of to the conqueror;
Against the which a moiety competent
Was gagèd by our King, which had return'd
To the inheritance of Fortinbras   90
Had he been vanquisher, as by the same co-mart
And carriage of the article design
His fell to Hamlet. Now, sir, young Fortinbras,
Of unimprovèd mettle, hot and full,
Hath in the skirts of Norway here and there   95
Shark'd up a list of lawless resolutes
For food and diet to some enterprise
That hath a stomach in't, which is no other,
As it doth well appear unto our state,
But to recover of us by strong hand   100
And terms compulsatory those foresaid lands
So by his father lost. And this, I take it,
Is the main motive of our preparations,
The source of this our watch, and the chief head
Of this post-haste and rummage in the land.   105

la-bourer (equiv. 2 syl.)

whisper – *rumour*

even (equiv. 1 syl.)

Thereto ... pride – *prompted by an excess of pride*   em-ulate (equiv. 2 syl.)
the combat – *single combat*   -bat in **which** (anapest); **val**-iant (equiv 2 syl.)
this ... world – *all of Europe*
seal'd compact – *sworn agreement*   -tin-bras **who**; by a **seal'd** (anapests)
ratified – *sanctioned*; law and heraldry – *heraldic law* (hendiadys – see Introduction)
                    Q2 – these, Q1/F – those
stood ... of – *held/possessed*
moiety competent – *equivalent portion of land*   **moie**-ty (equiv. 2 syl.)
gagèd – *wagered*   F – return'd Q2 – return

co-mart – *agreement*   Irregular – quartus paeon/hexameter
carriage – *fulfilment*; article design – *stated terms*   Pope – articles design'd
          Can be scanned with '-let. Now **sir**' or 'sir, young **For** –' as anapests
unimprovèd mettle – *untried/untamed spirit*; hot and full – *full of anger*
skirts – *outskirts*
Shark'd up – *seized*; list – *group*; resolutes – *resolute men*   Qq – lawless F – landless

stomach – *appetite*
our state – *the Danish authorities*   Q2 – As F – And
of us – *from us*; strong hand – *force*
compulsatory (com-**pul**-sa-**tory**) – *compulsory*   Q2 – compulsatory F –
                    compulsative

head – *origin*
post-haste – *urgency*; rummage – *disturbance*

BARNARDO

[I think it be no other but e'en so.
Well may it sort that this portentous figure
Comes armèd through our watch so like the King
That was and is the question of these wars.

HORATIO

A mote it is to trouble the mind's eye.   110
In the most high and palmy state of Rome
A little ere the mightiest Julius fell
The graves stood tenantless and the sheeted dead
Did squeak and gibber in the Roman streets;
At stars with trains of fire and dews of blood,   115
Disasters in the sun; and the moist star
Upon whose influence Neptune's empire stands
Was sick almost to doomsday with eclipse.
And even the like precurse of fear'd events,
As harbingers preceding still the fates   120
And prologue to the omen coming on,
Have heaven and earth together demonstrated
Unto our climatures and countrymen.]

Enter GHOST.

But soft, behold, lo where it comes again;
I'll cross it though it blast me. Stay, illusion.   125

[He] spreads his arms.

If thou hast any sound or use of voice,
Speak to me.
If there be any good thing to be done
That may to thee do ease and grace to me,
Speak to me.   130

be – *is*; e'en – *even*   Lines 105–22 are not in F or Q1
sort – *fit*; portentous – *ominous*

question – *cause*

mote – *piece of grit/dust*
palmy – *flourishing*
ere – *before*; Julius – *Julius Caesar*   **migh**-tiest (equiv. 2 syl.); **Ju**-lius (equiv. 2 syl.)
sheeted – *clad in winding sheets*   **tenant**-less (equiv. 2 syl.)
gibber – *talk nonsense*
trains of fire – *comet-like tails*; dews – *spots*
Disasters – *portents of disaster*; the moist star – *the moon* (controller of the tides)
Neptune – *the Roman god of the sea*   **in**-fluence (equiv. 2 syl.)
almost to doomsday – *almost as if it were the end of the world*
the like – *similar*; precurse – *warning signs*   even (equiv. 1 syl.)
harbingers – *those who go before*; still – *always*; fates – *the three goddesses of destiny*
omen – *terrible event*
                                                       heaven (equiv.1 syl.)
climatures – *regions*

soft – *be quiet*; lo – *oh*
cross it – *cross its path*; blast – *destroy*

SD – it is not clear whether it is the Ghost or Horatio who performs this action

                                     Metre – line is short by 7 syl.

                                     Metre – line is short by 7 syl.

If thou art privy to thy country's fate
Which happily foreknowing may avoid,
O, speak.
Or if thou hast uphoarded in thy life
Extorted treasure in the womb of earth –   135
For which they say you spirits oft walk in death –
Speak of it, stay and speak.

The cock crows.
Stop it, Marcellus!

MARCELLUS
Shall I strike at it with my partisan?

HORATIO
Do, if it will not stand.

BARNARDO
'Tis here.   140

HORATIO
'Tis here.

[Exit Ghost.]

MARCELLUS
'Tis gone.
We do it wrong being so majestical
To offer it the show of violence,
For it is as the air, invulnerable,   145
And our vain blows malicious mockery.

BARNARDO
It was about to speak when the cock crew.

art privy to – *have private knowledge of*

happily – *perhaps/fortunately*; foreknowing – *advanced knowledge*

Metre – line is short by 8 syl.

uphoarded – *acumulated*

Extorted – *wrongfully obtained*

Q1/F – you Q2 – your; spirits (equiv. 1 syl.)

partisan – *long-handled spear*   F – at it Q2 – it

stand – *stay*   Metre – Lines 138–41 have an ambiguous metrical connection.

being so majestical – *given that it is a king*   being (equiv.1 syl.)

vi-o-**lence** (equiv. 3 syl.)

invulnerable – *incapable of being wounded*   in-**vul**-nera-**ble** (equiv. 4 syl.)

vain – *pointless*

HORATIO

And then it started like a guilty thing
Upon a fearful summons. I have heard
The cock that is the trumpet to the morn   150
Doth with his lofty and shrill-sounding throat
Awake the god of day and, at his warning,
Whether in sea or fire, in earth or air,
Th'extravagant and erring spirit hies
To his confine – and of the truth herein   155
This present object made probation.

MARCELLUS

It faded on the crowing of the cock.
Some say that ever 'gainst that season comes
Wherein our Saviour's birth is celebrated
This bird of dawning singeth all night long,   160
And then, they say, no spirit dare stir abroad,
The nights are wholesome, then no planets strike,
No fairy takes, nor witch hath power to charm,
So hallow'd and so gracious is that time.

HORATIO

So have I heard and do in part believe it.   165
But look, the morn in russet mantle clad
Walks o'er the dew of yon high eastward hill.
Break we our watch up and by my advice
Let us impart what we have seen tonight
Unto young Hamlet, for upon my life   170
This spirit dumb to us will speak to him.
Do you consent we shall acquaint him with it
As needful in our loves, fitting our duty?

MARCELLUS

Let's do't, I pray, and I this morning know
Where we shall find him most convenient.   *Exeunt.*

started – *moved suddenly*

trumpet – *herald*   Q2 – morn F – day
lofty – *high*
the god of day – *the sun god Phoebus Apollo* (see Myth)

extravagant and erring – *wandering out of bounds*; hies – *hurries*
confine – *proper home/place of confinement*; of . . . herein – *of the truth in this saying*
made probation – *is proof*   pro-**ba**-ti-**on** (equiv. 4 syl)

'gainst – *just before*; that season . . . celebrated – *late December*

This . . . dawning – *the cock*   Q2 – This Q1/F – The
abroad – *beyond its confine*   spirit (equiv.1 syl.); Q2 – dare stir F – can walk
strike – *cause destruction*
takes – *(possibly) takes a child leaving a changeling*   Qq – takes F – talks
hallow'd – *holy*   Qq – that F – the

in part – *partly*
russet mantle – *red cloak*
yon – *that*   Q2 – eastward F – eastern

consent – *agree that*
needful in our loves – *necessary because of the love we bear him*

convenient – *conveniently*   Q2 – convenient Q1/F – conveniently

1.2   *Flourish. Enter Claudius, Gertrude, Polonius, Laertes [and]*
     Hamlet, with others [including VOLTEMAND and CORNELIUS].

KING

Though yet of Hamlet our dear brother's death
The memory be green, and that it us befitted
To bear our hearts in grief, and our whole kingdom
To be contracted in one brow of woe,
Yet so far hath discretion fought with nature   5
That we with wisest sorrow think on him
Together with remembrance of ourselves.
Therefore our sometime sister, now our Queen,
Th'imperial jointress to this warlike state,
Have we, as 'twere with a defeated joy,   10
With an auspicious and a dropping eye,
With mirth in funeral and with dirge in marriage,
In equal scale weighing delight and dole,
Taken to wife. Nor have we herein barr'd
Your better wisdoms, which have freely gone   15
With this affair along. For all, our thanks.
Now follows that you know: young Fortinbras,
Holding a weak supposal of our worth
Or thinking by our late dear brother's death
Our state to be disjoint and out of frame –   20
Co-leaguèd with this dream of his advantage –
He hath not fail'd to pester us with message
Importing the surrender of those lands
Lost by his father with all bands of law
To our most valiant brother. So much for him.   25
Now for ourself, and for this time of meeting,
Thus much the business is: we have here writ
To Norway, uncle of young Fortinbras –
Who impotent and bedrid scarcely hears
Of this his nephew's purpose – to suppress   30

SD – In F, Ophelia is included in the entrance direction for this scene, although she does not speak.

SD – In F, Voltemand and Cornelius do not enter until after line 25.

green – *fresh*; us befitted – *would have been appropriate for us*   -ory be **green** (anapest – see 'A Note on Metre')

To . . . woe – *To be drawn together in a single expression of grieving* (personification)

discretion – *rational judgement*; nature – *natural feelings*

Together . . . of – *As well as remembering*   re-**mem**-brance (equiv. 3 syl.)

sometime – *former*, sister – *sister-in-law*   Q2 – sometime F – sometimes

jointress – *joint possessor*   Th'im-**per**-ial (equiv. 3 syl.); Q2 – to F – of

as 'twere . . . dole – *(parenthetical clause)*; defeated – *frustrated*

auspicious – *hopeful*; dropping – *downcast/tearful*   Q2 an . . . a F one . . . one **fu**-neral (equiv. 2 syl.)

In . . . dole – *Balancing joy and sorrow equally*

barr'd – *excluded*

you know – *which you know already/you need to know*   Punct. – Q2/F – no : after 'know'

Holding . . . worth – *supposing that our position is weak*

by – *because of*

disjoint – *fractured*; frame – *order*

Co-leaguèd with – *Reinforced by*; dream – *fantasy*   Q2 – this F – the

Importing – *Concerning*

bands – *binding agreements*   Q2 – bands F – bonds

-er. So **much** (anapest – see 'A Note on Metre')   SD – Corneilus and Voltemand enter here in F (after 'him')

Thus much – *This*

Norway – *the Norwegian King*

impotent – *incapable*

His further gait herein, in that the levies,
The lists and full proportions are all made
Out of his subject; and we here dispatch
You, good Cornelius, and you, Voltemand,
For bearers of this greeting to old Norway,   35
Giving to you no further personal power
To business with the King more than the scope
Of these delated articles allow.
Farewell, and let your haste commend your duty.

CORN., VOLT.
In that and all things will we show our duty.   40

KING
We doubt it nothing. Heartily farewell.

[Exeunt Voltemand and Cornelius.]

And now, Laertes, what's the news with you?
You told us of some suit – what is't, Laertes?
You cannot speak of reason to the Dane
And lose your voice. What wouldst thou beg, Laertes,   45
That shall not be my offer, not thy asking?
The head is not more native to the heart,
The hand more instrumental to the mouth,
Than is the throne of Denmark to thy father.
What wouldst thou have, Laertes?

LAERTES   My dread lord,   50
Your leave and favour to return to France,
From whence though willingly I came to Denmark
To show my duty in your coronation,
Yet now I must confess, that duty done,
My thoughts and wishes bend again toward France   55
And bow them to your gracious leave and pardon.

gait – *progress*; in that – *since*; levies – *costs*
lists – *enlistments*; full proportions – *forces*; made – *comprised*
his subject – *the subjects of the King of Norway*

For – *As*   Q2 – bearers F – bearing
                                              per-sonal (equiv. 2 syl.)

To business – *To negotiate*
delated – *committed*   Q2 – delated F – dilated
let . . . duty – *demonstrate your duty with your speed*

                    SP – F – this line is assigned to Voltemand alone

nothing – *not at all*

suit – *formal request*
speak of reason – *make a reasonable request*; the Dane – *the King of Denmark*
lose your voice – *not have your request granted/waste your words*
What . . . asking – *What would you ask that I wouldn't give before you requested it?*
native – *naturally connected*
instrumental – *useful*

dread – *respected*   Q2 – My dread F – Dread my
leave and favour – *favourable leave* (hendiadys – see Introduction)

in – *at*

                    toward (equiv. 1 syl.); Q2 – toward F – towards
bow them – *I submit my wishes*; leave – *permission*

KING

Have you your father's leave? What says Polonius?

POLONIUS

He hath, my lord, [wrung from me my slow leave
By laboursome petition, and at last
Upon his will I seal'd my hard consent.]   60
I do beseech you give him leave to go.

KING

Take thy fair hour, Laertes, time be thine
And thy best graces spend it at thy will.
But now, my cousin Hamlet, and my son –

HAMLET

A little more than kin, and less than kind.   65

KING

How is it that the clouds still hang on you?

HAMLET

Not so, my lord, I am too much in the 'son'.

QUEEN

Good Hamlet, cast thy nighted colour off
And let thine eye look like a friend on Denmark.
Do not for ever with thy vailèd lids   70
Seek for thy noble father in the dust.
Thou knowst 'tis common all that lives must die,
Passing through nature to eternity.

HAMLET

Ay, madam, it is common.

Lines 58.5 ('wrung from me') to 60 ('hard consent') are not in F

laboursome – *laborious*

will – *desire*; sealed – *gave*; hard – *reluctant*

fair hour – *opportunity whilst you are still young*; time be thine – *your time is your own*

And . . . will – *spend it according to your best qualities*

cousin – *kinsman*

kin – *a kinsman*   Prov. – 'The nearer in kin the less in kindness'

Note that Claudius uses 'you' to Hamlet in explicit contrast
to his use of 'thou' to Laertes (see Introduction)

in the 'son' – *(Pun on son/sun (favour))*   I am **too** (anapest – see 'A Note on Metre');

F – Not so Q2 – Not so much

nighted colour – *mourning clothes/melancholic behaviour*   Q2 – nighted F – nightly

Denmark – *the King/the country*

vailèd lids – *downcast eyes*

common – *usual*   Thou . . . eternity – Prov.; Q2/F – lives F2 – live

common – *commonplace/crude*

QUEEN   If it be
  Why seems it so particular with thee?   75

HAMLET
  'Seems', madam – nay it is, I know not 'seems'.
  'Tis not alone my inky cloak, good mother,
  Nor customary suits of solemn black,
  Nor windy suspiration of forc'd breath,
  No, nor the fruitful river in the eye,   80
  Nor the dejected haviour of the visage,
  Together with all forms, moods, shapes of grief,
  That can denote me truly. These indeed 'seem',
  For they are actions that a man might play,
  But I have that within which passes show,   85
  These but the trappings and the suits of woe.

KING
  'Tis sweet and commendable in your nature, Hamlet,
  To give these mourning duties to your father,
  But you must know your father lost a father,
  That father lost lost his, and the survivor bound   90
  In filial obligation for some term
  To do obsequious sorrow; but to persever
  In obstinate condolement is a course
  Of impious stubbornness, 'tis unmanly grief,
  It shows a will most incorrect to heaven,   95
  A heart unfortified, or mind impatient,
  An understanding simple and unschool'd;
  For what we know must be, and is as common
  As any the most vulgar thing to sense –
  Why should we in our peevish opposition   100
  Take it to heart? Fie, 'tis a fault to heaven,
  A fault against the dead, a fault to nature,
  To reason most absurd, whose common theme

particular – *personal*

good mother (*also alluding to step-mother*)   F – good mother Q2 – cold mother
customary suits – *conventional garments*
suspiration – *sighing*
fruitful – *copious*
dejected haviour – *downcast expression*; visage – *face*

                                                       Q2 – shapes F – shows
denote – *describe*   in-deed **seem** (anapest – see 'A Note on Metre')
might play – *could act*

                                                       Q2 – passes F – passeth

trappings – *superficial appearances*

and co-**mmen** (anapest – see A Note on Metre); co-**mmen**-dable (equiv. 3 syl.)

bound – *was obliged*   Irregular line – quartus paeon/as hexameter
filial – *sonly*   **fi**-lial (equiv. 2 syl.)
do . . . sorrow – *mourn as befits funeral ceremonies*   ob-**se**-quious (equiv. 3 syl.);
condolement – *grieving*   '–rrow but **to**' or 'to per-**sev**' (anapest)
impious – *irreligious*   **im**-pious (2 syl.); **stubborn**-ness (equiv. 2 syl.)
incorrect – *disobedient*
unfortified – *not strengthened*; impatient – *incapable of suffering*   Q2 – or F – a
simple – *childish*; unschool'd – *untaught*

As . . . sense – *As the most ordinary thing that can be conceived*
peevish – *foolish*

to nature – *against natural law*

Is death of fathers, and who still hath cried
From the first corpse till he that died today   105
'This must be so.' We pray you throw to earth
This unprevailing woe, and think of us
As of a father, for let the world take note
You are the most immediate to our throne,
And with no less nobility of love   110
Than that which dearest father bears his son
Do I impart toward you. For your intent
In going back to school in Wittenberg
It is most retrograde to our desire,
And we beseech you bend you to remain   115
Here in the cheer and comfort of our eye,
Our chiefest courtier, cousin, and our son.

QUEEN
Let not thy mother lose her prayers, Hamlet.
I pray thee stay with us, go not to Wittenberg.

HAMLET
I shall in all my best obey you, madam.   120

KING
Why, 'tis a loving and a fair reply.
Be as ourself in Denmark. Madam, come –
This gentle and unforc'd accord of Hamlet
Sits smiling to my heart, in grace whereof
No jocund health that Denmark drinks today   125
But the great cannon to the clouds shall tell
And the King's rouse the heaven shall bruit again,
Re-speaking earthly thunder. Come away.

Flourish. Exeunt all but Hamlet.

still – *always*

unprevailing – *ineffective*; us – *me* (royal plural)

                         Can be scanned with '-er for **let**' or 'let the **world**' anapests

You ... throne – *You are my heir*   i-**mme**-diate (equiv. 3 syl.)

nobility – *purity*

                              toward (equiv. 1 syl.); Q2 – toward F – towards

school – *university*; Wittenberg (Pron. **Vit**-en-**burg**) – *German city*

retrograde – *contrary*

bend you – *to incline yourself*

                                         pray-ers (equiv. 2 syl.)

                  Q2 – pray thee F – prithee; Metre – long line (12 syl.)

Be ... Denmark – *Behave as if you were king*

accord – *agreement*

Sits ... heart – *Makes me happy*; grace – *thanks*

jocund – *joyful*; Denmark – *the King of Denmark*

tell – *sound*

rouse – *ceremonial drinking*; bruit – *proclaim*   Q2 – heaven F – heavens (equiv. 1 syl.)

Re-speaking – *echoing*

soliloquy

HAMLET

    O that this too too sallied flesh would melt,
    Thaw and resolve itself into a dew,   130
    Or that the Everlasting had not fix'd
    His canon 'gainst self-slaughter. O God, God,
    How weary, stale, flat and unprofitable
    Seem to me all the uses of this world!
    Fie on't, ah, fie, 'tis an unweeded garden   135
    That grows to seed, things rank and gross in nature
    Possess it merely. That it should come to this:
    But two months dead – nay not so much, not two –
    So excellent a king, that was to this
    Hyperion to a satyr, so loving to my mother   140
    That he might not beteem the winds of heaven
    Visit her face too roughly. Heaven and earth,
    Must I remember? Why, she would hang on him
    As if increase of appetite had grown
    By what it fed on. And yet within a month   145
    (Let me not think on't – Frailty, thy name is Woman),
    A little month, or e'er those shoes were old
    With which she follow'd my poor father's body,
    Like Niobe, all tears. Why, she –
    O God, a beast that wants discourse of reason   150
    Would have mourn'd longer – married with my uncle,
    My father's brother (but no more like my father

dissolve   Than I to Hercules). Within a month,
    Ere yet the salt of most unrighteous tears
    Had left the flushing in her gallèd eyes,   155
    She married. O most wicked speed! To post
    With such dexterity to incestuous sheets,
    It is not, nor it cannot come to good;
    But break, my heart, for I must hold my tongue.

    Enter HORATIO, MARCELLUS and BARNARDO.

sallied – *besieged* Qq – sallied F – solid
resolve – *dissolve*

canon – *divine law* Q2 – O God, God F – God, O God!
un-**profit**-a-**ble** (equiv. 4 syl.)
uses – *customs* Q2 – Seem F – Seems
Fie – *(exclamation of disgust)* Q2 – ah fie F – oh, fie, fie
rank and gross – *coarsely vigorous in growth* (hendiadys – see Introduction)
merely – *completely* -ly, That **it** (anapest) F – to this Q2 – thus

to this – *compared to Claudius*
Hyperion ... satyr – (see Myth) Irregular line (14 syl.)
beteem – *allow*

Heaven (equiv. 1 syl.)
-ber? Why **she** (anapest – see 'A Note on Metre'); Q1/F – would Q2 – should
As ... fed on – *As if her desire for him has increased by being satisfied*
on. And **yet** (anapest – see 'A Note on Metre')
Frailty ... Woman – *Women personify frailty* (Prov.) –ty, thy **name** (anapest)
or e'er – *even before* Q2 – e'er F – ere

Niobe – (see Myth) Metre – line is short by 2 syl.; Q2 – she, F – she, even she
wants – *lacks*; discourse of reason – *the faculty of reasoning* Q2 – God F – Heaven
Q2 – my F – mine
-er (but **no** (anapest – see 'A Note on Metre')
Hercules – (see Myth)
Ere – *before*; unrighteous – *false/wicked*
flushing – *redness*; gallèd – *irritated/sore*
post – *move quickly*
dexterity – *skill*; incestuous – *for a man to marry his* dex-**teri**-ty (equiv. 3 sy.)
brother's wife might be perceived as incest

HORATIO
Hail to your lordship.

HAMLET   I am glad to see you well –   160
Horatio, or I do forget myself.

HORATIO
The same, my lord, and your poor servant ever.

HAMLET
Sir, my good friend, I'll change that name with you.
And what make you from Wittenberg, Horatio?
Marcellus!   165

MARCELLUS
My good lord.

HAMLET
I am very glad to see you. [*to Barnardo*] Good even, sir. –
But what in faith make you from Wittenberg?

HORATIO
A truant disposition, good my lord.

HAMLET
I would not hear your enemy say so,   170
Nor shall you do my ear that violence
To make it truster of your own report
Against yourself. I know you are no truant;
But what is your affair in Elsinore?
We'll teach you to drink deep ere you depart.   175

HORATIO
My lord, I came to see your father's funeral.

Irregular shared line – can be scanned with quartus paeon
(see 'A Note on Metre')

I'll . . . you – *You are my friend not my servant*
make you from – *are you doing away from*

Line is short by 7 syl.

Line is short by 7 syl.

I am **ver-**; you. Good **e-** (both anapests – see 'A Note on Metre')

in faith – *truly*

truant – *idle*

Q2 – hear F – have
Q2 – my F – mine; **vi**-o-**lence** (equiv. 3 syl.)

Pron. **El**-sin-**ore**
This line may be ironic since Hamlet deplores the heavy drinking culture
(1.4.13–38).   F – to drink deep Q2 – for to drink

fun-eral (equiv. 2 syl.)

33

HAMLET

    I prithee do not mock me, fellow student,

    I think it was to see my mother's wedding.

HORATIO

    Indeed, my lord, it follow'd hard upon.

HAMLET

    Thrift, thrift, Horatio, the funeral bak'd meats   180

    Did coldly furnish forth the marriage tables.

    Would I had met my dearest foe in heaven

    Or ever I had seen that day, Horatio.

    My father, methinks I see my father.

HORATIO

    Where, my lord?

HAMLET   In my mind's eye, Horatio.   185

HORATIO

    I saw him once – he was a goodly king.

HAMLET

    He was a man, take him for all in all,

    I shall not look upon his like again.

HORATIO

    My lord, I think I saw him yesternight.

HAMLET

    Saw, who?

HORATIO   My lord, the King your father.

Q2 – prithee F – pray thee

Thrift – *Economy*   –tio, the **fun-** (anapest – see 'A Note on Metre')

Did . . . tables – *The cold meats from the funeral were eaten at the wedding*

dearest – *most hated*

Or ever – *Before ever*   Q2 – Or ever I had F – Ere I had ever

        Metre – Irregular line (can be scanned with a syllable pause after 'father')

Q2 – Where F – Oh where; Metre – line is headless (see 'A Note on Metre')

Q1/F – he Q2 – 'a

He was a man – *(implies an ideal of manhood)*   Q1/F – He Q2 – 'A

yesternight – *last night*

Punct. – Qq – Saw, who? F – Saw? Who?

Metre – ambiguous metrical connection (see Series Introduction)

HAMLET   The King my father?   190

HORATIO
Season your admiration for a while
With an attent ear till I may deliver
Upon the witness of these gentlemen
This marvel to you.

HAMLET   For God's love let me hear!

HORATIO
Two nights together had these gentlemen,   195
Marcellus and Barnardo, on their watch
In the dead waste and middle of the night
Been thus encounter'd: a figure like your father
Armèd at point, exactly cap-à-pie,
Appears before them and with solemn march   200
Goes slow and stately by them; thrice he walk'd
By their oppress'd and fear-surprisèd eyes
Within his truncheon's length whilst they, distill'd
Almost to jelly with the act of fear,
Stand dumb and speak not to him. This to me   205
In dreadful secrecy impart they did,
And I with them the third night kept the watch
Where, as they had deliver'd, both in time,
Form of the thing, each word made true and good,
The apparition comes. I knew your father,   210
These hands are not more like.

HAMLET   But where was this?

MARCELLUS
My lord, upon the platform where we watch.

Season – *moderate*; admiration – *amazement*
attent – *attentive*

you. For **God**'s (anapest – see 'A Note on Metre')

Qq – God's F – Heaven's

dead waste and middle – *desolation of midnight* (hendiadys – see Introduction)
-ter'd a **fig-** (anapest – see 'A Note on Metre')
at point – *in readiness*; cap-à-pie – *from head to foot*   Q2 – Armèd at point
F – Arm'd at all points

slow – *slowly*
fear-surprisèd – *surprised by fear*
truncheon – *military staff*; distill'd – *dissolved*
act – *effect*

dreadful secrecy – *secrecy full of dread*

deliver'd – *reported*

These . . . like – *my hands are not more alike than the ghost was like your father*

platform – *battlements*; watch – *keep the watch*   Q2 – watch Q1/F – watch'd

HAMLET
  Did you not speak to it?

HORATIO   My lord, I did,
  But answer made it none. Yet once methought
  It lifted up it's head and did address   215
  Itself to motion like as it would speak.
  But even then the morning cock crew loud
  And at the sound it shrunk in haste away
  And vanish'd from our sight.

HAMLET   'Tis very strange.

HORATIO
  As I do live, my honour'd lord, 'tis true,   220
  And we did think it writ down in our duty
  To let you know of it.

HAMLET
  Indeed, indeed sirs, but this troubles me.
  Hold you the watch tonight?

HORATIO, MARCELLUS, BARNARDO
  We do, my lord.   225

HAMLET
  Arm'd, say you?

HORATIO, MARCELLUS, BARNARDO
  Arm'd, my lord.

HAMLET
  From top to toe?

methought – *I thought*
address . . . motion – *begin to move*   Q4 – it's Q2/F – it (old fashioned form)
like as – *as if*

writ down – *prescribed*

Metre – line is short by 4 syl.

Q1/F – Indeed, indeed Q2 – Indeed
Metre – There is an ambiguous metrical connection between lines 224 to 230
(see Series Introduction).

HORATIO, MARCELLUS, BARNARDO
My lord, from head to foot.

HAMLET
Then saw you not his face.   230

HORATIO
O yes, my lord, he wore his beaver up.

HAMLET
What look'd he – frowningly?

HORATIO
A countenance more in sorrow than in anger.

HAMLET
Pale, or red?

HORATIO
Nay, very pale.   235

HAMLET
And fix'd his eyes upon you?

HORATIO
Most constantly.

HAMLET
I would I had been there.

HORATIO
It would have much amaz'd you.

HAMLET
Very like. Stay'd it long?   240

Punct. – Q2 – face. (statement), F – face? (question)

beaver – *visor*

What – *how*   Metre – this line is short by 4 syl.
                         Punct. Q2 – What looked he F – What, looked he

countenance – *expression*   **coun**-tenance (equiv. 2 syl.)

Metre – There is an ambiguous metrical connection between
lines 234 to 240 (see Series Introduction).

would – *wish*

Very like – *perhaps/possibly*   Q2 – Very like Q1/F – Very like, very like

HORATIO
While one with moderate haste might tell a hundred.

MARCELLUS, BARNARDO
Longer, longer.

HORATIO   Not when I saw't.

HAMLET   His beard was grizzl'd, no?

HORATIO
It was as I have seen it in his life:
A sable silver'd.

HAMLET   I will watch tonight.
Perchance 'twill walk again.

HORATIO   I warrant it will.   245

HAMLET
If it assume my noble father's person
I'll speak to it, though hell itself should gape
And bid me hold my peace. I pray you all,
If you have hitherto conceal'd this sight
Let it be tenable in your silence still   250
And whatsomever else shall hap tonight
Give it an understanding but no tongue,
I will requite your loves. So, fare you well.
Upon the platform 'twixt eleven and twelve
I'll visit you.

HORATIO, MARCELLUS, BARNARDO
                Our duty to your honour.   255

tell – *count to*   **mod**-erate (equiv. 2 syl.)

Metre – Ambiguous metrical connection (see Series Introduction)

grizzl'd – *grey*   Q2 – grizzl'd F – grizzly

A sable-silver'd – *a mixture of black and silver*

Qq – I will F – I'll
Qq – walk F – wake

warrant – *guarantee*   Qq – warrant F – warrant you; warrant (equiv. 1 syl.)

assume . . . person – *take on the form of my father*
gape – *open its mouth*
hold my peace – *be silent*
hitherto – *up until now*
tenable – *able to be held*   **ten**-able (equiv. 2 syl.); Q2 – tenable F – treble
whatsomever – *whatever*; hap – *happen*   Q2 – whatsomever Q1/F – whatsoever
no tongue – *do not speak of it*
requite – *reward/repay*   Qq – you F – ye
'twixt – *between*   e-**leven** (equiv. 2 syl.)

HAMLET
Your loves, as mine to you, farewell.

Exeunt [all but Hamlet].

My father's spirit – in arms! All is not well;
I doubt some foul play. Would the night were come.
Till then sit still my soul – foul deeds will rise
Though all the earth o'erwhelm them to men's eyes.   260

Exit.

1.3 *Enter LAERTES and OPHELIA his sister.*

LAERTES
My necessaries are embark'd; farewell.
And sister, as the winds give benefit
And convey is assistant, do not sleep
But let me hear from you.

OPHELIA   Do you doubt that?

LAERTES
For Hamlet and the trifling of his favour,   5
Hold it a fashion and a toy in blood,
A violet in the youth of primy nature,
Forward, not permanent, sweet, not lasting,
The perfume and suppliance of a minute,
No more.

OPHELIA   No more but so.

LAERTES   Think it no more.   10
For nature crescent does not grow alone

loves – *(contradicting them by invoking their love, not duty)*   Qq – loves F – love;

Metre – line 256 is short by 2 syl.

spirit (equiv. 1 syl.)

doubt – *fear* (since the word now means the opposite to modern ears, a number of

rise – *be revealed*   productions alter to 'fear')

Though . . . eyes – *Though all the earth attempt to conceal them.*

necessaries – *luggage*; embark'd – *on board the ship*

as – *whenever*

convey is assistant – *means of conveyance is available*

But let – *Without letting*

For – *Regarding*; trifling . . . favour – *his playful attention towards you*   F – favours

Hold – *Consider*; fashion and a toy in blood – *passing fancy of feeling* (hendiadys)

primy – *in its prime*

Forward – *premature*   Q2 – Forward F – Froward

perfume and suppliance – *supplying scent* (hendiadys – see Introduction)

but so – *than that*

crescent – *growing*

In thews and bulks, but as this temple waxes
The inward service of the mind and soul
Grows wide withal. Perhaps he loves you now,
And now no soil nor cautel doth besmirch   15
The virtue of his will; but you must fear,
His greatness weigh'd, his will is not his own.
[For he himself is subject to his birth]
He may not, as unvalu'd persons do,
Carve for himself, for on his choice depends   20
The sanctity and health of this whole state,
And therefore must his choice be circumscrib'd
Unto the voice and yielding of that body
Whereof he is the head. Then if he says he loves you
It fits your wisdom so far to believe it   25
As he in his particular act and place
May give his saying deed, which is no further
Than the main voice of Denmark goes withal.
Then weigh what loss your honour may sustain
If with too credent ear you list his songs   30
Or lose your heart, or your chaste treasure open
To his unmaster'd importunity.
Fear it, Ophelia, fear it, my dear sister,
And keep you in the rear of your affection
Out of the shot and danger of desire.   35
The chariest maid is prodigal enough
If she unmask her beauty to the moon.
Virtue itself scapes not calumnious strokes.
The canker galls the infants of the spring
Too oft before their buttons be disclos'd,   40
And in the morn and liquid dew of youth
Contagious blastments are most imminent.
Be wary then: best safety lies in fear,
Youth to itself rebels, though none else near.

thews and bulks – *physical size* (hendiadys); temple waxes – *body grows*   Q2 – this
inward service – *inner life*   F – his
withal – *also*
soil nor cautel – *deceptive stain* (hendiadys – see Introduction); besmirch – *deface*
virtue – *sincerity*; will – *intentions*
His greatness weigh'd – *When you consider his high position*

Line 18 is only in F.

unvalu'd – *ordinary*
Carve for himself – *Make his own choices*
sanctity – *holiness*   F – sanctity Q2 – safety; Q2 – this F – the
circumscrib'd – *limited*
Unto – *By*; voice and yielding – *vocal consent* (hendiadys); body – *people*

Irregular line – can be scanned with quartus paeon/as hexameter

It . . . it – *It is wise to believe it only so far*
act and place – *role and situation*   Q2 – particular act and place F – peculiar sect and
give . . . deed – *act on his words*   force; par-**ti**-cular (equiv. 3 syl.)
Than . . . withal – *than the collective agreement of the country*
weigh – *consider*
credent – *trusting*; list – *listen to*
chaste treasure – *treasure of your chastity*
unmaster'd importunity – *undisciplined persistence*

keep . . . affection – *be restrained in spite of your feelings*   Q2 – you in F – within
shot and danger – *dangerous aim* (hendiadys – see Introduction)
chariest – *most cautious* (Pron. **chair**-iest); prodigal – *extravagant*
moon – *(symbol of chastity) (Elizabethan women masked their faces from the sun)*
scapes – *escapes*; calumnious – *slanderous*   ca-**lum**-nious (equiv. 3 syl.)
canker – *cankerworm*; galls the infants – *damages the buds/young flowers*
oft – *often*; buttons be disclos'd – *buds are open*   Q2 – their F – the
morn and liquid dew – *morning freshness* (hendiadys – see Introduction)
Contagious blastments – *Infectious blights*; imminent – *immediately threatening*

Youth . . . near – *young people are naturally rebellious*

OPHELIA

    I shall th' effect of this good lesson keep   45
    As watchman to my heart. But, good my brother,
    Do not as some ungracious pastors do
    Show me the steep and thorny way to heaven
    Whilst like a puff'd and reckless libertine,
    Himself the primrose path of dalliance treads   50
    And recks not his own rede.

LAERTES   O fear me not.
    I stay too long.

Enter POLONIUS.

           But here my father comes.
    A double blessing is a double grace:
    Occasion smiles upon a second leave.

POLONIUS

    Yet here, Laertes? Aboard, aboard for shame!   55
    The wind sits in the shoulder of your sail
    And you are stay'd for. There, my blessing with thee,
    And these few precepts in thy memory
    Look thou character: give thy thoughts no tongue
    Nor any unproportion'd thought his act.   60
    Be thou familiar but by no means vulgar;
    Those friends thou hast, and their adoption tried,
    Grapple them unto thy soul with hoops of steel,
    But do not dull thy palm with entertainment
    Of each new-hatch'd, unfledg'd courage. Beware   65
    Of entrance to a quarrel but, being in,
    Bear't that th'oppos'd may beware of thee.
    Give every man thy ear but few thy voice;
    Take each man's censure but reserve thy judgement.

effect – *meaning*   F – th'effect Q2 – the effect
watchman … heart – *guardian of my affections*
ungracious pastors – *irreligious priests*

puff'd – *bloated*; libertine – *licentious man*   F – Whilst like Q2 – Whiles
primrose … dalliance – *flower-strewn path of pleasure*
recks … rede – *ignores his own teaching*

fear me not – *don't worry about me*

Occasion … leave – *Fortune permits us a second farewell*

Yet – *Still*
The wind … sail – *You have a following wind*
stay'd for – *awaited*   Qq – thee F – you
precepts – *rules of conduct*
character – *write*; give … tongue – *don't speak your mind*   Q2 – Look F – See
Nor … act – *Do not act on an undeveloped thought*
familiar – *friendly*; vulgar – *promiscuous*   fa-**mi**-liar (equiv. 3 syl.)
adoption tried – *suitability as friends proven*   Qq – Those F – The
Grapple – *Fasten*   Grapple (equiv. 1 syl.); Q2 – unto, Q1/F – to
dull thy palm – *callous your hand*; entertainment – *greeting* (by shaking hands)
new … courage – *new, untried fellow*   F – unhatch'd; Qq – courage F – comrade
                                                                 quarrel (equiv. 1 syl.)
Bear't that – *manage it so that*; th'oppos'd – *your opponent*
                                                                 Q2 – thy ear F – thine ear
censure – *opinion*

Costly thy habit as thy purse can buy   70
But not express'd in fancy – rich, not gaudy;
For the apparel oft proclaims the man
And they in France of the best rank and station
Are of all most select and generous chief in that.
Neither a borrower nor a lender be,   75
For loan oft loses both itself and friend
And borrowing dulls the edge of husbandry.
This above all, to thine own self be true
And it must follow as the night the day
Thou canst not then be false to any man.   80
Farewell, my blessing season this in thee.

LAERTES
Most humbly do I take my leave, my lord.

POLONIUS
The time invites you. Go, your servants tend.

LAERTES
Farewell, Ophelia, and remember well
What I have said to you.

OPHELIA   'Tis in my memory lock'd   85
And you yourself shall keep the key of it.

LAERTES
Farewell.   *Exit.*

POLONIUS
What is't, Ophelia, he hath said to you?

OPHELIA
So please you, something touching the Lord Hamlet.

habit – *dress*

fancy – *frivolous fashion*; rich – *expensive*; gaudy – *ostentatious*

the ... man – *a man's clothes often indicates his true nature*

Are of **all**; most sel-**ect** (anapests); **gen**-erous

select ... chief – *distinguished* (equiv. 2 syl.)

bo-rrower (equiv. 2 syl.); F – be Q2 – boy

For ... friend – *You often lose the loan and the friend you lent it to*

husbandry – *good household management*   **bo**-rrowing (equiv. 2 syl.); F – dulls the

edge Q2 – dulleth th'edge

as ... day – *as day follows night*

season – *mature*; this – *my advice*

tend – *are waiting*   F – invites Q2 – invests

Irregular shared line – Can be scanned with quartus paeon/as
hexameter (see 'A Note on Metre')

Metre – line is short by 8 syl.

touching – *concerning*

POLONIUS
Marry, well bethought.   90
'Tis told me he hath very oft of late
Given private time to you, and you yourself
Have of your audience been most free and bounteous.
If it be so – as so 'tis put on me,
And that in way of caution – I must tell you   95
You do not understand yourself so clearly
As it behoves my daughter and your honour.
What is between you? Give me up the truth.

OPHELIA
He hath, my lord, of late made many tenders
Of his affection to me.   100

POLONIUS
Affection? Pooh, you speak like a green girl
Unsifted in such perilous circumstance.
Do you believe his 'tenders', as you call them?

OPHELIA
I do not know, my lord, what I should think.

POLONIUS
Marry, I will teach you; think yourself a baby   105
That you have ta'en these tenders for true pay
Which are not sterling. Tender yourself more dearly
Or – not to crack the wind of the poor phrase,
Wronging it thus – you'll tender me a fool.

OPHELIA
My lord, he hath importun'd me with love   110
In honourable fashion.

Marry – *By the Virgin Mary*; bethought – *thought of*   Metre – line is short by 5 syl.
oft – *often*; of late – *recently*

                                                    Given (equiv. 1 syl.)

audience – *attention*; bounteous – *generous*   **au**-dience (equiv. 2 syl.)
put on me – *suggested to me*
And that . . . caution – *as a means of warning*
yourself – *your position*
behoves – *is appropriate for*; honour – *reputation*
Give me up – *Tell me*

tenders – *offers*
affection – *passion*   Metre – line is short by 3 syl.

green – *innocent*
Unsifted – *Inexperienced*; perilous (**pe**-rilous) circumstance – *dangerous matters*

                                Marry (equiv. 1 syl.); Q2 – I will F – I'll
ta'en – *taken*   ta'en (equiv. 1 syl.); Q2 – these F – his
sterling – *genuine currency*; Tender (equiv. 1 syl.) – *protect/value*; dearly – *carefully/costly*
crack . . . phrase – *ruin the phrase with overworking*
                         Pope – Wronging Collier – Running Theobald – Wringing

importun'd me – *persistently solicited*   Pron. im-**por**-tun'd
fashion – *manner*   Metre – line is short by 3 syl.

POLONIUS

Ay, 'fashion' you may call it. Go to, go to.

OPHELIA

And hath given countenance to his speech, my lord,
With almost all the holy vows of heaven.

POLONIUS

Ay, springes to catch woodcocks – I do know   115
When the blood burns how prodigal the soul
Lends the tongue vows. These blazes, daughter,
Giving more light than heat, extinct in both
Even in their promise as it is a-making,
You must not take for fire. From this time   120
Be something scanter of your maiden presence;
Set your entreatments at a higher rate
Than a command to parley. For Lord Hamlet,
Believe so much in him that he is young
And with a larger tether may he walk   125
Than may be given you. In few, Ophelia,
Do not believe his vows, for they are brokers
Not of that dye which their investments show
But mere implorators of unholy suits
Breathing like sanctified and pious bonds   130
The better to beguile. This is for all;
I would not in plain terms from this time forth
Have you so slander any moment leisure
As to give words or talk with the Lord Hamlet.
Look to't, I charge you. Come your ways.   135

OPHELIA

I shall obey, my lord.   *Exeunt.*

fashion – *passing fancy*; Go to (*dismissive expression*)   it. Go **to** (anapest)

countenance (**count**-enance) – *support*   And hath **giv**- (anapest)

springes (rhymes with hinges) – *traps*; woodcocks – *birds thought easy to catch*
When ... burns – *When sexual desire is aroused*; prodigal – *lavishly*
blazes – *flashes of rhetoric*   Irregular line (short by 1 syl.); Q2 – Lends F – Gives
extinct ... making – *the promise of light and heat vanishes as soon as it is made*
                                                                Even (equiv. 1 syl.)
fi-re (equiv. 2 syl.); Q2 – From F – For; Q2 – time F – time Daughter
something scanter – *somewhat more sparing*   Q2 – something F – somewhat
Set ... parley – *Don't let him see you whenever he wants to*
                                                       F – parley Q2 – parle
in – *of*
larger – *longer*; tether – *rope*
In few – *In brief*
brokers – *go-betweens*
dye – *colour*; investments – *garments*
implorators – *solicitors*; unholy suits – *wicked requests*   im-**ploro**-tors (equiv. 3 syl.)
Breathing – *Speaking*   Q2/F – bonds Theobald – bawds
beguile – *deceive*; This is for all – *This is the only time I will say this*
forth – *forward*
slander – *abuse*; moment leisure – *moment's leisure*   Q2/F – moment, Q3 – moment's
words – *written words*
Look to't – *pay attention to this*; Come your ways – *Come away*   Metre – line
                                                                is short by 2 syl.

                                          Metre – line is short by 4 syl.

1.4 *Enter HAMLET, HORATIO and MARCELLUS.*

HAMLET
The air bites shrewdly; it is very cold.

HORATIO
It is a nipping, and an eager air.

HAMLET
What hour now?

HORATIO   I think it lacks of twelve.

MARCELLUS   No, it is struck.

HORATIO
Indeed, I heard it not. It then draws near the season
Wherein the spirit held his wont to walk.   5

A flourish of trumpets and two pieces goes off.

What does this mean, my lord?

HAMLET
The King doth wake tonight and takes his rouse,
Keeps wassail and the swaggering upspring reels,
And as he drains his draughts of Rhenish down
The kettledrum and trumpet thus bray out   10
The triumph of his pledge.

HORATIO   Is it a custom?

HAMLET   Ay, marry is't,
But to my mind, though I am native here

shrewdly – *bitterly*

eager – *sharp* F – a nipping Q2 – nipping

ho-ur (equiv. 2 syl.) Metre – Ambiguous metrical connection
(see Series Introduction)
lacks of – *is just before*

season – *time* Irregular – Can be scanned with quartus paeon/as hexameter;
held his wont – *was accustomed to* Q2 – It then F – Then it

Metre – line is short by 4 syl.

wake – *stay up late*; takes his rouse – *drinks deeply*
Keeps wassail – *drinks many toasts*; the . . . reels – *dances wildly* **swagg**-ering
draughts – *quantities*; Rhenish – *wine from Rhine region of Germany* (equiv. 2 syl.)
bray out – *loudly announce*
triumph – *success*; pledge – *toast* Metre – Ambiguous metrical connection
(see Series Introduction)

marry – *by Mary* (mild oath)

Q2 – But F – And

And to the manner born, it is a custom
More honour'd in the breach than the observance.
[This heavy-headed revel east and west   15
Makes us traduc'd and tax'd of other nations:
They clepe us drunkards and with swinish phrase
Soil our addition, and indeed it takes
From our achievements, though perform'd at height,
The pith and marrow of our attribute.   20
So oft it chances in particular men
That, for some vicious mole of nature in them,
As in their birth wherein they are not guilty
(Since nature cannot choose his origin),
By their o'ergrowth of some complexion   25
Oft breaking down the pales and forts of reason,
Or by some habit that too much o'erleavens
The form of plausive manners – that these men,
Carrying, I say, the stamp of one defect
(Being Nature's livery or Fortune's star),   30
His virtues else, be they as pure as grace,
As infinite as man may undergo,
Shall in the general censure take corruption
From that particular fault: the dram of eale
Doth all the noble substance of a doubt   35
To his own scandal –]

Enter GHOST.

HORATIO   Look, my lord, it comes.

HAMLET
Angels and ministers of grace defend us!
Be thou a spirit of health or goblin damn'd,
Bring with thee airs from heaven or blasts from hell,
Be thy intents wicked or charitable,   40

To ... born – *accustomed to this tradition from birth*
breach – *breaking*; observance – *observing*
heavy-handed revel – *drunken revelling*   Lines 15 to 36 are not in Q1/F.
traduc'd – *slandered*; tax'd – *blamed*; of – *by*
clepe – *call*; swinish (pron. **swine**-ish) phrase – *calling us pigs*
Soil our addition – *mar our reputation*; takes – *takes away*
perform'd at height – *they may be outstanding*
pith – *essence*; marrow – *core*; attribute – *good name*
So oft – *As often*; chances – *happens*; particular – *certain*   par-**tic**-ular (equiv. 3 syl.)
vicious mole of nature – *natural blemish*
As – *For example*; in– *caused by*
his – *its*
By ... complexion (com-**plex**-i-**on**) – *overbalance of one humour*
Oft – *Often*; pales and forts – *defences*
too much o'erleavens – *ruins* (as an excess of yeast)
plausive – *pleasing*
stamp – *mark*   **Carry**-ing (equiv.2 syl.)
Nature's livery – *a congenital defect*; star – *blemish*   Being (equiv. 1 syl.)
else – *otherwise*; be they – *even if they are*
undergo – *enjoy*
general censure – *public opinion*; take corruption – *become corrupted*
From – *Because of*; dram – *tiny amount*; eale – *evil*   par-**tic**-ular (equiv. 3 syl.)
Doth ... scandal – *Brings him into disrepute*

Angels ... grace – *Angels who minister grace* (hendiadys – see note)
spirit of health – *good spirit*; goblin – *demon*   spirit (equiv. 1 syl.)
                                                           heaven (equiv. 1 syl.)
intents – *intentions*   Qq – intents F – events; **charit**-a-**ble** (equiv. 3 syl.)

Thou com'st in such a questionable shape
That I will speak to thee. I'll call thee Hamlet,
King, father, royal Dane. O answer me,
Let me not burst in ignorance but tell
Why thy canoniz'd bones hearsèd in death   45
Have burst their cerements, why the sepulchre
Wherein we saw thee quietly interr'd
Hath op'd his ponderous and marble jaws
To cast thee up again. What may this mean
That thou, dead corpse, again in complete steel,   50
Revisits thus the glimpses of the moon,
Making night hideous, and we fools of nature
So horridly to shake our disposition
With thoughts beyond the reaches of our souls?
Say why is this? Wherefore? What should we do?   55

[Ghost] beckons.

HORATIO
It beckons you to go away with it
As if it some impartment did desire
To you alone.

MARCELLUS   Look with what courteous action
It waves you to a more removèd ground,
But do not go with it.

HORATIO   No, by no means.   60

HAMLET
It will not speak: then I will follow it.

HORATIO
Do not, my lord.

questionable – *inviting questions*

Qq – O F – Oh, oh

in – *with*

canoniz'd (can-**on**-iz'd) – *consecreated*; hearsèd – *enclosed in a coffin*

cerements – *grave-clothes*; sepulchre – *tomb*   **cere**-ments (equiv. 2 syl)

interr'd – *buried*   **qui**-et-**ly** (equiv. 3 syl.); Q2 – interr'd F – enurn'd

op'd – *opened*; ponderous and marble – *heavy* (because made of marble) (hendiadys)

in complete steel – *dressed in full armour*

glimpses – *pale gleams*

we . . . nature – *making us weak mortals*   **hi**-deous (equiv. 2 syl.)

disposition – *composure*

reaches – *capacities*

Wherefore – *For what?*

impartment – *communication*

cour-teous (equiv. 2 syl.)

waves – *beckons*; removèd – *secluded*   Qq – waves F – wafts

Q2 – I will Q1/F – will I

HAMLET   Why, what should be the fear?
I do not set my life at a pin's fee,
And for my soul – what can it do to that,
Being a thing immortal as itself?   65
It waves me forth again. I'll follow it.

HORATIO
What if it tempt you toward the flood, my lord,
Or to the dreadful summit of the cliff
That beetles o'er his base into the sea,
And there assume some other horrible form   70
Which might deprive your sovereignty of reason
And draw you into madness? Think of it:
[The very place puts toys of desperation
Without more motive into every brain
That looks so many fathoms to the sea   75
And hears it roar beneath.]

HAMLET
It waves me still. Go on, I'll follow thee.

MARCELLUS
You shall not go, my lord.

HAMLET   Hold off your hands.

HORATIO
Be rul'd, you shall not go.

HAMLET   My fate cries out
And makes each petty artery in this body   80
As hardy as the Nemean lion's nerve.
Still am I call'd – unhand me, gentlemen –
By heaven I'll make a ghost of him that lets me!
I say away! – Go on! I'll follow thee.

what . . . fear – *what is there to fear?*
set – *value*; a pin's fee – *the worth of a pin*

flood – *sea*   toward (equiv. 1 syl.)

beetles o'er – *overhangs*; his – *its*
                                    Qq – assume F – assumes; **horri**-ble (equiv. 2 syl.)
your . . . reason – *you of the supremacy of reason/your highness of reason*   **sov**-ereign-**ty**
                                                                      (equiv. 3 syl.)
toys of desperation – *thoughts of despair/suicide*   Lines 73–6 are not in Q1/F.

fathoms – *nautical measures of around six feet*
                                    Metre – line is short by 4 syl.

Q2 – hands F – hand

My . . . out – *My destiny calls*
each petty – *every insignificant*   **ar**-tery (equiv. 2 syl.)
Nemean (**Ne**-meean) lion – *a supposedly invulnerable beast killed by Hercules*
call'd – *summoned*; unhand me – *let go of me*
make a ghost – *kill*; lets – *stops* (often changed in performance)   heaven (equiv. 1 syl.)

Exeunt Ghost and Hamlet.

HORATIO
He waxes desperate with imagination.   85

MARCELLUS
Let's follow. 'Tis not fit thus to obey him.

HORATIO
Have after. To what issue will this come?

MARCELLUS
Something is rotten in the state of Denmark.

HORATIO
Heaven will direct it.

MARCELLUS   Nay, let's follow him.

Exeunt.

1.5 *Enter GHOST and HAMLET.*

HAMLET
Whither wilt thou lead me? Speak! I'll go no further.

GHOST
Mark me.

HAMLET   I will.

GHOST   My hour is almost come
When I to sulphurous and tormenting flames
Must render up myself.

waxes – *grows*   **des**-perate (equiv. 2 syl.)

fit – *appropriate*

Have after – *Let's go after him*; issue – *outcome*

state – *kingdom*

it – *the outcome*   Heaven (equiv.1 syl.)

Whither – *Where*   Qq – Whither F – Where; Whither (equiv. 1 syl.)

Mark – *Listen to*

My . . . come – *It is nearly dawn*
sulphurous (**sul**-phurous) and tormenting – *painfully sulphurous* (hendiadys)
render – *give*

HAMLET   Alas, poor ghost.

GHOST
Pity me not, but lend thy serious hearing   5
To what I shall unfold.

HAMLET   Speak, I am bound to hear.

GHOST
So art thou to revenge when thou shalt hear.

HAMLET
What?

GHOST
I am thy father's spirit,
Doom'd for a certain term to walk the night   10
And for the day confin'd to fast in fires
Till the foul crimes done in my days of nature
Are burnt and purg'd away. But that I am forbid
To tell the secrets of my prison-house
I could a tale unfold whose lightest word   15
Would harrow up thy soul, freeze thy young blood,
Make thy two eyes like stars start from their spheres,
Thy knotted and combinèd locks to part
And each particular hair to stand on end
Like quills upon the fearful porpentine –   20
But this eternal blazon must not be
To ears of flesh and blood. List, list, O list,
If thou didst ever thy dear father love –

HAMLET
O God!

ser-ious (equiv. 2 syl.)

Irregular shared line – can be scanned with quartus paeon/as hexameter (see 'A Note on Metre')

bound – *committed*

Metre – this line is short by 9 syl.

Metre – this line is short by 3 syl.

walk the night – *walk throughout the night*

days of nature – *natural life*
burnt and purg'd – *purged with burning* (hendiadys)   Irregular line (12 syl.)

harrow – *tear*
start – *jump*; spheres – *sockets*
knotted and combinèd – *knotted together* (hendiadys)   Qq – knotted F – knotty
par-**tic**-ular (equiv. 3 syl.)

fearful – *terrifying/terrified*; porpentine – *porcupine*   Q2 – fearful Q1/F – fretful
eternal blazon – *description of the afterlife*; be – *be told*
list – *listen*   Q2 – List, list, O list F – Hamlet, O list

Qq – God, F – Heaven; Metre – line is short by 8 syl.

GHOST
  – Revenge his foul and most unnatural murder!   25

HAMLET
  Murder!

GHOST
  Murder most foul – as in the best it is –
  But this most foul, strange and unnatural.

HAMLET
  Haste me to know't that I with wings as swift
  As meditation or the thoughts of love   30
  May sweep to my revenge.

GHOST   I find thee apt.
  And duller shouldst thou be than the fat weed
  That roots itself in ease on Lethe wharf
  Wouldst thou not stir in this. Now, Hamlet, hear:
  'Tis given out that, sleeping in my orchard,   35
  A serpent stung me. So the whole ear of Denmark
  Is by a forgèd process of my death
  Rankly abus'd. But know, thou noble youth,
  The serpent that did sting thy father's life
  Now wears his crown.   40

HAMLET
  O my prophetic soul! My uncle!

GHOST
  Ay, that incestuous, that adulterate beast,
  With witchcraft of his wits, with traitorous gifts –
  O wicked wit and gifts that have the power
  So to seduce – won to his shameful lust   45

Metre – line is short by 8 syl.

as . . . is – *as even the best are*

un-**nat**-u-**ral** (equiv. 4 syl.)

know't (equiv. 1 syl.)

apt – *ready*
fat – *gross*
Lethe (Pron. **Lee**-thee) – *a river of the Classical underworld*; wharf – *banks*

given out – *reported*; orchard – *garden*   Qq – 'Tis F – It's; Qq – my F – mine
                                                                                        the whole **ear** (anapest – see 'A Note on Metre')
forgèd process – *false account*
Rankly – *Grossly*
that . . . life – *that poisoned your father*
                              Ambiguous lineation – some editions link 'Now wears his crown/
                                                                                O my prophetic soul'

prophetic – *foreknowing*   Qq – my F – mine; Punct. Q1 – uncle! Q2/F – uncle?

a-**dul**-terate (equiv. 3 syl.) – *stained by adultery/corrupted*; in-**ces**-tuous (equiv.3 syl.)
gifts – *qualities*   Qq – with F – hath

          Q2 – his F – this

The will of my most seeming-virtuous Queen.
O Hamlet, what a falling off was there,
From me whose love was of that dignity
That it went hand in hand even with the vow
I made to her in marriage, and to decline   50
Upon a wretch whose natural gifts were poor
To those of mine.
But Virtue, as it never will be mov'd
Though Lewdness court it in a shape of heaven,
So Lust, though to a radiant angel link'd,   55
Will sate itself in a celestial bed
And prey on garbage.
But soft, methinks I scent the morning air.
Brief let me be. Sleeping within my orchard –
My custom always of the afternoon –   60
Upon my secure hour thy uncle stole
With juice of cursèd hebona in a vial
And in the porches of my ears did pour
The leperous distilment whose effect
Holds such an enmity with blood of man   65
That swift as quicksilver it courses through
The natural gates and alleys of the body
And with a sudden vigour it doth possess
And curd like eager droppings into milk
The thin and wholesome blood. So did it mine   70
And a most instant tetter bark'd about
Most lazar-like with vile and loathsome crust
All my smooth body.
Thus was I sleeping by a brother's hand
Of life, of crown, of queen at once dispatch'd,   75
Cut off even in the blossoms of my sin,
Unhousel'd, disappointed, unanel'd,
No reckoning made but sent to my account
With all my imperfections on my head.

will – *sexual desire* **vir**-tuous (equiv. 2 syl.)

falling off – *decline in standards* F – what a Q2 – what

dignity – *worth*

even . . . vow – *with the very vow* even (equiv. 1 syl.)

to – *that she should* -riage, and **to** (anapest – see 'A Note on Metre')

Upon – *To*

To those of – *Compared to* Metre – line is short by 6 syl.

court – *woo*

 ra-diant (equiv. 2 syl.)

sate – *satiate* (and be unable to find further pleasure)

garbage – *entrails* Metre – line is short by 5 syl.

soft – *wait* Q2 – morning Q1/F – morning's

 Qq – my F – mine

secure – *free from care*

juice . . . hebona (**he**-bona) – *poison*; vial – *small container* Qq – hebona F – hebenon

porches – *entrance-ways* Qq – my F – mine

leperous distilment – *distillation causing scaly skin* **lep**-er-**ous** (equiv. 3 syl.)

Holds . . . with – *Is such an enemy to the*

quicksilver – *liquid mercury*

possess – *take control of* vigour (equiv. 1 syl.); Q2 – possess F – posset

curd – *congeal*; eager – *acid*

thin and wholesome – *wholesomely thin* (hendiadys – see note)

tetter – *scaly rash*; bark'd about – *covered like bark*

lazar-like – *leper-like*

 Metre – line is short by 5 syl.

dispatch'd – *deprived* Qq – of queen F – and queen

in . . . sin – *in the height of sin* even (equiv. 1 syl.)

Unhousel'd . . . unanel'd – *Without proper spiritual preparation*

No reckoning (**reck**-oning) made – *Without confessing my sins*; my account – *judgement*

With . . . head – *liable for all my faults*

O horrible, O horrible, most horrible!   80
If thou hast nature in thee bear it not,
Let not the royal bed of Denmark be
A couch for luxury and damned incest.
But howsoever thou pursues this act
Taint not thy mind nor let thy soul contrive   85
Against thy mother aught; leave her to heaven
And to those thorns that in her bosom lodge
To prick and sting her. Fare thee well at once:
The glow-worm shows the matin to be near
And 'gins to pale his uneffectual fire.   90
Adieu, adieu, adieu, remember me.   [*Exit.*]

HAMLET
O all you host of heaven, O earth – what else? –
And shall I couple hell? O fie! Hold, my heart,
And you, my sinews, grow not instant old
But bear me swiftly up. Remember thee?   95
Ay, thou poor ghost, while memory holds a seat
In this distracted globe. Remember thee?
Yea, from the table of my memory
I'll wipe away all trivial fond records,
All saws of books, all forms, all pressures past   100
That youth and observation copied there
And thy commandment all alone shall live
Within the book and volume of my brain
Unmix'd with baser matter. Yes, by heaven,
O most pernicious woman,   105
O villain, villain, smiling damnèd villain,
My tables! Meet it is I set it down
That one may smile and smile and be a villain –
At least I am sure it may be so in Denmark.
So, uncle, there you are. Now to my word.   110

Metre – irregular line (12 syl.)/hexameter

nature – *natural feeling*

luxury – *lechery*   Pron. damned may be pronounced with an accented èd, or without

Q1/F – howsoever Q2 – howsomever; Q2 – pursues F – pursuest

Taint . . . mind – *Don't let your mind become corrupted*; contrive – *plot*

aught – *anything*

at once – *immediately*

The glow-worm – *the diminishing light of the glow-worm*; matin – *morning*

'gins – *begins*

Adieu – *Farewell*   Q2 – Adieu, adieu, adieu F – Adieu, adieu, Hamlet

heaven (equiv. 1 syl.)

couple – *join*   O fie! **Hold** (anapest); F – Hold Q2 – Hold, hold,

sinews – *muscles*; instant old – *suddenly feeble*

Q2 – swiftly F – stiffly

holds a seat – *is a force*   **mem**-ory (equiv. 2 syl.); F – while Q2 – whiles

distracted globe – *confused head/shattered world/theatre*

table – *wax tablet*

fond – *foolish*   **tri**-vial (equiv. 2 syl.); Metre suggests Pron. – re-**cords**

saws of books – *sayings from books*; forms – *formulas*; pressures – *impressions*

youth and observation (hendiadys – see Introduction)

book and volume – *spacious book* (hendiadys – see Introduction)

baser – *less valuable*   Q2 – Yes Q1/F – Yes, yes

pernicious – *evil*   Metre – line is short by 3 syl.

tables – *tablet/notebook*; Meet – *appropriate*   Qq – tables F – tables my tables

I am **sure** (anapest – see 'A Note on Metre'); Qq – I am F – I'm

word – *promise*

It is 'Adieu, adieu, remember me.'
I have sworn't.

Enter HORATIO and MARCELLUS.

HORATIO
My lord, my lord!

MARCELLUS
Lord Hamlet!

HORATIO
Heavens secure him!   115

HAMLET
So be it.

MARCELLUS
Illo, ho, ho, my lord!

HAMLET
Hillo, ho, ho, boy, come and come!

MARCELLUS
How is't, my noble lord?

HORATIO
What news, my lord?   120

HAMLET
O, wonderful.

HORATIO
Good my lord, tell it.

Metre – the next 14 lines have an ambiguous metrical connection (see Series Introduction) – somewhere between VERSE and PROSE, possibly indicative of the lines tumbling over one another (see Introduction)

secure – *save*   Qq – Heavens F – Heaven

Illo – *Hello*

Hillo – *Hello*   Q2 – and F – bird

How is't – *How are you?*

HAMLET
No, you will reveal it.

HORATIO
Not I, my lord, by heaven.

MARCELLUS
Nor I, my lord.   125

HAMLET
How say you then – would heart of man once think it? –
But you'll be secret?

HORATIO, MARCELLUS   Ay, by heaven, my lord.

HAMLET
There's never a villain dwelling in all Denmark
But he's an arrant knave.

HORATIO
There needs no ghost, my lord, come from the grave   130
To tell us this.

HAMLET   Why, right, you are in the right!
And so without more circumstance at all
I hold it fit that we shake hands and part –
You as your business and desire shall point you
(For every man hath business and desire   135
Such as it is) and for my own poor part
I will go pray.

HORATIO
These are but wild and whirling words, my lord.

Q2 – you will Q1/F – you'll

would heart of man once think it? – *would man ever believe it?*

Ay – *Yes*   F – heaven, my lord; Q – heaven

                                        never (equiv. 1 syl.); Qq – never F – ne'er
arrant – *downright*   Metre – line is short by 4 syl.

                you are **in** (anapest – see 'A Note on Metre'); Q2 – in the, F – i'th'
circumstance – *elaborate speech*
hold it fit – *consider it appropriate*; shake hands – *(gesture of parting)*
point – *direct*   **bus**-iness (equiv. 2 syl.); Q2 – desire Q1/F – desires
                                        Qq – hath F – has
                                        Qq – my F – mine
        Q2 – I will F – Look you, I'll; Metre – the line is short by 6 syl.

wild and whirling – *wildly whirling* (hendiadys – see Introduction), whirling
– *extravagant*   Qq – whirling F – hurling

HAMLET
I am sorry they offend you – heartily,
Yes, faith, heartily.

HORATIO   There's no offence, my lord.   140

HAMLET
Yes, by Saint Patrick, but there is, Horatio,
And much offence too. Touching this vision here
It is an honest ghost – that let me tell you.
For your desire to know what is between us
O'ermaster't as you may. And now, good friends,   145
As you are friends, scholars and soldiers,
Give me one poor request.

HORATIO
What is't, my lord? We will.

HAMLET
Never make known what you have seen tonight.

HORATIO, MARCELLUS
My lord, we will not.   150

HAMLET
Nay, but swear't.

HORATIO
In faith, my lord, not I.

MARCELLUS
Nor I, my lord, in faith.

I am **so**- (anapest – see 'A Note on Metre'); Qq – I am F – I'm (metrically regular)
heart-ily (equiv. 2 syl.)

Saint Patrick – *keeper of purgatory*   Qq – Horatio F – my Lord
Touching – *concerning*   Can be scanned with o-ffence **too** or -ching this **vis**- as anapest

is – *has passed*
O'ermaster't – *Overcome it*   O'er-**mast**-er't (equiv. 3 syl.)
sol-di-**ers** (equiv. 3 syl.)
Metre – line is short by 4 syl.

Metre – line is short by 4 syl.

Metre – the next 8 lines have an ambiguous metrical connection

not I – *I will not make known what I have seen*

HAMLET
Upon my sword.

MARCELLUS
We have sworn, my lord, already.   155

HAMLET
Indeed, upon my sword, indeed.

GHOST *(Cries under the stage.)*
Swear.

HAMLET
Ha, ha, boy, sayst thou so? Art thou there, truepenny?
Come on, you hear this fellow in the cellarage?
Consent to swear.

HORATIO   Propose the oath, my lord.   160

HAMLET
Never to speak of this that you have seen,
Swear by my sword.

GHOST
Swear.

HAMLET
Hic et ubique? Then we'll shift our ground.
Come hither, gentlemen, and lay your hands   165
Again upon my sword. Swear by my sword
Never to speak of this that you have heard.

GHOST
Swear by his sword.

truepenny (**true**-penny) – *honest fellow* sayst (equiv. 1 syl.); Qq – Ha, ha F – Ah ha
cellarage – *cellar*   **cell**-arage (equiv. 2 syl.)

Metre – line is short by 6 syl.

Metre – line is short by 9 syl.

Hic et ubique (**oo**-bi-quay) – *here and everywhere* (Latin)   –bi -que? **Then** (anapest)

Metre – line is short by 6 syl.

HAMLET

Well said, old mole, canst work i'th' earth so fast?
A worthy pioner! Once more remove, good friends.   170

HORATIO

O day and night, but this is wondrous strange.

HAMLET

And therefore as a stranger give it welcome:
There are more things in heaven and earth, Horatio,
Than are dreamt of in your philosophy. But come,
Here as before: never – so help you mercy,   175
How strange or odd some'er I bear myself
(As I perchance hereafter shall think meet
To put an antic disposition on) –
That you at such times seeing me never shall
With arms encumber'd thus, or this headshake,   180
Or by pronouncing of some doubtful phrase
As 'Well, well, we know', or 'We could an if we would',
Or 'If we list to speak', or 'There be an if they might',
Or such ambiguous giving out to note
That you know aught of me. This not to do,   185
So grace and mercy at your most need help you.

GHOST

Swear.

HAMLET

Rest, rest, perturbèd spirit. So, gentlemen,
With all my love I do commend me to you,
And what so poor a man as Hamlet is   190
May do t'express his love and friending to you
God willing shall not lack. Let us go in together
And still your fingers on your lips, I pray.

i'th' (equiv. 1 syl.); Qq – earth F – ground

pioner (Pron. **pio**-ner) – *solider who digs to lay mines*; remove – *move*

Can be scanned with '-ner! Once **more**' or 'more re-**move**' as anapests

heaven (equiv. 1 syl.)

philosophy – *knowledge* Than are **dreamt**; of in **your** (anapests); Qq – your F – our

so help you – *as you hope to obtain*

some'er – *soever*   Q2 – some'er Q1/F – so ere

perchance – *perhaps*; hereafter – *at a future time*; think meet – *think it appropriate*

antic disposition – *bizarre behaviour*

seeing (equiv. 1 syl.); Qq – times F – time

encumber'd – *folded*   Qq – this F – thus

doubtful – *ambiguous*

an if – *if*   As 'Well, **well**'; or 'We **could**' (anapests); Qq – Well, well F – well

list – *wished*; 'be . . . might' – *are those could tell if they wanted.*   Irregular (13 syl.)

giving out – *pronouncement*; note – *indicate*   am-**big**-uous (equiv. 3 syl.)

aught – *anything*   Q1/F – This not to do Q2 – This do swear

at your most need – *when you most need them*

Metre – line is short by 9 syl.

perturbèd – *restless*   spirit (equiv. 1 syl)

commend me – *give trust*

friending – *friendship*

Irregular (13 syl.) – can be scanned with quartus paeon/as hexameter

still – *always*

The time is out of joint; O cursèd spite
That ever I was born to set it right!   195
Nay, come, let's go together.   *Exeunt.*

2.1   *Enter old POLONIUS with his man [REYNALDO]*

POLONIUS
Give him this money and these notes, Reynaldo.

REYNALDO
I will, my lord.

POLONIUS
You shall do marvellous wisely, good Reynaldo,
Before you visit him to make inquire
Of his behaviour.

REYNALDO   My lord, I did intend it.   5

POLONIUS
Marry, well said, very well said. Look you, sir,
Inquire me first what Danskers are in Paris,
And how, and who, what means, and where they keep,
What company, at what expense, and finding
By this encompassment and drift of question   10
That they do know my son, come you more nearer
Than your particular demands will touch it;
Take you as 'twere some distant knowledge of him,
As thus, 'I know his father and his friends
And in part him' – do you mark this, Reynaldo?   15

REYNALDO
Ay, very well, my lord.

spite – *fortune*

Metre – line is short by 3 syl.

SD – Q2 includes an additional '*or two*' in the entrance but no other character speaks.

notes – *letters*   Qq – this F – his

Metre – line is short by 6 syl.

shall do – *should be sure to do*; marvellous – *marvellously*   **mar**-vellous (equiv. 2 syl.)
inquire – *inquiry*   Q2 – to make inquire F – you make inquiry

-viour/My **lord** (anapest – see 'A Note on Metre')

me – *for me*; Danskers – *Danes*
how – *how they live*; what means – *what are their resources*; keep – *frequent*

encompassment – *roundabout manner of talking*; drift – *general direction*
come . . . nearer – *come closer to the topic*
Than . . . demands – *Than these particular questions*
Take you – *Assume*

in part – *partly*; mark – *listen to*

Metre – line is short by 4 syl.

POLONIUS

   'And in part him, but', you may say, 'not well.
   But if't be he I mean he's very wild,
   Addicted so and so', and there put on him
   What forgeries you please. Marry, none so rank   20
   As may dishonour him – take heed of that –
   But, sir, such wanton, wild and usual slips
   As are companions noted and most known
   To youth and liberty.

REYNALDO   As gaming, my lord?

POLONIUS

   Ay, or drinking, fencing, swearing,   25
   Quarrelling, drabbing – you may go so far.

REYNALDO

   My lord, that would dishonour him.

POLONIUS

   Faith, as you may season it in the charge.
   You must not put another scandal on him
   That he is open to incontinency –   30
   That's not my meaning – but breathe his faults so quaintly
   That they may seem the taints of liberty,
   The flash and outbreak of a fiery mind,
   A savageness in unreclaimèd blood
   Of general assault.

REYNALDO   But my good lord –   35

POLONIUS

   Wherefore should you do this?

Addicted so and so – *devoted to such and such pursuits*
forgeries – *inventions*; rank – *offensive*   Marry (equiv. 1 syl.)

wanton – *boisterous*; usual slips – *common failings*
noted – *well known*
youth and liberty – *the unrestrained behaviour of young men* (hendiadys – see
Introduction)
gaming – *gambling*   -ing my **lord** (anapest – see 'A Note on Metre')

                                  Metre – line is short by 2 syl.
drabbing – *patronising prostitutes*   **Quarre**-lling (equiv. 2 syl.)

                                  Metre – line is short by 2 syl.

as . . . charge – *It depends how you modify the accusation.*   Q2 – Faith F – Faith no

incontinency – *excessive sexual licence*   Pron. in-**con**-tinen-**cy**/in-**con**-tin-**en**-cy
breathe – *utter*; quaintly – *artfully*   -ing but **breathe** (anapest – see 'A Note on Metre')
taints of liberty – *faults of too much freedom*

savageness – *wildness*; unreclaimèd – *untamed*
Of general assault – *which affects most men*   **gen**-er-**al** (equiv. 3 syl.)

Wherefore – *For what purpose*   Metre – The shared line is short by 1 syl.

REYNALDO   Ay, my lord,
　I would know that.

POLONIUS   Marry, sir, here's my drift –
　And I believe it is a fetch of wit –
　You laying these slight sallies on my son
　As 'twere a thing a little soil'd with working,   40
　Mark you, your party in converse (him you would sound)
　Having ever seen in the prenominate crimes
　The youth you breathe of guilty, be assur'd
　He closes with you in this consequence:
　'Good sir' (or so), or 'friend' or 'gentleman',   45
　According to the phrase or the addition
　Of man and country.

REYNALDO   Very good, my lord.

POLONIUS
　And then, sir, does he this, he does –
　What was I about to say? [By the mass], I was about to
　say something! Where did I leave?   50

REYNALDO
　At 'closes in the consequence'.
　[At friend, or so, and gentleman.]

POLONIUS
　At 'closes in the consequence', ay, marry.
　He closes thus: 'I know the gentleman,
　I saw him yesterday, or th'other day,   55
　Or then, or then, with such or such, and as you say
　There was he gaming, there o'ertook in's rouse,
　There falling out at tennis', or perchance
　'I saw him enter such a house of sale',

drift – *plan*

fetch of wit – *witty strategy*   Q2 – wit F – warrant

sallies – *criticisms*   Q2 – sallies F – sullies

As 'twere – *As if he were*; soil'd – *dirtied*; working – *handling*   Q2 – with F – i'th'

Mark … converse – *Listen, the person you're talking to*; sound – *probe*   Irregular

Having – *if he has ever seen*; pre-**nom**-inate – *aforementioned*   Having (equiv. 1 syl.)

breathe of – *speak about*

closes with you – *confides in you*; consequence – *manner*

or so – *or whatever*

phrase … addition – *form of address* (hendiadys – see Introduction)   Q2 – or F – and

man and country – *the man's country* (hendiadys – see Introduction)

Metre – line is short by 2 syl.; F – he … he Q2 – 'a … 'a
Polonius seems to briefly move from VERSE to PROSE for
these two lines; Q2 – 'By the mass' (oath) – not in F

Metre – line is short by 2 syl.
This line is only in F. (short by 2 syl.)

Q2 – closes (metrically regular), F – closes with you
th'o-ther (equiv. 2 syl.); Q2 – th'other F – t'other
Metre – Irregular. Can be scanned with quartus paeon/as hexameter; Q2 – or F – and
o'ertook – *overcome*; rouse – *carousing/drinking*   in's (equiv. 1 syl.); F – he Q2 – a'
at – *over*

Videlicet a brothel, or so forth. See you now   60
Your bait of falsehood take this carp of truth,
And thus do we of wisdom and of reach,
With windlasses and with assays of bias,
By indirections find directions out:
So by my former lecture and advice   65
Shall you my son. You have me, have you not?

REYNALDO
My lord, I have.

POLONIUS   God buy ye, fare ye well.

REYNALDO   Good my lord.

POLONIUS
Observe his inclination in yourself.

REYNALDO
I shall, my lord.

POLONIUS   And let him ply his music.

REYNALDO   Well, my lord.

POLONIUS
Farewell. How now, Ophelia, what's the matter?   70

Exit Reynaldo.

Enter OPHELIA.

OPHELIA
O my lord, my lord, I have been so affrighted.

Videlicit – namely   Vid-e-li;-cet a **bro-;** thel or **so** (anapests)

carp – *fish*   F – takes Q2 – take

reach – *wide understanding*

windlasses – *roundabout ways*; assays of bias – *indirect attempts*

indirections – *indirect methods*; directions – *information*

lecture and advice – *teaching* (hendiadys – see Introduction)

have me – *understand me*

Metre – Ambiguous metrical connection (see Series Introduction)

God buy ye – *God be with you*   Q2 – ye … ye F – you … you

Observe … yourself – *Observe his behaviour in person/go along with his inclination*

Metre – Ambiguous metrical connection (see Series Introduction)

ply his music – *practice his music/go his own way* (metaphorically)

Well – *very well*

O my **lord** (anapest – see 'A Note on Metre'); Q2 – O my lord F – Alas

POLONIUS
　　With what, i'th' name of God?

OPHELIA
　　My lord, as I was sewing in my closet
　　Lord Hamlet, with his doublet all unbrac'd,
　　No hat upon his head, his stockings fouled,　　　　75
　　Ungarter'd and down-gyvèd to his ankle,
　　Pale as his shirt, his knees knocking each other,
　　And with a look so piteous in purport
　　As if he had been loosèd out of hell
　　To speak of horrors, he comes before me.　　　　80

POLONIUS　Mad for thy love?

OPHELIA　　　　　　　　　　My lord, I do not know,
　　But truly I do fear it.

POLONIUS　　　　　　　　What said he?

OPHELIA
　　He took me by the wrist and held me hard,
　　Then goes he to the length of all his arm
　　And with his other hand thus o'er his brow　　　　85
　　He falls to such perusal of my face
　　As he would draw it. Long stay'd he so;
　　At last, a little shaking of mine arm
　　And thrice his head thus waving up and down,
　　He raised a sigh so piteous and profound　　　　90
　　As it did seem to shatter all his bulk
　　And end his being. That done, he lets me go
　　And with his head over his shoulder turned
　　He seemed to find his way without his eyes
　　(For out o'doors he went without their help)　　　　95
　　And to the last bended their light on me.

Metre – line is short by 4 syl.; Q2 – i'th' F – in the; Q2 – God F – Heaven

closet – *private chamber*   Q2 – closet F – chamber
doublet – *jacket*; unbrac'd – *undone*
fouled – *unwashed*
Ungarter'd – *untied*; down-gyvèd – *falling down* (like shackles)

purport (Pron. per-**port**) – *meaning*   **pi**-teous (equiv. 2 syl.)
loosèd – *released*

Then . . . arm – *Then he backed off an arm's length*
o'er – *over*   o'er (equiv. 1 syl.)
perusal – *detailed examination*
As – *As if*   Metre – line is short by 1 syl. (possibly at the caesura); F – he would
                                                              Q2 – 'a would
thrice – *three times*
raised – *uttered*   **pi**-teous (equiv. 2 syl.)
As – *That*; bulk – *body*   Q2 – As F – That
                              -ing. That **done** (anapest – see 'A Note on Metre')
                                              Qq – shoulder F – shoulders

o'doors – *of doors*   Q1/F – help Q2 – helps
bended their light – *directed their gaze*

POLONIUS

Come, go with me: I will go seek the King.
This is the very ecstasy of love,
Whose violent property fordoes itself
And leads the will to desperate undertakings   100
As oft as any passions under heaven
That does afflict our natures. I am sorry –
What, have you given him any hard words of late?

OPHELIA

No, my good lord, but as you did command
I did repel his letters and denied   105
His access to me.

POLONIUS   That hath made him mad.
I am sorry that with better heed and judgement
I had not quoted him. I feared he did but trifle
And meant to wrack thee – but beshrew my jealousy –
By heaven it is as proper to our age   110
To cast beyond ourselves in our opinions
As it is common for the younger sort
To lack discretion. Come, go we to the King:
This must be known which, being kept close, might move
More grief to hide than hate to utter love.   115
[Come].   *Exeunt.*

2.2 *Flourish. Enter* KING *and* QUEEN, *ROSENCRANTZ and*
GUILDENSTERN [and other Courtiers]

KING

Welcome, dear Rosencrantz and Guildenstern.
Moreover that we much did long to see you
The need we have to use you did provoke
Our hasty sending. Something have you heard

ecstasy – *madness*

property – *nature*; fordoes – *destroys*

                                          des-perate (equiv. 2 syl.)

oft – *often*   Q2 – passions F – passion

of late – *recently*   given (equiv. 1 syl.); any (equiv. 1 syl.)

His – *him*

heed and judgement – *careful judgement* (hendiadys)   Q2 – heed F – speed

quoted – *observed*   Irregular line – can be scanned with quartus paeon/hexameter

wrack – *dishonour*; beshrew my jealousy – *curse my suspicions*   Irregular line (12 syl.)

as . . . age – *typical of old men*   heaven (equiv. 1 syl.); Qq – By heaven F – It seems

cast beyond ourselves – *miss the mark*

                        Can be scanned with '-tion. Come, **go**' or 'to the **King**' as anapests

close – *secret*   being (equiv. 1 syl.)

to hide – *by hiding it*; hate to utter love – *distress to reveal it*

                                      Come – not in F

                      SD – The additional courtiers are not listed in Q2.

Moreover – *Besides*

sending – *summons*

Of Hamlet's transformation – so I call it   5
Sith nor th'exterior nor the inward man
Resembles that it was. What it should be
More than his father's death, that thus hath put him
So much from th'understanding of himself
I cannot dream of. I entreat you both   10
That, being of so young days brought up with him
And since so neighbour'd to his youth and haviour,
That you vouchsafe your rest here in our Court
Some little time, so by your companies
To draw him on to pleasures and to gather   15
So much as from occasion you may glean,
[Whether aught to us unknown afflicts him thus]
That open'd lies within our remedy.

QUEEN
Good gentlemen, he hath much talk'd of you
And sure I am two men there are not living   20
To whom he more adheres. If it will please you
To show us so much gentry and good will
As to expend your time with us awhile
For the supply and profit of our hope,
Your visitation shall receive such thanks   25
As fits a king's remembrance.

ROSENCRANTZ   Both your majesties
Might by the sovereign power you have of us
Put your dread pleasures more into command
Than to entreaty.

GUILDENSTERN   But we both obey
And here give up ourselves in the full bent   30

F – so I call it Q2 – so call it

Sith nor – *Since neither*   Q2 – Sith nor F – Since not; th'ex-**te**-rior (equiv. 3 syl.)

Q2 – dream F – deem

of – *from*   being (equiv. 1 syl.)

neighbour'd … haviour – *familiar with his youthful behaviour* (hendiadys)   F – since

vouchsafe your rest – *agree to stay*   Q2 – sith; Q2 – haviour F – humour

companies – *companionship*

draw him on – *encourage him to participate in*

occasion – *opportunity*; glean – *pick up*   Q2 – occasion F – occasions

aught – *anything*   This line is not in F; Whether (equiv. 1 syl.)

open'd – *if revealed*

F – are Q2 – is

more adheres – *is more attached*

gentry – *courtesy*

expend – *spend*

supply and profit – *profitable fulfilment* (hendiadys – see Introduction)

Metre – irregular shared line (12 syl.)

of – *over*

dread pleasures – *respected wishes*; into – *into the form of a*

to – *into the form of an*

Q2 – But we F – We

in the full bent – *to the fullest extent*

To lay our service freely at your feet
To be commanded.

KING

Thanks, Rosencrantz, and gentle Guildenstern.

QUEEN

Thanks, Guildenstern, and gentle Rosencrantz.
And I beseech you instantly to visit   35
My too much changèd son. Go some of you
And bring these gentlemen where Hamlet is.

GUILDENSTERN

Heavens make our presence and our practices
Pleasant and helpful to him.

QUEEN   Ay, amen.

*Exeunt ROSENCRANTZ, GUILDENSTERN [and one or more
Courtiers].*

Enter POLONIUS.

POLONIUS

Th'ambassadors from Norway, my good lord,   40
Are joyfully returned.

KING

Thou still hast been the father of good news.

POLONIUS

Have I, my lord? I assure my good liege
I hold my duty as I hold my soul,
Both to my God and to my gracious King;   45

Q2 – service F – services
Metre – line is short by 5 syl.

The Queen's line is sometimes played as though the King has confused the two men.

some – *some/one*

practices – *actions*   Heavens (equiv. 1 syl.)
Pleasant – *pleasing*

Th'am-**bass**-a-**dors** (equiv. 4 syl.)
Metre – line is short by 4 syl.

still – *always*

Q2 – I assure my good liege F – Assure you, my good liege (metrically regular)
hold – *regard*

And I do think, or else this brain of mine
Hunts not the trail of policy so sure
As it hath used to do, that I have found
The very cause of Hamlet's lunacy.

KING

O, speak of that, that do I long to hear.   50

POLONIUS

Give first admittance to th'ambassadors.
My news shall be the fruit to that great feast.

KING

Thyself do grace to them and bring them in.
He tells me, my dear Gertrude, he hath found
The head and source of all your son's distemper.   55

QUEEN

I doubt it is no other but the main –
His father's death and our hasty marriage.

KING

Well, we shall sift him.

Enter VOLTEMAND and CORNELIUS.

Welcome, my good friends.
Say, Voltemand, what from our brother Norway?

VOLTEMAND

Most fair return of greetings and desires.   60
Upon our first he sent out to suppress
His nephew's levies, which to him appear'd

Hunts ... sure – *doesn't pursue the path of statecraft*

Q2 – it hath F – I have

Q2 – do I F – I do

th'am-**bass**-a-**dors** (equiv. 4 syl.)

fruit – *dessert*

grace – *honour*

Q2 – dear Gertrude F – sweet Queen that

head – *origins*; distemper – *illness*

doubt – *suspect*; main – *chief concern*

ou-r (equiv. 2 syl.); Q2 – hasty F – o'er-hasty

sift him – *interrogate him*

our brother – *our fellow monarch*

desires – *good wishes*
Upon our first – *when we first raised the matter*

To be a preparation 'gainst the Polack;
But, better looked into, he truly found
It was against your highness; whereat, griev'd   65
That so his sickness, age and impotence
Was falsely borne in hand, sends out arrests
On Fortinbras, which he in brief obeys,
Receives rebuke from Norway and, in fine,
Makes vow before his uncle never more   70
To give th'assay of arms against your majesty.
Whereon old Norway, overcome with joy,
Gives him three thousand crowns in annual fee
And his commission to employ those soldiers
So levied (as before) against the Polack,   75
With an entreaty herein further shown
That it might please you to give quiet pass
Through your dominions for this enterprise
On such regards of safety and allowance
As therein are set down.

KING   It likes us well,   80
And at our more consider'd time we'll read,
Answer and think upon this business;
Meantime, we thank you for your well-took labour.
Go to your rest, at night we'll feast together.
Most welcome home.

Exeunt Voltemand, Cornelius [and Courtiers].

POLONIUS   This business is well ended.   85
My liege and madam, to expostulate
What majesty should be, what duty is,
Why day is day, night night, and time is time,
Were nothing but to waste night, day and time;
Therefore, since brevity is the soul of wit   90

the Polack – *the King of Poland*

impotence – *frailty*
falsely borne in hand – *tricked*

in fine – *in conclusion*

give th'assay of arms – *mount a war*   th'a-**ssay** – (equiv. 2 syl.); **maj**-esty (equiv. 2 syl.)

fee – *income*; threescore – *sixty*   Q1/F – three Q2 – threescore
commission – *authority*
levied – *enlisted*; (as before) – *as mentioned before/as enlisted before*
herein – *in this paper*
quiet pass – *safe passage*
                                                    do-**min**-ions (equiv. 3 syl.); Q2 – this F – his
On ... allowance – *On such conditions of your realm's safety*

likes – *pleases*
at out more consider'd time – *when we have more time for consideration*
                                                            bus-i-**ness** (equiv. 3 syl.)
well-took – *well-undertaken*

                                                            bus-iness (equiv.2 syl)
expostulate – *debate*

wit – *intellect*   -vi-ty **is** (anapest – see 'A Note on Metre'); F – since brevity Q2 – brevity

And tediousness the limbs and outward flourishes.
I will be brief: your noble son is mad.
Mad call I it, for to define true madness,
What is't but to be nothing else but mad?
But let that go.

QUEEN   More matter with less art.   95

POLONIUS
Madam, I swear I use no art at all.
That he is mad, 'tis true, 'tis true 'tis pity,
And pity 'tis 'tis true: a foolish figure!
But farewell it, for I will use no art.
Mad let us grant him then, and now remains   100
That we find out the cause of this effect –
Or rather say the cause of this defect,
For this effect defective comes by cause.
Thus it remains, and the remainder thus.
Perpend,   105
I have a daughter – have while she is mine –
Who in her duty and obedience, mark,
Hath given me this. Now gather and surmise.
[*Reads.*] *To the celestial and my soul's idol, the most
beautified Ophelia* – that's an ill phrase, a vile phrase,   110
'beautified' is a vile phrase, but you shall hear – *thus in
her excellent white bosom, these*, etc.

QUEEN
Came this from Hamlet to her?

POLONIUS
Good madam, stay awhile: I will be faithful.
[*Reads.*]   *Doubt thou the stars are fire,*   115
            Doubt that the sun doth move,

limbs and flourishes – *rhetorical devices*   **te**-dious-**ness** (equiv. 3 syl.); **flou**-rishes
                                                                                          (equiv. 2 syl.)
for . . . madness – *it would be mad to try to define true madness*

matter – *substance*; art – *artfulness*

                                                  F – he is (metrically regular) Q2 – he's
figure – *figure of speech*   Q2 – 'tis 'tis F – it is

effect – *behaviour*
defect – *disability*
effect defective comes by cause – *defective behaviour has a cause*
Thus . . . thus – *thus it is, and now for the rest*
Perpend – *consider*   Ambiguous lineation – Perpend is on the previous line in F
while she is mine – *until she marries*   Qq – while F – whilst
                                                                        o-**be**-dience (equiv. 3 syl.)
gather and surmise – *draw your conclusions/draw nearer and look*   given (equiv. 1 syl.)
celestial – *heavenly*   Polonius moves into PROSE for the next 4 lines
beautified – *beautiful*
                                                          Q2 – hear – *thus* F – hear these

                                                          Metre – line is short by 3 syl.

stay – *wait*; I will be faithful – *I will accurately read the letter*
                                        Metre – Hamlet's poem is in iambic trimeter

> *Doubt truth to be a liar,*
> *But never doubt I love.*
> *O dear Ophelia, I am ill at these numbers. I have not art*
> *to reckon my groans, but that I love thee best, O most*   120
> *best, believe it. Adieu. Thine evermore, most dear lady,*
> *whilst this machine is to him. Hamlet.*
> This in obedience hath my daughter shown me;
> And more about hath his solicitings
> As they fell out, by time, by means and place,   125
> All given to my ear.

KING   But how hath she
    Receiv'd his love?

POLONIUS   What do you think of me?

KING
    As of a man faithful and honourable.

POLONIUS
    I would fain prove so. But what might you think
    When I had seen this hot love on the wing –   130
    As I perceiv'd it (I must tell you that)
    Before my daughter told me – what might you,
    Or my dear majesty your Queen here, think
    If I had played the desk or table-book,
    Or given my heart a working mute and dumb,   135
    Or look'd upon this love with idle sight,
    What might you think? No, I went round to work
    And my young mistress thus I did bespeak:
    'Lord Hamlet is a prince out of thy star.
    This must not be.' And then I prescripts gave her   140
    That she should lock herself from his resort,
    Admit no messengers, receive no tokens;

Doubt – *suspect* (shifts meaning in this line)

ill . . . numbers – *bad at writing verse*   The letter is in PROSE.
to reckon my groans – *count my groans/render my groans in verse*
Adieu – *farewell*
machine is – *body belongs* (i.e. he is alive)

Q2 – shown F – showed

more about – *in addition*; solicitings – *entreaties/approaches*   Q2 – about F – above
fell out – *occurred*

hon-oura-**ble** (equiv. 3 syl.)

fain – *be glad to*
hot – *impetuous*; on the wing – *developing quickly*
perceiv'd – *noticed*

play'd the desk or table book – *remained silent/conveyed messages between them*
given . . . dumb – *forced my heart to remain silent*   given (equiv. 1 syl.); Q2 – working
with idle sight – *complacently*   F – winking
round – *directly*
bespeak – *address*
out of thy star – *above your sphere*
prescripts – *instructions*   Q2 – prescripts F – precepts
resort – *visits*

Which done, she took the fruits of my advice,
And he, repellèd, a short tale to make,
Fell into a sadness, then into a fast,   145
Thence to a watch, thence into a weakness,
Thence to lightness, and by this declension
Into the madness wherein now he raves,
And all we mourn for.

KING   Do you think 'tis this?

QUEEN   It may be, very like.

POLONIUS
Hath there been such a time – I would fain know that –   150
That I have positively said 'tis so
When it proved otherwise?

KING   Not that I know.

POLONIUS
Take this from this if this be otherwise.
If circumstances lead me I will find
Where truth is hid, though it were hid indeed   155
Within the centre.

KING   How may we try it further?

POLONIUS
You know sometimes he walks four hours together
Here in the lobby?

QUEEN   So he does, indeed.

POLONIUS
At such a time I'll loose my daughter to him.

fruits – *benefits*

a . . . make – *to cut a long story short*   Q2 – repellèd F – repulsèd

into (first occurrence) (equiv. 1 syl.)

a watch – *insomnia*

a lightness – *dizziness*; declension – *decline*

all we – *all of us*   Q2 – mourn F – wail; Metre – Ambiguous metrical connection

(see General Introduction)

F – Do you think 'tis this? Q2 – Do you think this?

like – *likely*   Q2 – like F – likely

Q2 – I would F – I'd

Take this from this – *separate my head from my shoulders*

circumstances – *relevant evidence*

the centre – *the centre of the earth*

try – *test*   may we **try** (anapest – see 'A Note on Metre')

together – *at a time*

loose – *set loose*

Be you and I behind an arras then,   160
Mark the encounter: if he love her not
And be not from his reason fallen thereon
Let me be no assistant for a state
But keep a farm and carters.

KING   We will try it.

Enter HAMLET.

QUEEN
But look where sadly the poor wretch comes reading.   165

POLONIUS
Away, I do beseech you both, away.
I'll board him presently. O, give me leave.

Exeunt King and Queen.

How does my good lord Hamlet?

HAMLET
Well, God-a-mercy.

POLONIUS
Do you know me, my lord?   170

HAMLET
Excellent well, you are a fishmonger.

POLONIUS
Not I, my lord.

HAMLET
Then I would you were so honest a man.

arras – *tapestry*
Mark – *Listen to*
thereon – *on that account*
assistant for a state – *councillor of state*
carters – *cart drivers*

sadly – *gravely*

board him presently – *accost him immediately*

*See Introductory note about the placement of 'To be or not to be'.

The scene moves into PROSE at this point.

God-a-mercy – *God have mercy on you* (greeting with inferiors)

fishmonger – *(punning on the slang meaning of 'pimp')*   Q2 – Excellent
                                                                 F – Excellent, excellent

POLONIUS
Honest, my lord?

HAMLET
Ay, sir, to be honest as this world goes is to be   175
one man picked out of ten thousand.

POLONIUS
That's very true, my lord.

HAMLET
For if the sun breed maggots in a dead dog,
being a good kissing carrion – have you a daughter?

POLONIUS
I have, my lord.   180

HAMLET
Let her not walk i'th'sun: conception is a
blessing but as your daughter may conceive, friend –
look to't.

POLONIUS [*aside*]
How say you by that? Still harping on my daughter.
Yet he knew me not at first, he said I was a fishmonger!   185
He is far gone; and truly, in my youth I suffered much
extremity for love, very near this. I'll speak to him
again. – What do you read, my lord?

HAMLET
Words, words, words.

POLONIUS
What is the matter, my lord?   190

one ... thousand – Prov. Qq – ten F – two

good kissing carrion – *good piece of decaying flesh to kiss*

i'th'sun – *(lest she breed, like maggots – pun on 'son')*; conception ... conceive – *(pun on formation of ideas/pregnancy.)*   Q2 – but F – but not
look to't – *take care*

How ... that? – *What do you say to that?* (addressed to the audience); harping – *dwelling*
                                                           F – he said Q2 – 'a said
far gone – *seriously affected*   F – He Q2 – 'A; Q2 – far gone F – far gone, far gone
extremity – *stress*

matter – *content*

HAMLET
Between who?

POLONIUS
I mean the matter that you read, my lord.

HAMLET
Slanders, sir. For the satirical rogue says here
that old men have grey beards, that their faces are
wrinkled, their eyes purging thick amber and plumtree   195
gum, and that they have a plentiful lack of wit together
with most weak hams – all which, sir, though I most
powerfully and potently believe, yet I hold it not
honesty to have it thus set down. For yourself, sir, shall
grow old as I am – if, like a crab, you could go   200
backward.

POLONIUS [*aside*]
Though this be madness yet there is
method in't. – Will you walk out of the air, my lord?

HAMLET
Into my grave.

POLONIUS [*aside*]
Indeed, that's out of the air. How pregnant sometimes   205
his replies are – a happiness that often madness hits
on, which reason and sanity could not so prosperously
be delivered of. I will leave him and [suddenly contrive
the means of meeting between him, and] my daughter. –
My lord, I will take my leave of you.   210

HAMLET
You cannot take from me anything that I will

Between who – *(Hamlet deliberately interprets matter as problem/quarrel)*

Q2 – that you read Q1/F – you read

Slanders – *false statements*   Q2 – rogue F – slave

purging – *discharging*; thick . . . gum – *resin*   Q2 – amber and F – amber, or
wit – *wisdom*
hams – *thighs*   Q2 – most weak F – weak
potently – *strongly*
honesty – *honourable*   Q2 – yourself F – you your self; Q2 – shall grow F – should be
old – *as old*

out of the air – *indoors/out of the draught*

pregnant – *meaningful*   Qq – that's F – that is
happiness – *appropriateness*
prosperously – *effectively*

suddenly . . . and – only in F
Qq – My F – My honourable; Q2 – will take F – will most humbly take

Q2 – cannot F – cannot Sir

more willingly part withal – except my life, except
my life, except my life.

POLONIUS
Fare you well, my lord.

HAMLET
These tedious old fools.   215

Enter GUILDENSTERN *and* ROSENCRANTZ.

POLONIUS
You go to seek the Lord Hamlet? There he is.

ROSENCRANTZ [*to Polonius*]
God save you, sir.   [*Exit Polonius*]

GUILDENSTERN
My honoured lord.

ROSENCRANTZ
My most dear lord.

HAMLET
My excellent good friends. How dost thou,   220
Guildenstern? Ah, Rosencrantz! Good lads, how do
you both?

ROSENCRANTZ
As the indifferent children of the earth.

GUILDENSTERN
Happy, in that we are not ever happy.
On Fortune's cap we are not the very button.   225

withal – *with*   F – more willingly Q2 – not more willingly

Q2 – except my life F – my life; SD – In Q2, Rosencrantz and Guildenstern are directed to enter here.

Q2 – the Lord Hamlet F – my Lord Hamlet

Q2 – My F – Mine

Q2 – Ah F – Oh

[Q2 – you F – ye]

indifferent – *ordinary*   Lines 223–5 are in VERSE; in-**diff**-erent (equiv. 3 syl.)

Happy – *Fortunate*; ever – *always*   Q2 – ever F – over

button – *top*   we are **not** (anapest – see 'A Note on Metre')

HAMLET
Nor the soles of her shoe.

ROSENCRANTZ
Neither, my lord.

HAMLET
Then you live about her waist, or in the middle
of her favours.

GUILDENSTERN
Faith, her privates we.   230

HAMLET
In the secret parts of Fortune? O, most true –
she is a strumpet. What news?

ROSENCRANTZ
None, my lord, but the world's grown
honest.

HAMLET
Then is doomsday near – but your news is not true.   235
[Let me question more in particular. What have
you, my good friends, deserved at the hands of Fortune
that she sends you to prison hither?

GUILDENSTERN
Prison, my lord?

HAMLET
Denmark's a prison.   240

ROSENCRANTZ
Then is the world one.

The scene moves back into PROSE

Q2 – favours F – favour

privates – *pun on private parts/men of no rank/intimate friends*

strumpet – *whore*   Q2 – What news? F – What's the news?

Q2 – but the F – but that the

in particular – *in detail*   Lines 236 to 265 are only in F.

HAMLET

A goodly one, in which there are many confines,
wards and dungeons – Denmark being one o'th'worst.

ROSENCRANTZ

We think not so, my lord.

HAMLET

Why, then 'tis none to you; for there is nothing   245
either good or bad, but thinking makes it so. To me it is
a prison.

ROSENCRANTZ

Whey, then your ambition makes it one:
'tis too narrow for your mind.

HAMLET

O God, I could be bounded in a nutshell and   250
count myself a king of infinite space – were it not that
I have bad dreams.

GUILDENSTERN

Which dreams, indeed, are ambition;
for the very substance of the ambitious is merely the
shadow of a dream.   255

HAMLET

A dream itself is but a shadow.

ROSENCRANTZ

Truly, and I hold ambition of so airy and
light a quality that it is but a shadow's shadow.

HAMLET

Then are our beggars bodies, and our monarchs

confines – *places of confinement*
wards – *prison cells*

'tis none – *it isn't one*

bounded – *enclosed*

substance of the ambitious – *material of which ambitious men are made/material that fuels them*

are our beggars bodies – *our beggars have bodies; and our ... shadows – and kings and heroes are merely shadows*

and outstretched heroes the beggars' shadows. Shall we   260
to th'Court? For, by my fay, I cannot reason.

ROSENCRANTZ, GUILDENSTERN
We'll wait upon you.

HAMLET
No such matter. I will not sort you with the rest
of my servants, for, to speak to you like an honest man,
I am most dreadfully attended.]   265
But, in the beaten way of friendship, what make
you at Elsinore?

ROSENCRANTZ
To visit you, my lord, no other occasion.

HAMLET
Beggar that I am, I am ever poor in thanks, but
I thank you, and sure, dear friends, my thanks are too   270
dear a halfpenny. Were you not sent for? Is it your own
inclining? Is it a free visitation? Come, come, deal justly
with me. Come, come, nay speak.

GUILDENSTERN
What should we say, my lord?

HAMLET
Anything but to th' purpose. You were sent for,   275
and there is a kind of confession in your looks, which
your modesties have not craft enough to colour. I know
the good King and Queen have sent for you.

ROSENCRANTZ
To what end, my lord?

fay – *faith*

wait upon – *accompany*

No such matter – *I'll have no such thing*; sort – *class*

dreadfully attended – *poorly served*
beaten way – *well-trodden track* (plain words); make you – *are you doing*

Q2 – ever F – even
too dear a halfpenny – *too expensive at half a penny*

inclining – *inclination*; free – *voluntary*   Q2 – Come, come, deal F – come deal

but – *except*   Q2 – Anything but F – Why any thing. But (note difference in punctuation)
modesties – *decent natures*; colour – *disguise*

HAMLET

That you must teach me. But let me conjure   280
you, by the rights of our fellowship, by the consonancy
of our youth, by the obligation of our ever-preserved
love, and by what more dear a better proposer can
charge you withal, be even and direct with me whether
you were sent for or no.   285

ROSENCRANTZ

What say you?

HAMLET

Nay then, I have an eye of you. If you love me,
hold not off.

GUILDENSTERN

My lord, we were sent for.

HAMLET

I will tell you why. So shall my anticipation   290
prevent your discovery and your secrecy to the King
and Queen moult no feather. I have of late, but
wherefore I know not, lost all my mirth, forgone all
custom of exercises and, indeed, it goes so heavily with
my disposition that this goodly frame the earth seems   295
to me a sterile promontory, this most excellent canopy
the air, look you, this brave o'erhanging firmament, this
majestical roof fretted with golden fire, why it
appeareth nothing to me but a foul and pestilent
congregation of vapours. What a piece of work is a man   300
– how noble in reason; how infinite in faculties, in form
and moving; how express and admirable in action; how
like an angel in apprehension; how like a god; the
beauty of the world; the paragon of animals. And yet to

conjure – *entreat*
consonancy – *friendship*

what more dear – *whatever more significant*   Q2 – can F – could
charge you withal – *impose on you*; even – *straightforward*
or no – *or not*

                This line is probably addressed to Guildenstern.

of – *on*
hold not off – *don't hesitate to tell me*

anticipation – *saying it first*

moult no feather – *remain unimpaired*; of late – *lately*
wherefore – *for what reason*; mirth – *happiness*; forgone – *neglected*
custom of exercises – *customary activities*   Q2 – exercises F – exercise
it … disposition – *I am so heavy with melancholy*; frame – *structure* (possibly also a
sterile promontory – *barren headland*   reference to the Globe playhouse)
brave o'erhanging firmament – *fine overhanging sky* (possibly a reference to the
fretted – *decorated*   heavens of the Globe)
   Q2 – appeareth F – appears; Q2 – nothing to me but F – no other thing to me than
congregation – *mass*; piece of work – *masterpiece of creation*   F – What a Q2 – What
faculties – *capabilities*; form and moving – *physical form*;   Punct. – F – faculty?
express and admirable – *admirably precise* (both hendiadys)
apprehension – *understanding*   Punct. – F – admirable? … angel? … God?
paragon – *supreme example*

me what is this quintessence of dust? Man delights not 305
me – nor woman neither, though by your smiling you
seem to say so.

ROSENCRANTZ
My lord, there was no such stuff in my
thoughts.

HAMLET
Why did ye laugh then, when I said man 310
delights not me?

ROSENCRANTZ
To think, my lord, if you delight not in
man what lenten entertainment the players shall receive
from you; we coted them on the way and hither are they
coming to offer you service. 315

HAMLET
He that plays the King shall be welcome – his majesty
shall have tribute of me – the Adventurous Knight shall
use his foil and target, the Lover shall not sigh gratis,
the Humorous Man shall end his part in peace, and [the
clown shall make those laugh whose lungs are tickled 320
a'th'sere, and] the Lady shall say her mind freely or the
blank verse shall halt for't. What players are they?

ROSENCRANTZ
Even those you were wont to take such
delight in, the tragedians of the city.

HAMLET
How chances it they travel? Their residence, 325
both in reputation and profit, was better both ways.

quintessence – *concentration*

Q2 – nor Q1/F – no nor; Q1/F – woman Q2 – women

Q2 – ye laugh then F – you laugh

lenten entertainment – *mean reception* (as at Lent – a period of fasting and penitence)
coted – *passed*; hither – *here*

tribute – *payment/praise*; of – *from*   Q1/F – of Q2 – on
foil and target – *sword and shield*; gratis – *for nothing*
Humorous – *prone to excess of one of the four humours*

the ... and – only in F

or ... halt for't – *the metre will be interrupted*

were wont – *used*   Q2 – take such delight Q1/F – take delight
tragedians – *actors* (not only of tragedies)

chances it – *come*; travel – *tour*; residence – *(in the city)*
both ways – *for reputation and financial gain*

ROSENCRANTZ

I think their inhibition comes by the
means of the late innovation.

HAMLET

Do they hold the same estimation they did
when I was in the city? Are they so followed?   330

ROSENCRANTZ

No, indeed are they not.

[HAMLET

How comes it? Do they grow rusty?

ROSENCRANTZ

Nay, their endeavour keeps in the wonted
pace. But there is, sir, an eyrie of childen, little eyases
that cry out on the top of question and are most   335
tyranically clapped for't. These are now the fashion,
and so berattle the common stages (so they call them)
that many wearing rapiers are afraid of goose-quills and
dare scarce come thither.

HAMLET

What, are they children? Who maintains 'em?   340
How are they escotted? Will they pursue the quality no
longer than they can sing? Will they not say afterwards
if they should grow themselves to common players – as
it is most like if their means are no better – their
writers do them wrong to make them exclaim against   345
their own succession?

ROSENCRANTZ

Faith, there has been much to-do on both
sides, and the nation holds it no sin to tar them to

inhibition – *hindrance/official prohibition*
the late innovation – *recent events/fashion*

estimation – *reputation*
Are . . . followed? – *do they still draw audiences?*

Q2 – are they F – they are

Do . . . rusty? – *Have their skills become impaired?*   Lines 332–57 are only in F

endeavour – *efforts*; keeps . . . pace – *continue as before*
eyrie – *brood*; eyases – *young hawks*
cry . . . question – *shout down others in the debate*
tyrannically – *excessively*
berattle – *clamour against*; common stages – *public theatres*
wearing rapiers – *fashionable young men*; goose-quills – *pens* (of authors writing for
scarce – *hardly*; dare . . . thither – *(for fear of being mocked)*   the boys)

escotted – *provided for*; pursue the quality – *follow the profession of acting*
no . . . sing – *only until their voices break*
to – *into*; common – *adult* (on the public stages)
like – *likely*; if their means. . . better – *if they have no better way of making money*

succession – *future profession*

This is a reference to the Wars of the Theatres between the adult companies and
tar – *incite*   the Children of the Chapel.

controversy. There was for a while, no money bid for
argument unless the poet and the player went to cuffs   350
in the question.

HAMLET
Is't possible?

GUILDENSTERN
O, there has been much throwing
about of brains.

HAMLET
Do the boys carry it away?   355

ROSENCRANTZ
Ay, that they do, my lord – Hercules and
his load too.]

HAMLET
It is not very strange, for my uncle is King of
Denmark, and those that would make mouths at him
while my father lived give twenty, forty, fifty, a hundred 360
ducats apiece for his picture in little. ['Sblood], there is
something in this more than natural if philosophy
could find it out.

A flourish

GUILDENSTERN
There are the players!

HAMLET
Gentlemen, you are welcome to Elsinore. Your   365
hands, come, [then!] Th'appurtenance of welcome is

bid – *paid*
argument – *a new play*; went to cuffs – *became violently involved*
question – *dispute*

throwing . . . brains – *expenditure of mental effort*

carry it away – *win the day*

his load – *the world* (which Hercules carried on his shoulders) (the emblem for the Globe theatre)

Q2 – very strange F – strange; Q2 – my F – mine
make mouths – *make faces*   Q2 – mouths F – mowes
                    Q2 – forty, fifty, a hundred F – forty, an hundred
picture in little – *miniature portrait*; 'Sblood – *God's blood* (oath) – not in F
more than natural – *abnormal*; philosophy – *science*

Your hands – *Give me your hands*
Th'appurtenance – *the proper accompaniment*   then – not in F; Q2 – Th' F – The

fashion and ceremony. Let me comply with you in this
garb lest my extent to the players, which I tell you
must show fairly outwards, should more appear like
entertainment than yours. You are welcome. But my   370
uncle-father and aunt-mother are deceived.

GUILDENSTERN
In what, my dear lord?

HAMLET
I am but mad north-north-west. When the
wind is southerly I know a hawk from a handsaw.

Enter POLONIUS.

POLONIUS
Well be with you, gentlemen.   375

HAMLET
Hark you, Guildenstern, and you too – at each
ear a hearer. That great baby you see there is not yet out
of his swaddling clouts.

ROSENCRANTZ
Happily he is the second time come to
them, for they say an old man is twice a child.   380

HAMLET
I will prophesy he comes to tell me of the
players. Mark it. – You say right, sir, o'Monday
morning, 'twas then indeed.

POLONIUS
My lord, I have news to tell you.

fashion and ceremony – *formal ceremony* (hendiadys); comply with – *follow accepted form*
this garb – *this manner*, extent – *extension of welcome*

Q2 – outwards F – outward

entertainment – *welcome*

aunt-mother – *(by marrying his uncle, Gertrude has become his aunt as well as his mother)*

but mad north-north-west – *Only mad when the wind is NNW/Only one fraction of*
handsaw – *small saw*/hernshaw – *a heron*   *the compass away from sanity*

Well . . . you – *I wish you well*

at . . . hearer – *stand close to me on either side*

swaddling clouts – *swaddling clothes*   Qq – swaddling F – swathing

Happily – *Perhaps*   Q2 – he is F – he's
an old . . . child – Prov.

Punct. – Q2 – prophesy F – prophesy.
Mark it – *Observe the outcome*; o' – *on*   Q2 – 'o F – for a
You . . . indeed – *(Hamlet pretends to be mid-conversation)*   Q2 – then Q1/F – so

HAMLET
My lord, I have news to tell you. When Roscius   385
was an actor in Rome –

POLONIUS
The actors are come hither, my lord.

HAMLET
Buzz, buzz.

POLONIUS
Upon my honour.

HAMLET
– Then came each actor on his ass.   390

POLONIUS
The best actors in the world, either for
tragedy, comedy, history, pastoral, pastoral-comical,
historical-pastoral, scene individable or poem
unlimited. Seneca cannot be too heavy nor Plautus too
light for the law of writ and the liberty. These are the   395
only men.

HAMLET
O Jephthah, judge of Israel, what a treasure hadst
thou?

POLONIUS
What a treasure had he, my lord?

HAMLET
Why,   400
         One fair daughter and no more,
         The which he lovèd passing well.

Roscius (**Ross**-key-**us**) – Quintus Roscius – *a famous Classical Roman actor*

hither – *here*

Buzz, buzz – *(dismissive expression)*

Q2 – my F – mine

Then . . . ass – *(possibly a line from a popular ballad)*

Q2 – pastoral . . . historical-pastoral; F – pastoral-comical-historical-pastoral: scene individable – *play with no breaks*   tragical-historical: unlimited – *not conforming to rules*   tragical-comical-historical-pastoral Seneca (**Sen**-e-**ca**) – . . . Plautus (**Plor**-tus) – *leading Roman tragic and comic dramatists* the law . . . liberty – *for plays which conform to or flout classical rules;* These – *these actors*

Jephthah (**Jepp**-tha) – *Old Testament figure who sacrificed his virgin daughter*

One . . . well – *(lines from a seventeenth-century ballad)*   Metre – Iambic tetrameter

POLONIUS [*aside*]
   Still on my daughter.

HAMLET
   Am I not i'th' right, old Jephthah?

POLONIUS
   If you call me Jephthah, my lord, I have a   405
   daughter that I love passing well.

HAMLET
   Nay, that follows not.

POLONIUS
   What follows then, my lord?

HAMLET
   Why,
          As by lot,   410
          God wot
   and then, you know,
          It came to pass,
          As most like it was
   The first row of the pious chanson will show you more,   415
   for look where my abridgement comes.

Enter the Players.

You are welcome, masters, welcome all. I am glad to see
thee well. Welcome, good friends. O old friend, why,
thy face is valanced since I saw thee last! Com'st thou to
beard me in Denmark? What, my young lady and   420
mistress! By'r Lady, your ladyship is nearer to heaven
than when I saw you last by the altitude of a chopine.

passing – *extremely*

Nay . . . not – *That's not necessarily true/That's not the next line*

lot – *chance*
wot – *knows*

like – *likely*
row – *line*; pious chanson – *religious song*
abridgement – *entertainment/interruption*   Qq – abridgement comes
                                                      F – abridgements come

                                      Q2 – old friend, why Q1/F – my old friend
valanced – *draped* (bearded)
beard me – *show me your beard/defy me*; my young lady – *(the boy player)*
By'r – *By our*; nearer to heaven – *taller/older*   Q2 – to heaven F – heaven
altitude – *height*; chopine – *platform shoe*

Pray God your voice, like a piece of uncurrent gold, be
not cracked within the ring. Masters, you are all
welcome. We'll e'en to't like French falconers –   425
fly at anything we see. We'll have a speech straight.
Come, give us a taste of your quality. Come, a
passionate speech.

1 PLAYER
What speech, my good lord?

HAMLET
I heard thee speak me a speech once – but it was   430
never acted, or, if it was, not above once, for the play I
remember pleased not the million, 'twas caviare to the
general. But it was, as I received it, and others whose
judgements in such matters cried in the top of mine, an
excellent play, well digested in the scenes, set down   435
with as much modesty as cunning. I remember one said
there were no sallets in the lines to make the matter
savoury nor no matter in the phrase that might indict
the author of affection, but called it an honest method,
[as wholesome as sweet, and by very much more   440
handsome than fine.] One speech in't I chiefly loved –
'twas Aeneas' tale to Dido, and thereabout of it
especially when he speaks of Priam's slaughter. If it live
in your memory begin at this line – let me see, let me
see –   445
The ruggèd Pyrrhus like th' Hyrcanian beast . . .
– 'Tis not so. It begins with Pyrrhus.
The ruggèd Pyrrhus, he whose sable arms,
Black as his purpose, did the night resemble
When he lay couchèd in the ominous horse,   450
Hath now this dread and black complexion smear'd
With heraldry more dismal, head to foot.

like ... ring – *(if the outside ring of a gold coin was cracked it was no longer legal tender)*

e'en to it – *get to work at once*; French falconers – *enthusiastic/expert in the sport*;
fly – *launch our birds*; straight – *immediately*
quality – *acting skill*

Qq – good lord F – lord

me – *for me*; it – *the play*

caviare to the general – *a delicacy not appreciated by the common people*

cried ... mine – *excelled mine*   Qq – judgements F – judgement
well digested in the scenes – *well organised into scenes*
modesty – *restraint*; cunning – *skill*
sallets – *salty dishes/embellishments*
savoury – *pleasing*; no ... phrase – *nothing in the expression*; indict – *accuse*
affection – *affectation*; honest method – *straightforward composition*   F – affectation
very ... fine – *natural rather than artful*   Q2 – as ... fine – not in F
          Q2 – One F – One chief; Q2 – in't Q1/F – in it
Aeneas ... Dido – (see Myth); Aeneas' tale – *story of Troy's fall*   Q1/F – tale Q2 – talk
Priam – (see Myth) (Source: Virgil's *Aeneid*, Book 2)   Q2 – when Q1/F – where

The speech is in VERSE.
ruggèd – *fierce*; Pyrrhus – (see Myth); th'Hyrcanian (th'Er-**cane**-ian) beast – *tiger*
          This interjection is in PROSE; Qq – 'Tis F – It is
sable arms – *black armour*

couchèd – *crouched/hidden*; ominous (**o**-minous) – *unlucky*   Q1/F – the Q2 – th'
this – *this already*; dread – *terrifying*
heraldry – *heraldic colours* (blood)

Now is he total gules, horridly trick'd
With blood of fathers, mothers, daughters, sons,
Bak'd and impasted with the parching streets   455
That lend a tyrannous and a damnèd light
To their lord's murder; roasted in wrath and fire
And thus o'ersizèd with coagulate gore,
With eyes like carbuncles, the hellish Pyrrhus
Old grandsire Priam seeks.   460
[So proceed you.]

POLONIUS
'Fore God, my lord, well spoken – with good
accent and good discretion.

1 PLAYER   *Anon he finds him,*
Striking too short at Greeks. His antique sword,   465
Rebellious to his arm, lies where it falls,
Repugnant to command. Unequal match'd,
Pyrrhus at Priam drives, in rage strikes wide,
But with the whiff and wind of his fell sword
Th'unnervèd father falls. [Then senseless Ilium]   470
Seeming to feel this blow, with flaming top
Stoops to his base and with a hideous crash
Takes prisoner Pyrrhus' ear. For lo, his sword
Which was declining on the milky head
Of reverend Priam seem'd i'th' air to stick.   475
So as a painted tyrant Pyrrhus stood
And like a neutral to his will and matter,
Did nothing.
But as we often see against some storm
A silence in the heavens, the rack stand still,   480
The bold winds speechless and the orb below
As hush as death, anon the dreadful thunder

total gules – *red all over*; trick'd – *decorated*

Bak'd – *Cooked*; impasted – *made into pastry*; with – *by*; parching – *fiery*
tyrannous . . . damnèd – *damnedly fierce* (hendiadys)   **tyra**-nnous (equiv. 2 syl.)
lord's – *Priam's*   -ted in **wrath** (anapest); Q2 – lord's murder F – vild murders
o'ersizèd – *coated with* (*liquid used to prepare paint canvases*)   co-**ag**-ulate (equiv. 3 syl.)
carbuncles – *large red gems*
grandsire – *grandfather*   Hamlet ends the speech mid-line. The line is 4 syl. short
                    Lines 461–3 – in PROSE; So proceed you – not in F.

'Fore – *Before*
accent – *pronunciation*; discretion – *judgement*

Anon – *Soon*   The Player resumes the verse line left off by Hamlet.
                    antique – Pron. **an**-tique
                    Re-**be**-llious (equiv. 3 syl.)
Repugnant to command – *refusing to do his business*   Q2 – match'd F – match
drives – *aims with his sword*
whiff and wind – *whiff of wind* (hendiadys – see Introduction); fell – *cruel*
Th'unnervèd – *the enfeebled*; Ilium – *Troy*   F – Then senseless Ilium – not in Q2
                    Q2 – this F – his
Stoops . . . base – *Collapses*; his – *its*   **hi**-deous (equiv. 2 syl.)
Takes . . . ear – *Distracts Pyrrhus' attention*   **pris**-oner (equiv. 2 syl.)
declining – *descending*; milky – *white-haired*
                    i'th' (equiv. 1 syl.)
painted – *as if in a painting/covered in blood*
like . . . to – *like one unable to act according to*   F – And like Q2 – Like
                    Metre – this line is short by 7 syl.
see – *experience*; against – *before*
rack – *clouds*   heavens (equiv.1 syl.)
orb – *earth*
anon – *soon*

Doth rend the region, so after Pyrrhus' pause
A rousèd vengeance sets him new a-work
And never did the Cyclops' hammers fall   485
On Mars's armour, forg'd for proof eterne,
With less remorse than Pyrrhus' bleeding sword
Now falls on Priam.
Out, out, thou strumpet Fortune! All you gods
In general synod take away her power,   490
Break all the spokes and fellies from her wheel
And bowl the round nave down the hill of heaven
As low as to the fiends.

POLONIUS
This is too long.

HAMLET
It shall to the barber's with your beard. Prithee   495
say on – he's for a jig, or a tale of bawdry, or he sleeps.
Say on, come to Hecuba.

1 PLAYER
But who – ah woe – had seen the mobled queen –

HAMLET
'The mobled queen'!

POLONIUS
That's good. [Inobled queen is good.]   500

1 PLAYER
– Run barefoot up and down, threatening the flames
With bisson rheum, a clout upon that head
Where late the diadem stood and, for a robe,
About her lank and all-o 'erteemèd loins,

rend – *tear through*; region – *sky*   -ion, so **af**- (anapest – see 'A Note on Metre')

Cyclops – (see Myth)
Mars – (see Myth); for proof eterne – *to endure forever*
bleeding – *dripping with blood*

                                Metre – this line is short by 5 syl.

strumpet – *whore*
general synod – *general assembly*
fellies – *bent wood forming the rim of a wheel*; wheel – *(Fortune is often depicted with*
nave – *wheel hub*; hill of heaven – *Mount Olympus*   *a wheel)*

Lines 494–7 – in PROSE

for – *in favour of*; jig – *musical entertainment at the end of a tragedy*; bawdry – *rudeness*
Hecuba – (see Myth)

mobled – *muffled*   Q2 – ah woe Q1/F – O who; Q2 – mobled F – inobled

Q2 – mobled F – inobled; Lines 499–500 – in PROSE

Inobled queen is good – not in Q2

threate-**ning** (equiv. 2 syl.); Q2 – flames F – flame
bisson rheum – *blinding tears*; clout – *cloth*   Q2 – upon F – about
diadem – *crown*   **dia**-dem (equiv. 2 syl.)
lank – *shrunken*; o 'erteemèd – *worn out with childbirth*

A blanket in the alarm of fear caught up.   505
Who this had seen, with tongue in venom steep'd,
'Gainst Fortune's state would treason have pronounc'd.
But if the gods themselves did see her then
When she saw Pyrrhus make malicious sport
In mincing with his sword her husband's limbs,   510
The instant burst of clamour that she made
(Unless things mortal move them not at all)
Would have made milch the burning eyes of heaven
And passion in the gods.

POLONIUS

Look where he has not turned his colour and   515
has tears in's eyes. – Prithee no more!

HAMLET

'Tis well. I'll have thee speak out the rest of this
soon. [*to Polonius*] Good my lord, will you see the
players well bestowed? Do you hear, let them be well
used, for they are the abstract and brief chronicles of   520
the time: after your death you were better have a bad
epitaph than their ill report while you live.

POLONIUS

My lord, I will use them according to their
desert.

HAMLET

God's bodkin, man, much better! Use every   525
man after his desert and who shall scape whipping? Use
them after your own honour and dignity – the less they
deserve the more merit is in your bounty. Take them in.

POLONIUS
Come, sirs.

the a-**larm** (anapest – see 'A Note on Metre'); Q2 – the alarm F – th'alarum
Who ... seen – *Whoever had seen this*; in venom steep'd – *steeped in poison*
Fortune's state – *the rule of Fortune*; treason ... pronounc'd – *have uttered treason*

mincing – *chopping up*   Q1/F – husband's Q2 – husband
clamour – *noise*

milch – *milky/moist*
And passion – *And aroused passion*   Metre – line is short by 4 syl.

       The dialogue between Hamlet and Polonius resumes in PROSE
Look where – *See whether*; his colour – *pale*
       Q2 – Prithee F – Pray you

       F – rest of this soon; Q2 – rest soon

bestowed – *accommodated*   Q2 – you F – ye
used – *treated*; abstract ... chronicles – *brief summarisers*   Q2 – abstract F – abstracts
you were better have – *it would be better for you if you had*
       Qq – live F – lived

use – *treat*
desert – *deserving*

bodkin – *dear body*   Q2 – bodkin F – bodykins; Q2 – much better F – better
scape – *escape*; whipping – *(punishment for vagabonds)*   Q2 – shall Q1/F – should
after – *according to*
bounty – *generosity*

HAMLET

   Follow him, friends. We'll hear a play   530
tomorrow. [*aside to First Player*] Dost thou hear me, old
friend? Can you play The Murder of Gonzago?

1 PLAYER

   Ay, my lord.

HAMLET

   We'll ha't tomorrow night. You could for need
study a speech of some dozen lines, or sixteen lines,   535
which I would set down and insert in't, could you not?

1 PLAYER

   Ay, my lord.

HAMLET

   Very well. Follow that lord – and look you mock
him not. [*to other Players*] My good friends, I'll leave
you till night. You are welcome to Elsinore.   540

ROSENCRANTZ

   Good my lord.

HAMLET

   Ay so, God buy to you.   *Exeunt* [*all but Hamlet*].

                Now I am alone.
O, what a rogue and peasant slave am I!
Is it not monstrous that this player here,
But in a fiction, in a dream of passion,   545
Could force his soul so to his own conceit
That from her working all his visage wann'd
– Tears in his eyes, distraction in his aspect,

Dost thou hear me – *Can I have a word with you*

ha't – *have it*; for need – *as required*   Q2 – for Q1/F – for a
study – *learn*   Q2 – dozen lines Q1/F – dozen
set down – *write down*   Q2 – you F – ye

Good my lord – *Farewell my lord*

                                                      The scene moves into VERSE.
God buy – *Goodbye*   Q2 – God buy to you F – God buy'ye;
                                                      to you./**Now** (anapest – see 'A Note on Metre')

monstrous – *shocking*
But – *merely*
so ... conceit – *to conform to the imagined situation*   Q2 – own F – whole
her – *the soul's*; visage wann'd – *face grew pale*   Q2 – wann'd F – warm'd
distraction – *frenzy*; aspect – *appearance*   Q2 – in his aspect F – in's aspect

A broken voice, and his whole function suiting
With forms to his conceit – and all for nothing –   550
For Hecuba?
What's Hecuba to him, or he to Hecuba,
That he should weep for her? What would he do
Had he the motive and the cue for passion
That I have? He would drown the stage with tears   555
And cleave the general ear with horrid speech,
Make mad the guilty and appal the free,
Confound the ignorant and amaze indeed
The very faculties of eyes and ears. Yet I,
A dull and muddy-mettl'd rascal, peak   560
Like John-a-dreams, unpregnant of my cause,
And can say nothing. No, not for a king
Upon whose property and most dear life
A damn'd defeat was made. Am I a coward?
Who calls me villain, breaks my pate across,   565
Plucks off my beard and blows it in my face,
Tweaks me by the nose, gives me the lie i'th' throat
As deep as to the lungs? Who does me this,
Ha? 'Swounds, I should take it. For it cannot be
But I am pigeon-liver'd and lack gall   570
To make oppression bitter, or ere this
I should ha' fatted all the region kites
With this slave's offal – bloody, bawdy villain,
Remorseless, treacherous, lecherous, kindless villain.
[Oh vengeance!]   575
Why, what an ass am I: this is most brave,
That I, the son of a dear murderèd,
Prompted to my revenge by heaven and hell,
Must like a whore unpack my heart with words
And fall a-cursing like a very drab,   580
A stallion! Fie upon't, foh! About, my brains!

function – *way of being*
With forms – *in expression*; conceit – *imaginings*

Metre – line is short by 6 syl.

Q1/F – he to Hecuba Q2 – he to her; Irregular line (12 syllables)

F – the cue Q2 – that

cleave – *split*; general – *people's*; horrid – *causing horror*
appal the free – *horrify the innocent*
Confound – *Devastate*; amaze – *bewilder*   **ig**-norant (equiv. 2 syl.)
very faculties – *proper functions*   Irregular line – quartus paeon/as hexameter
dull – *slow*; muddy-mettl'd – *poor-spirited*; peak – *mope about*
John-a-dreams – *a dreamy, inactive man*; unpregnant – *not stimulated by*

property – *rightful sovereignty*
defeat – *overthrow*
pate – *head*

gives . . . throat – *accuses me of lying* (Prov.)   by the **nose** (anapest), I'th' (equiv. 1 syl.);
Who . . . this – *Who does this to me*   Q2 – by the F – by'th'
'Swounds – *God's wounds* (oath)   I should **take** (anapest); Q2 – 'Swounds F – Why
pigeon . . . gall – *(pigeons were thought to be gentle because their livers lacked gall)*
ere – *before*
ha' – *have*; region kites – *sky's birds of prey*   Q2 – ha' F – have
offal – *entrails*; bawdy – *lewd* Q2 – offal – bloody, bawdy F – offal, bloody: a bawdy
kindless – *lacking natural feelings*   **treach**-erous; **lech**-erous, (both equiv. 2 syl.)
                                                Oh vengeance! – only in F
brave – *admirable* (sarcastic)   Qq – Why F – Who?
           Q2 – a dear murderèd F – the dear murderèd Q3 – a dear father murder'd
                                                heaven (equiv. 1 syl.)
unpack – *unload*
drab – *whore*
sta-llion – *male whore* (equiv. 2 syl.); About – *get to work*   upon't (equiv. 1 syl.)
           Q2 – stallion F – scullion; Q2 – brains Q1/F – brain

Hum, I have heard
That guilty creatures sitting at a play
Have by the very cunning of the scene
Been struck so to the soul that presently   585
They have proclaim'd their malefactions.
For murder, though it have no tongue, will speak
With most miraculous organ. I'll have these players
Play something like the murder of my father
Before mine uncle. I'll observe his looks,   590
I'll tent him to the quick. If he but blench
I know my course. The spirit that I have seen
May be a devil, and the devil hath power
T'assume a pleasing shape. Yea, and perhaps
Out of my weakness and my melancholy,   595
As he is very potent with such spirits,
Abuses me to damn me! I'll have grounds
More relative than this. The play's the thing
Wherein I'll catch the conscience of the King.   *Exit.*

3.1 *Enter KING, QUEEN, POLONIUS, OPHELIA, ROSENCRANTZ,
GUILDENSTERN [and] Lords.*

KING
And can you by no drift of conference
Get from him why he puts on this confusion,
Grating so harshly all his days of quiet
With turbulent and dangerous lunacy?

ROSENCRANTZ
He does confess he feels himself distracted   5
But from what cause he will by no means speak.

GUILDENSTERN
Nor do we find him forward to be sounded

Ambiguous lineation – different editions divide ll. 581–2 differently; Hum - not in F

creatures – *people*

cunning – *ingenuity*; scene – *performance*

presently – *immediately*

malefactions – *ill deeds*   malefactions – metre suggests **mal**-e-**fac**-ti-**ons**

For ... speak – *Murder will out* (Prov.)

miraculous organ – *supernatural tongue*   mir-**ac**-ulous (equiv. 3 syl.);

                                        – gan. I'll **have** (anapest – see 'A Note on Metre')

tent – *probe*; quick – *most sensitive point*; blench – *flinch*   F – he but Q2–'a do

                                        -rit that **I** (anapest – see 'A Note on Metre')

                    Q2 – a Q1/F – the; F – devil Q2 – de'il; devil (second time) (equiv. 1 syl.)

Out of – *By exploring*

potent – *influential*; such spirits – *those who are melancholy*

Abuses – *Deceives*

relative – *relevant*; this – *the word of the ghost*

drift of conference (**con**-fer-**ence**) – *course of conversation*   Q2 – conference

puts on – *assumes*; confusion – *mental disturbance*   F – circumstance

Grating – *Disturbing/Wearing away*

                                        dan-gerous (equiv. 2 syl.)

distracted – *seriously disturbed*

                                        F – he Q2 – 'a

forward – *inclined*; sounded – *questioned*

But with a crafty madness keeps aloof
When we would bring him on to some confession
Of his true state.

QUEEN   Did he receive you well?

ROSENCRANTZ   Most like a gentleman.   10

GUILDENSTERN
But with much forcing of his disposition.

ROSENCRANTZ
Niggard of question, but of our demands
Most free in his reply.

QUEEN
Did you assay him to any pastime?

*/ concern
for son's
health*

ROSENCRANTZ
Madam, it so fell out that certain players   15
We o'erraught on the way. Of these we told him
And there did seem in him a kind of joy
To hear of it. They are here about the Court
And, as I think, they have already order
This night to play before him.

POLONIUS   'Tis most true,   20
And he beseeched me to entreat your majesties
To hear and see the matter.

KING
With all my heart, and it doth much content me
To hear him so inclined.
Good gentlemen, give him a further edge   25
And drive his purpose into these delights.

crafty – *cunning*; aloof – *at a distance*

Metre – Ambiguous metrical connection (see Series Introduction)

disposition – *mood*

Niggard of question – *Reluctant to initiate conversation*; demands – *questions*
Metre – line is short by 4 syl.

assay him – *encourage him to try*

o'erraught – *overtook*

They are **here** (anapest); Q2 – are here about F – are about
have already – *already have*

ma-jesties (equiv. 2 syl.)
Metre – in F this line is short by 3 syl.
Ambiguous lineation – lines 23 to 26 are lineated differently in Q2 and F
(implying different links)
Metre – in Q2 this line is short by 4 syl.

a further edge – *incite him more forcefully*
drive ... delights – *encourage him to undertake these pleasures*   Q2 – into F – on/To

ROSENCRANTZ
   We shall, my lord.

   Exeunt Rosencrantz and Guildenstern [and Lords].

KING   Sweet Gertrude, leave us two.
   For we have closely sent for Hamlet hither
   That he, as 'twere by accident, may here
   Affront Ophelia. Her father and myself –   30
   Will so bestow ourselves that, seeing unseen,
   We may of their encounter frankly judge
   And gather by him as he is behav'd
   If't be th'affliction of his love or no
   That thus he suffers for.

QUEEN   I shall obey you.   35
   And for your part, Ophelia, I do wish
   That your good beauties be the happy cause
   Of Hamlet's wildness. So shall I hope your virtues
   Will bring him to his wonted way again
   To both your honours.

OPHELIA   Madam, I wish it may.   40

   [Exit Queen.]

POLONIUS
   Ophelia, walk you here. (Gracious, so please you,
   We will bestow ourselves.) Read on this book
   That show of such an exercise may colour
   Your loneliness. We are oft too blame in this –
   'Tis too much prov'd that with devotion's visage   45
   And pious action we do sugar o'er
   The devil himself.

two – *presumably referring to himself and Polonius*   Q2 – two F – too
closely – *secretly*; hither – *to this place*

                                       Q2 – here F – there

Affront – *come face to face with*   -lia. Her **fa**- (anapest'); F – myself (lawful espials)
bestow – *position*   F – Will Q2 – We'll; seeing (equiv. 1 syl.)

by … behav'd – *from his behaviour*

                                       If't (equiv. 1 syl.)

                        shall I **hope** (anapest – see 'A Note on Metre')
wonted way – *normal behaviour*   wonted – Pron. – **wohn**-ted

                        -am, I **wish** (anapest – see 'A Note on Metre')

Gracious – *Your grace* (addressed to the King)   Q2 – please you F – please ye
bestow – *hide*; this book – *(a prayer book)*
an exercise – *private devotion*; colour/Your loneliness – *account for your being alone*
oft – *often*; too blame – *blameworthy*   We are **oft** (anapest – see 'A Note on Metre')
much – *often*; devotion's visage – *the pretence of religion*
sugar o'er – *cover up with sweetness*

                                    devil (equiv. 1 syl.)

KING   O, 'tis too true.
   [*aside*] How smart a lash that speech doth give my
     conscience!
   The harlot's cheek beautied with plastering art
   Is not more ugly to the thing that helps it   50
   Than is my deed to my most painted word.
   O heavy burden!

reveal truth that he's guilty

POLONIUS
   I hear him coming, let's withdraw, my lord.

[King and Polonius hide behind an arras.]

Enter HAMLET.

HAMLET
   To be, or not to be – that is the question;
   Whether 'tis nobler in the mind to suffer   55
   The slings and arrows of outrageous fortune
   Or to take arms against a sea of troubles
   And by opposing end them; to die: to sleep –
   No more, and by a sleep to say we end
   The heartache and the thousand natural shocks   60
   That flesh is heir to: 'tis a consummation
   Devoutly to be wished – to die: to sleep –
   To sleep, perchance to dream – ay, there's the rub,
   For in that sleep of death what dreams may come
   When we have shuffl'd off this mortal coil   65
   Must give us pause: there's the respect
   That makes calamity of so long life.
   For who would bear the whips and scorns of time,
   Th'oppressor's wrong, the proud man's contumely,
   The pangs of dispriz'd love, the law's delay,   70
   The insolence of office and the spurns

Metre – shared line is short by 2 syl.; Q2 – too true F – true
smart – *stinging*

beautied – *made beautiful*; plastering art – *make-up*
to – *in comparison to*; the . . . it – *the make-up*

Metre – line is short by 5 syl.

F – let's withdraw Q2 – withdraw

See Introduction for details of the placement of 'To be or not to be' and the nunnery scene in Q1.

slings – *catapults*; outrageous – *excessively wicked*

sea of troubles – Prov.
opposing – *fighting against them*   them; to **die** (anapest – see 'A Note on Metre')
No more – *(i.e. death is no more than sleep)*

That . . . to – *That are common to all humans*; consummation – *ending*

rub – *difficulty*
what – *the thought of what*
mortal coil – *mortal flesh/turmoil of living*
give – *make*; there's – *that's*; respect – *consideration*   Metre – short by 2 syl.
calamity . . . life – *a calamitous life continue for so long*
scorns – *insults*; time – *life*
contumely – *insolence*   Q2 – proud F – poor
dispriz'd – *unvalued*   F – dispriz'd Q2 – despis'd
office – *officials*

That patient merit of th'unworthy takes,
When he himself might his quietus make
With a bare bodkin. Who would fardels bear
To grunt and sweat under a weary life   75
But that the dread of something after death
(The undiscover'd country from whose bourn
No traveller returns) puzzles the will
And makes us rather bear those ills we have
Than fly to others that we know not of.   80
Thus conscience does make cowards of us all
And thus the native hue of resolution
Is sicklied o'er with the pale cast of thought,
And enterprises of great pitch and moment
With this regard their currents turn awry   85
And lose the name of action. Soft you now,
The fair Ophelia! Nymph, in thy orisons
Be all my sins remember'd.

OPHELIA   Good my lord,
How does your honour for this many a day?

HAMLET
I humbly thank you, well.   90

OPHELIA
My lord, I have remembrances of yours
That I have longèd long to redeliver.
I pray you now receive them.

HAMLET
No, not I. I never gave you aught.

OPHELIA
My honour'd lord, you know right well you did,   95

patient merit . . . takes – *a deserving person receives from a worthless one*
his quietus make – *end his life* (paying his debts)
bare bodkin – *unsheathed dagger*, fardels – *burdens*   Q2 – would F – would these

But that – *Except that*
bourn – *boundary*
puzzles – *confuses*

conscience – *consciousness*   F – cowards of us all Q2 – cowards
native hue – *natural colour*
sicklied o'er – *unhealthily covered over*, cast – *colour*   F – sicklied Q2 – sickled
pitch – *height*, moment – *significance*   Q2 – pitch F – pith
With this regard – *On this account*, turn awry – *alter*   Q2 – awry F – away
Soft you – *Wait a moment*
orisons – *prayers*   Punct. Q2 – fair Ophelia F – fair Ophelia?;
                                        in thy **or-** (anapest – see 'A Note on Metre')

How . . . day – *How have you been for the last few days?*   -ny a **day** (anapest –
                                        see 'A Note on Metre')

                Hamlet moves into PROSE; Q2 – well F – well, well, well

remembrances – *gifts/love tokens*

                                Metre – line is short by 3 syl.

aught – *anything*   Q2 – No, not I F – No, no

                                Q2 – you know F – I know

And with them words of so sweet breath compos'd
As made these things more rich. Their perfume lost,
Take these again, for to the noble mind
Rich gifts wax poor when givers prove unkind.
There, my lord.   100

HAMLET
Ha! Ha! Are you honest?

OPHELIA
My lord?

HAMLET
Are you fair?

OPHELIA
What means your lordship?

HAMLET
That if you be honest and fair you should admit   105
no discourse to your beauty.

OPHELIA
Could Beauty, my lord, have better commerce
than with Honesty?

HAMLET
Ay, truly. For the power of Beauty will sooner
transform Honesty from what it is to a bawd than the   110
force of Honesty can translate Beauty into his likeness.
This was sometime a paradox, but now the time gives it
proof. I did love you once.

OPHELIA
Indeed, my lord, you made me believe so.

words . . . compos'd – *such charming words*

Their perfume lost – *Now their attraction has gone*   Q2 – these F – the

                                                    to the noble . . . unkind – Prov.

wax – *turn*

                                                    Metre – line is short by 7 syl.

Here Ophelia moves into PROSE as well

Q2 – you . . . beauty F – your honesty should admit no discourse to your beauty

you . . . beauty – *your honesty should not allow anyone to converse with your beauty*

commerce – *dealings*

bawd – *pimp/pander*

translate – *transform*

sometime – *once*; paradox – *seemingly absurd statement*

HAMLET

    You should not have believed me. For virtue   115
cannot so inoculate our old stock but we shall relish
of it. I loved you not.

look back

OPHELIA

    I was the more deceived.

HAMLET

    Get thee to a nunnery! Why wouldst thou be a
breeder of sinners? I am myself indifferent honest but   120
yet I could accuse me of such things that it were better
my mother had not borne me. I am very proud,
revengeful, ambitious, with more offences at my beck
than I have thoughts to put them in, imagination to give
them shape, or time to act them in. What should such   125
fellows as I do crawling between earth and heaven? We
are arrant knaves all – believe none of us. Go thy ways to
a nunnery. Where's your father?

conflicting

OPHELIA

    At home, my lord.

HAMLET

    Let the doors be shut upon him that he may   130
play the fool nowhere but in's own house. Farewell.

OPHELIA [*aside*]

    O help him, you sweet heavens!

HAMLET

    If thou dost marry, I'll give thee this plague for
thy dowry: be thou as chaste as ice, as pure as snow,
thou shalt not escape calumny. Get thee to a nunnery.   135

For virtue ... it – *Virtue cannot be grafted onto a sinful tree without some element of sin remaining.*

nunnery – *convent* (possibly also slang for brothel)
indifferent honest – *reasonably virtuous*
me – *myself*

beck – *command*

Q2 – earth and heaven Q1/F – heaven and earth
arrant – *downright*; Go thy ways – *Go away*   Q1/F – knaves all Q2 – knaves
IN PERFORMANCE – this is often the point where Hamlet realises that he is being watched – note the change of address from 'thou'/'thy' to 'you'/'your' (see Introduction)

in's – *in his*

plague – *curse*

calumny – *slander*

Farewell. Or, if thou wilt needs marry, marry a fool, for
wise men know well enough what monsters you make
of them. To a nunnery go, and quickly too. Farewell.

OPHELIA [*aside*]
Heavenly powers restore him.

HAMLET
I have heard of your paintings well enough.   140
God hath given you one face and you make yourselves
another. You jig and amble and you lisp, you
nickname God's creatures and make your wantonness
ignorance. Go to, I'll no more on't. It hath made me
mad. I say we will have no more marriage. Those that   145
are married already – all but one – shall live. The rest
shall keep as they are. To a nunnery, go!   *Exit.*

OPHELIA
O, what a noble mind is here o'erthrown!
The courtier's, soldier's, scholar's eye, tongue, sword,
Th'expectancy and rose of the fair state,   150
The glass of fashion and the mould of form,
Th'observed of all observers, quite, quite down.
And I, of ladies most deject and wretched,
That sucked the honey of his musick'd vows,
Now see that noble and most sovereign reason   155
Like sweet bells jangl'd out of time and harsh –
That unmatch'd form and feature of blown youth
Blasted with ecstasy. O woe is me
T'have seen what I have seen, see what I see.

[*King and Polonius step forward from behind the arras.*]

KING
Love! His affections do not that way tend.   160

not love sick

Q2 – Farewell F – Go, farewell
monsters – *cuckolds* (men with unfaithful wives were thought to grow horns)

Q2 – Heavenly F – O, heavenly

paintings – *use of make-up*　　Q2 – paintings Q1 – paintings too F – pratlings too
　　　　　　　　　　　　　Q2/Q1 – hath F – has; Q2/Q1 – yourselves F – yourself
lisp – *speak in an affected way*　　Q2 – jig and ... lisp, you F – jig, you ... lisp, and
your wantonness ignorance – *use ignorance as an excuse for wanton behaviour*
I'll – *I'll put up with*; on't – *of it*　　　　Q2 – ignorance Q1/F – your ignorance;
　　　　　　　　　　　　　　　　　Q2 – marriage Q1/F – marriages
all but one – *(presumably the King)*

o'erthrown – *overthrown*　　　　　　　The scene moves into VERSE.

th'expectancy and rose – *rose-like hope* (hendiadys) F – expectancy Q2 – expectation
glass – *model*; mould of form – *pattern of behaviour*
Th'observed ... observers – *the one watched by everyone*
deject – *down-cast*
musick'd – *music-like*　　　　　　　　　　Q2 – musick'd F – music
　　　　　　　　　　　　　　　　　　　F – that Q2 – what
　　　　　　　　　　　　　　　　　　　Q2 – time F – tune
blown – *blooming*　　　　　　　　　　　F – feature Q2 – stature
Blasted with ecstasy – *Destroyed by madness*

affections – *emotions*

[handwritten annotation: not mad]

Nor what he spake, though it lack'd form a little,
Was not like madness. There's something in his soul
O'er which his melancholy sits on brood
And I do doubt the hatch and the disclose
Will be some danger – which for to prevent   165
I have in quick determination
Thus set it down. He shall with speed to England
For the demand of our neglected tribute.
Haply the seas and countries different
With variable objects shall expel   170
This something-settled matter in his heart
Whereon his brains still beating puts him thus
From fashion of himself. What think you on't?

POLONIUS
It shall do well. But yet do I believe
The origin and commencement of his grief   175
Sprung from neglected love. How now, Ophelia?
You need not tell us what Lord Hamlet said –
We heard it all. My lord, do as you please,
But if you hold it fit after the play
Let his Queen-mother all alone entreat him   180
To show his grief. Let her be round with him
And I'll be plac'd, so please you, in the ear
Of all their conference. If she find him not,
To England send him or confine him where
Your wisdom best shall think.

KING   It shall be so.   185
Madness in great ones must not unwatch'd go.   *Exeunt.*

3.2 *Enter* HAMLET *and three of the Players.*

HAMLET
Speak the speech, I pray you, as I pronounced

-ness. There's **some-** (anapest – see 'A Note on Metre')

sits on brood – *sits brooding* (like a hen on eggs)

doubt – *fear*; hatch and the disclose – *outcome* (hendiadys – see Introduction)

for to – *in order to*

determination – metre suggests de-**ter**-min-a-ti-**on** (6 syl.)

set it down – *decided*

For the demand – *To demand*; tribute – *peace money paid by one state to another*

Haply – *Perhaps*   different – metre suggests **diff**-er-**ent** (3 syl.)

variable objects – *a change of scene*

something-settled – *somewhat obsessive*

still beating – *(with concentration)*

fashion of himself – *his usual behaviour*

o-rigin (equiv. 2 syl.)

hold it – *consider it*

round – *severe*   Q2 – grief F – griefs

in the ear/Of – *so as to hear*

find him not – *fails to find out what is troubling him*   **con**-ference (2 syl.)

The scene begins in PROSE.

it to you – trippingly on the tongue. But if you mouth
it as many of our players do, I had as lief the town-crier
spoke my lines. Nor do not saw the air too much with
your hand, thus, but use all gently; for, in the very   5
torrent, tempest and, as I may say, whirlwind of your
passion, you must acquire and beget a temperance that
may give it smoothness. O, it offends me to the soul to
hear a robustious periwig-pated fellow tear a passion to
tatters, to very rags, to split the ears of the groundlings,   10
who for the most part are capable of nothing but
inexplicable dumb-shows and noise. I would have such
a fellow whipped for o'erdoing Termagant – it out-
Herods Herod. Pray you avoid it.

PLAYER
I warrant your honour.   15

HAMLET
Be not too tame neither, but let your own
discretion be your tutor. Suit the action to the word, the
word to the action, with this special observance – that
you o'erstep not the modesty of nature. For anything so
o'erdone is from the purpose of playing whose end,   20
both at the first and now, was and is to hold as 'twere
the mirror up to Nature to show Virtue her feature,
Scorn her own image, and the very age and body of the
time his form and pressure. Now this overdone, or
come tardy off, though it makes the unskilful laugh,   25
cannot but make the judicious grieve, the censure of
which one must in your allowance o'erweigh a whole
theatre of others. O, there be players that I have seen
play and heard others praised – and that highly – not to
speak it profanely, that neither having th'accent of   30
Christians nor the gait of Christian, pagan nor man

trippingly – *fast/rhythmically*; mouth – *declaim*

as lief – *rather*   Q2 – our Q1/F – your; Q2 – town-crier F – town-crier had

thus – *like this*; use all gently – *do everything in moderation*

                                                Q2 – whirlwind of your F – the whirlwind of

beget – *create*; temperance – *moderation*

robustious – *boisterous*; periwig-pated – *wearing a styled wig*   Q2/Q1 – hear F – see

groundlings – *those who stood at ground level in the theatre* (paying the lowest price)

capable of – *capable of understanding*

inexplicable dumb-shows – *meaningless mimed spectacles*   Q2/Q1 – would F – could

Termagant – *imaginary deity represented as loud and overbearing*

Herod – *King of Judea at Christ's birth* (represented in Mystery plays as a raging

tyrant)

warrant – *can assure*

tame – *understated*

discretion – *judgement*; action – *gesture*

modesty – *restraints*

from – *far from*; playing – *acting*; end – *objective*   Q2 – o'erdone F – over done

feature – *appearance*   Q2 – her feature F – her own feature

Scorn . . . image – *a scornful person how they appear to others*; age and body – *aged*

pressure – *impression*   *body* (hendiadys)

come tardy off – *performed inadequately*   Q2 – makes F – make

the censure of which one – *the judgement of whom*   Q2 – of F – of the

in your allowance – *by your admission*

                                                      Q2 – praised F – praise

profanely – *irreverently*; accent – *pronunciation*   Q2 – th'accent F – the accent

gait – *bearing*

have so strutted and bellowed that I have thought some
of Nature's journeymen had made men, and not made
them well, they imitated humanity so abhominably.

PLAYER

I hope we have reformed that indifferently with us.   35

HAMLET

O, reform it altogether, and let those that play
your clowns speak no more than is set down for them.
For there be of them that will themselves laugh to set
on some quantity of barren spectators to laugh too,
though in the meantime some necessary question of the   40
play be then to be considered. – That's villainous and
shows a most pitiful ambition in the fool that uses it.
Go, make you ready.   [*Exeunt Players.*]

Enter POLONIUS, GUILDENSTERN and ROSENCRANTZ.

How now, my lord, will the King hear this piece of
work?   45

POLONIUS

And the Queen too, and that presently.

HAMLET

Bid the players make haste.
Will you two help to hasten them?

ROSENCRANTZ

Ay, my lord.

Exeunt Rosencrantz and Guildenstern.

HAMLET

What ho, Horatio!

Nature's journeyman – *Nature's hired, low-skilled, workers* (rather than Nature herself)

indifferently – *a little*   Q2 – us F – us, sir

set down – *written*
of them that – *amongst them those who*
set on – *incite*; barren – *lacking in judgement*
necessary question – *important aspect*

uses – *practices*

presently – *immediately*

SP – in F this line is spoken by ROSENCRANTZ and GUILDENSTERN
                                       Q2 – Ay F – We will

The scene moves into VERSE at this point.

Enter HORATIO.

HORATIO   Here, sweet lord, at your service.   50

HAMLET
Horatio, thou art e'en as just a man
As e'er my conversation coped withal.

HORATIO
O my dear lord –

HAMLET   Nay, do not think I flatter,
For what advancement may I hope from thee
That no revenue hast but thy good spirits   55
To feed and clothe thee? Why should the poor be flattered?
No, let the candied tongue lick absurd pomp
And crook the pregnant hinges of the knee
Where thrift may follow fawning. Dost thou hear?
Since my dear soul was mistress of her choice   60
And could of men distinguish her election
Sh'ath sealed thee for herself. For thou hast been
As one in suffering all that suffers nothing –
A man that Fortune's buffets and rewards
Hast ta'en with equal thanks. And blest are those   65
Whose blood and judgement are so well co-meddl'd
That they are not a pipe for Fortune's finger
To sound what stop she please. Give me that man
That is not passion's slave and I will wear him
In my heart's core – ay, in my heart of heart –   70
As I do thee. Something too much of this:
There is a play tonight before the King –
One scene of it comes near the circumstance
Which I have told thee of my father's death.
I prithee when thou seest that act afoot,   75

at your **ser**- (anapest – see 'A Note on Metre')

e'en – *absolutely*; just – *honourable/judicious*
my conversation coped withal – *I encountered in my dealings with others*

revenue – *income*   re-**ven**-ue – metre suggests emphasis on 2nd syl.
                                      should the **poor** (anapest – see 'A Note on Metre')
candied – *flattering*   Q2 – tongue lick F – tongue, like
crook – *bend*; pregnant – *ready*; crook . . . knee – *kneel*
thrift – *profit*; follow – *stem from*

                                      Q2 – her F – my
of . . . election – *choose between men*
sealed – *chosen*   Q5 – Sh'ath Q2 – S'hath F – Hath
As – *like*; that suffers – *that seems to suffer*   **suff**-ering (equiv. 2 syl.)
buffets – *blows*
ta'en – *taken*   Q2 – Hast F – Hath
blood – *passion*; co-meddl'd – *mixed together*   Q2 – co-meddl'd F – co-mingl'd
pipe – *(musical instrument)*
stop – *note*; That they . . . please – *That Fortune cannot manipulate them*

core – *centre*; heart of hearts – *(a play on core sounding like the Latin word for heart – cor)*
Something – *Altogether*

circumstance – *events*

act – *action*; afoot – *being performed*

Even with the very comment of thy soul
Observe my uncle. If his occulted guilt
Do not itself unkennel in one speech
It is a damnèd ghost that we have seen
And my imaginations are as foul   80
As Vulcan's stithy. Give him heedful note,
For I mine eyes will rivet to his face
And after we will both our judgements join
In censure of his seeming.

HORATIO   Well, my lord
If he steal aught the whilst this play is playing   85
And scape detecting I will pay the theft.

Enter Trumpets and Kettledrums, KING, QUEEN, POLONIUS,
OPHELIA [ROSENCRANTZ and GUILDENSTERN].

HAMLET [*to Horatio*]
They are coming to the play. I must be idle. Get you
a place.

KING
How fares our cousin Hamlet?

HAMLET
Excellent, i'faith! Of the chameleon's dish – I   90
eat the air, promise-crammed. You cannot feed capons so.

KING
I have nothing with this answer, Hamlet. These
words are not mine.

HAMLET
No, nor mine now, my lord. [*to Polonius*] You
played once i'th' university, you say?   95

the very . . . soul – *your most careful attention*   Even (equiv. 1 syl.); Q2 – thy F – my
occulted – *concealed*   Q2 – my F – mine; Can be scanned with '-cle. If **his**' or
itself unkennel – *reveal itself*   'his o-**ccul**' as anapest

imaginations – *suspicions*
Vulcan – (see Myth); stithy – *forge*; heedful – *attentive*   Q2 – heedful F – needful
rivet – *fix*

censure of his seeming – *assessing his behaviour*   Q2 – In F – To

steal aught – *get away with anything*   F – he Q2 – 'a
scape – *escape*   F – detecting Q2 – detected

                                    The scene moves into PROSE.
be idle – *resume my mad behaviour*; Get you a place – *Find yourself somewhere to sit*

fares – *is*

Of . . . dish – *I eat the same food as a chameleon* (thought to be air)
promised-crammed – *I am stuffed with promises*; capons – *castrated cockerels fattened
for eating*

I have nothing with – *gain nothing from*
words are not mine – *nothing to do with my question*

                        Punct. – Q2 – nor mine now F – nor mine. Now

POLONIUS
That did I, my lord, and was accounted a good
actor.

HAMLET
What did you enact?

POLONIUS
I did enact Julius Caesar. I was killed i'th'
Capitol. Brutus killed me.   100

HAMLET
It was a brute part of him to kill so capital a calf
there. Be the players ready?

ROSENCRANTZ
Ay, my lord, they stay upon your
patience.

QUEEN
Come hither, my dear Hamlet, sit by me.   105

HAMLET
No, good mother, here's metal more attractive.

POLONIUS [*to King*]
O ho, do you mark that!

HAMLET
Lady, shall I lie in your lap?

OPHELIA
No, my lord.

[HAMLET
I mean, my head upon your lap?   110

accounted – *reported/considered to be*   Q2 – did I F – I did

Q2/Q1 – What F – And what

brute part – *brutal action* (puns on Brutus and actor's part); capital a calf – *such a prize fool* (with pun on Capitol)

stay ... patience – *are waiting for you to tell them to start*

hither – *here*   The Queen's line is in VERSE.

metal more attractive – *a more magnetic metal/*   Q2 – dear F – good
a more appealing proposition

mark – *note*

Lines 110 and 111 are only in F.

OPHELIA
Ay my lord.]

HAMLET
Do you think I meant country matters?

OPHELIA
I think nothing, my lord.

HAMLET
That's a fair thought to lie between maids' legs.

OPHELIA
What is, my lord?   115

HAMLET
Nothing.

OPHELIA
You are merry, my lord.

HAMLET
Who, I?

OPHELIA
Ay, my lord.

HAMLET
O God, your only jig-maker! What should a   120
man do but be merry, for look you how cheerfully my
mother looks, and my father died within's two hours!

OPHELIA
Nay, 'tis twice two months, my lord.

country matters – *something vulgar* (with pun on cunt)

fair – *reasonable*

Nothing – *(with pun on 'no-thing' – vagina)*

only jig-maker – *best comedian/clown*

within's – *within this*

twice two months – *four months*

HAMLET

So long? Nay, then, let the devil wear black, for
I'll have a suit of sables! O heavens – die two months   125
ago and not forgotten yet? Then there's hope a great
man's memory may outlive his life half a year! But, by'r
Lady, he must build churches then, or else shall he suffer
not thinking on – with the hobby-horse whose epitaph
is 'For O! For O! The hobby-horse is forgot!'   130

The trumpets sounds. Dumb-show follows.

Enter [Players as] a king and a queen, the queen embracing
him and he her. He takes her up and declines his head upon
her neck. He lies him down upon a bank of flowers. She
seeing him asleep leaves him. Anon come in [a Player as]
another man, takes off his crown, kisses it, pours poison in
the sleeper's ears and leaves him. The queen returns, finds
the king dead, makes passionate action. The poisoner with
some three or four [Players] come in again, seem to condole
with her. The dead body is carried away. The poisoner woos
the queen with gifts. She seems harsh awhile but in the end
accepts love.   [*Exeunt.*]

OPHELIA

What means this, my lord?

HAMLET

Marry, this is miching mallico! It means
mischief.

OPHELIA

Belike this show imports the argument of the
play.   135

Enter [a Player as the] Prologue.

let … sables – *the devil can wear my mourning clothes and I will wear furs*

by'r Lady – *by Our Lady* (the Virgin Mary)

build churches – *(i.e. in which to be remembered/buried)*   F – he … he Q2 – 'a … 'a

suffer … on – *shall be forgotten*; hobby-horse – *pantomime horse left out of festivities because of Puritan disapproval*; For O … forgot – *(a line from a ballad and a common saying)*

Q2 – *The trumpets sounds.* F – *Hoboyes* [oboes] *play.*

The Dumb Show is often left out in performance since it duplicates the action of the play, and the King does not react to it.

takes her up – raises her from a kneeling position; *declines* – lays

another man – (the King's nephew)

passionate action – actions to portray her shock/grief

condole – sympathise

harsh awhile – unresponsive for a bit

miching mallico – *sneaking wickedness*   F/Q1 – this is Q2 – this; F – miching

Q2 – munching; Q2 – It F/Q1 – That

Belike – *perhaps*; argument – *plot*

HAMLET
We shall know by this fellow. The players
cannot keep council – they'll tell all.

OPHELIA
Will they tell us what this show meant?

HAMLET
Ay, or any show that you will show him. Be not
you ashamed to show, he'll not shame to tell you what   140
it means.

OPHELIA
You are naught, you are naught. I'll mark the
play.

PROLOGUE
For us and for our tragedy,
Here stooping to your clemency,   145
We beg your hearing patiently.   [*Exit.*]

HAMLET
Is this a prologue or the posy of a ring?

OPHELIA
'Tis brief, my lord.

HAMLET
As woman's love.

Enter [Player] King and [Player] Queen.

PLAYER KING
Full thirty times hath Phoebus' cart gone round   150

Q2/Q1 – this fellow F – these fellows

keep council – *keep a secret*

F – they Q2 – 'a

show – *sexual display*; Be not you – *if you are not*   Q2 – you will F/Q1 – you'll

naught – *offensive*

Metre – the Prologue is in iambic tetrameter

stooping – *bowing*; clemency – *mercy*

the posy of a ring – *short rhyme inscribed inside a ring*

Phoebus – (see Myth)   The play is in VERSE

Neptune's salt wash and Tellus' orbèd ground
And thirty dozen moons with borrowed sheen
About the world have times twelve thirties been
Since love our hearts and Hymen did our hands
Unite commutual in most sacred bands.   155

PLAYER QUEEN
So many journeys may the sun and moon
Make us again count o'er ere love be done.
But woe is me, you are so sick of late,
So far from cheer and from your former state,
That I distrust you. Yet, though I distrust,   160
Discomfort you, my lord, it nothing must.
[For women fear too much, even as they love,]
And women's fear and love hold quantity –
In neither aught, or in extremity.
Now what my love is proof hath made you know   165
And, as my love is sized, my fear is so.
[Where love is great, the littlest doubts are fear,
Where little fears grow great, great love grows there.]

PLAYER KING
Faith, I must leave thee, love, and shortly too,
My operant powers their functions leave to do,   170
And thou shalt live in this fair world behind
Honour'd, belov'd, and haply one as kind
For husband shalt thou –

PLAYER QUEEN   *O, confound the rest!*
Such love must needs be treason in my breast.
In second husband let me be accurst: 175
None wed the second but who killed the first.

Neptune's salt wash – *the sea*; Tellus' orbèd ground – *the earth* (see Myth)
borrowed sheen – *light reflected from the sun*
twelve thirties – *(suggesting thirty years, rather than the days implied in the first line)*
Hymen – (see Myth)
commutual – *together*

ere – *before*

from cheer ... state – *from your former cheerfulness* (hendiadys)
distrust you – *fear for you*
Discomfort ... must – *It must not concern you*

                                                           Line 162 is not in F.
hold quantity – *are in proportion to each other*   Q2 – And F – For; Q2 – hold F – holds
In ... extremity – *either there is nothing or*   F – In neither aught
both in the extreme   Q2 – Either none, in neither aught

                                                   Lines 167–8 are not in F.

operant powers – *faculties*; leave to do – *stop performing*   **op**-erant (equiv. 2 syl.);
                                                               Q2 – their F – my

The Player Queen's interruption seems to prevent the Player King from completing
the rhyme with 'find'.
confound – *don't say*

In – *In taking a*; accurst – *cursed*

HAMLET
That's wormwood!

PLAYER QUEEN
The instances that second marriage move
Are base respects of thrift, but none of love.
A second time I kill my husband dead   180
When second husband kisses me in bed.

PLAYER KING
I do believe you think what now you speak.
But what we do determine oft we break.
Purpose is but the slave to memory,
Of violent birth but poor validity,   185
Which now like fruit unripe sticks on the tree
But fall unshaken when they mellow be.
Most necessary 'tis that we forget
To pay ourselves what to ourselves is debt.
What to ourselves in passion we propose,   190
The passion ending doth the purpose lose.
The violence of either grief or joy
Their own enactures with themselves destroy.
Where joy most revels grief doth most lament,
Grief joys, joy grieves, on slender accident.   195
This world is not for aye, nor 'tis not strange
That even our loves should with our fortunes change,
For 'tis a question left us yet to prove
Whether Love lead Fortune or else Fortune Love.
The great man down, you mark his favourite flies,   200
The poor advanc'd makes friends of enemies,
And hitherto doth Love on Fortune tend,
For who not needs shall never lack a friend,
And who in want a hollow friend doth try
Directly seasons him his enemy.   205

wormwood – *bitter* (like the plant)   Hamlet's interjection is in PROSE;
Q2 – *That's wormwood!* F – *Wormwood, Wormwood.*

instances . . . move – *things that motivate second marriage*
respects of thrift – *considerations of profit*

determine – *resolve*
Purpose . . . memory – *our intentions are easily forgotten*
of violent birth – *passionate at the start*; poor validity – *lacking endurance*
Which – *i.e. Purpose* (which is like unripe fruit)
mellow – *ripe*
necessary – *inevitable*
To pay . . . debt – *to pay the debts we owe to ourselves*
passion – *a state of passion*

vi-o-**lence** (equiv. 3 syl.)

enactures – *actions*

Grief . . . accident – *Grief turns to joy and vice versa at the slightest provocation*
aye – *ever*

even (equiv. 1 syl.)

prove – *answer*
lead – *is stronger than*   Whether (equiv. 1 syl.)
mark – *notice*; down – *fallen in favour*; favourite – *favourite supporter*; flies – *runs away*
poor advanc'd – *poor man who gains advancement*
hitherto – *up to this point*; tend – *serve*
who not needs – *the person who needs nothing*
who – *the person who*; try – *test*
seasons him – *turns him into*

But orderly to end where I begun,
Our wills and fates do so contrary run
That our devices still are overthrown.
Our thoughts are ours, their ends none of our own:
So think thou wilt no second husband wed   210
But die thy thoughts when thy first lord is dead.

PLAYER QUEEN
Nor earth to me give food nor heaven light,
Sport and repose lock from me day and night.
[To desperation turn my trust and hope
And anchor's cheer in prison be my scope.]   215
Each opposite that blanks the face of joy
Meet what I would have well and it destroy.
Both here and hence pursue me lasting strife
If once a widow ever I be wife.

HAMLET
If she should break it now!   220

PLAYER KING
'Tis deeply sworn. Sweet, leave me here awhile.
My spirits grow dull, and fain I would beguile
The tedious day with sleep.

PLAYER QUEEN   Sleep rock thy brain,
And never come mischance between us twain.

                    Exit. [He sleeps.]

HAMLET
Madam, how like you this play?   225

QUEEN
The lady doth protest too much, methinks.

orderly – *properly*

devices – *plans*; still – *always*
ends – *outcomes*

die thy thoughts – *let your thoughts die/your thoughts may die*

Nor – *Neither*   Q2 – me give F – give me
Sport – *Recreation*; repose – *rest*

                                                     Lines 214–15 are not in F.

anchor's cheer – *the food of an anchorite* (hermit); scope – *desire*
opposite – *opposing force*; blanks – *makes pale*
what I would have well – *everything good that I desire*
here and hence – *in this world and the next*
once a widow – *once I am a widow*   F – If once a widow, ever I be wife
                                        Q2 – If once I be a widow ever I be a wife

                                     Hamlet's interjection is in PROSE.

fain – *willingly*; beguile – *while away*

                                        te-dious (equiv. 2 syl.)

mischance – *ill fortune*; twain – *two*

        This exchange is in PROSE, excepting the Queen's line which is VERSE.

doth protest too much – *makes too many protestations*

HAMLET

O, but she'll keep her word.

KING

Have you heard the argument? Is there no offence
in't?

HAMLET

No, no, they do but jest. Poison in jest. No   230
offence i'th' world.

KING

What do you call the play?

HAMLET

The Mousetrap. Marry, how tropically! This
play is the image of a murder done in Vienna. Gonzago
is the duke's name, his wife Baptista. You shall see anon   235
'tis a knavish piece of work, but what of that? Your
majesty and we that have free souls – it touches us not.
Let the galled jade wince, our withers are unwrung.

Enter Lucianus.

This is one Lucianus, nephew to the king.

OPHELIA

You are as good as a chorus, my lord.   240

HAMLET

I could interpret between you and your love if I
could see the puppets dallying.

OPHELIA

You are keen, my lord, you are keen.

argument – *(of the play)*; offence – *offensive matter*

jest – *pretend*

how tropically – *what an appropriate trope*
image – *mirror image*
anon – *soon*

free souls – *souls free from guilt*
galled jade – *saddle-sore horse*; withers – *part of a horse's back*; unwrung – *not chafed*

Qq – as good as a chorus F – a good chorus

interpret between – *commentate on*
dallying – *performing* (as in a puppet show)

keen – *sharp*

HAMLET
It would cost you a groaning to take off mine
edge.   245

OPHELIA
Still better and worse.

HAMLET
So you mistake your husbands. Begin,
murderer: leave thy damnable faces and begin. Come,
'the croaking raven doth bellow for revenge'.

LUCIANUS
Thoughts black, hands apt, drugs fit, and time agreeing,   250
Considerate season else no creature seeing,
Thou mixture rank, of midnight weeds collected,
With Hecate's ban thrice blasted, thrice infected,
Thy natural magic and dire property
On wholesome life usurps immediately.   255

[Pours the poison in his ears.]

HAMLET
He poisons him i'th' garden for his estate. His
name's Gonzago. The story is extant and written in
very choice Italian. You shall see anon how the
murderer gets the love of Gonzago's wife.

OPHELIA
The King rises.   260

[HAMLET
What, frighted with false fire.]

a groaning – *cries of a woman losing her virginity/in labour*   Q2 – mine F – my
take off mine edge – *blunt my wit or my sexual desire*

better and worse – *wittier and more offensive*

mistake your husbands – *(i.e. by taking them 'for better or for worse' in marriage)*
    Q2 – leave F/Q1 – pox, leave

Con-**si**-derate (equiv. 3 syl.) – *Appropriate*; else … seeing –   Q2 – Considerate
and no one else to see me   F/Q1 – Confederate
Hecate – (see Myth); ban – *curse*
dire – *dreadful power*
usurps – *takes unjustly*   im-**me**-diate-**ly** (equiv. 4 syl.)

estate – *wealth*   This exchange is in PROSE; F/Q1 – He Q2 – 'A
extant – *current/in vogue*   Q2 – written F – writ
anon – *soon*   Q2 – very choice F – choice

Line 261 is only in F.

QUEEN
How fares my lord?

POLONIUS
Give o'er the play.

KING
Give me some light, away.

POLONIUS
Lights! Lights! Lights!   265

Exeunt all but Hamlet and Horatio.

HAMLET
Why let the stricken deer go weep,
The hart ungallèd play,
For some must watch while some must sleep.
Thus runs the world away.
Would not this, sir, and a forest of feathers, if the rest   270
of my fortunes turn Turk with me, with provincial
roses on my razed shoes, get me a fellowship in a cry of
players?

HORATIO
Half a share.

HAMLET
A whole one, I.   275
For thou dost know, O Damon dear,
This realm dismantl'd was
Of Jove himself, and now reigns here
A very, very pajock.

Give o'er – *abandon*

SP – Q2 – POLONIUS F – ALL

Metre – Hamlet's rhyme is in common metre (alternating lines of eight
stricken – *wounded*   and six syllables)
hart – *male deer*; ungallèd – *uninjured*
watch – *stay awake*
Thus . . . away – *This is the way of the world*   Q2/Q1 – Thus F – So
this – *the play*; forest of feathers – *elaborate plumes on a hat*
turn . . . me – *desert me*   Q2 – with provincial F – with two provincial
provincial roses – *French-style roses*; razed – *fashionably cut*;   Q2 – players
fellowship – *partnership* (as a sharer); cry – *group*   F – players sir

Damon – *ideal friend* (see Myth)   Metre – *Hamlet's rhyme is in*
dismantl'd – *stripped*   *common metre* (as above)
Jove – (see Myth)
pajock – *peacock or patchcock* (ragamuffin)

HORATIO

You might have rhymed.   280

HAMLET

O good Horatio, I'll take the Ghost's word for a
thousand pound. Didst perceive?

HORATIO

Very well, my lord.

HAMLET

Upon the talk of the poisoning.

HORATIO

I did very well note him.   285

HAMLET

Ah ha! Come, some music! Come, the
recorders!
     For if the King like not the comedy
     Why then belike he likes it not, perdie.
Come, some music!   290

Enter ROSENCRANTZ and GUILDENSTERN.

GUILDENSTERN

Good my lord, vouchsafe me a word
with you.

HAMLET

Sir, a whole history.

GUILDENSTERN

The King, sir –

You ... rhymed – *(the expected rhyme is 'ass')*

Metre – This rhyme is in iambic pentameter.

belike – *perhaps*; perdie – *by god*

SD – the entrance for Rosencrantz and Guildenstern in F comes after line 282

vouchsafe – *permit*

history – *story*

HAMLET
Ay, sir, what of him?   295

GUILDENSTERN
– is in his retirement marvellous
distempered.

HAMLET
With drink, sir?

GUILDENSTERN
No, my lord, with choler.

HAMLET
Your wisdom should show itself more richer to   300
signify this to the doctor, for for me to put him to his
purgation would perhaps plunge him into more choler.

GUILDENSTERN
Good my lord, put your discourse into
some frame and start not so wildly from my affair.

HAMLET
I am tame, sir, pronounce.   305

GUILDENSTERN
The Queen your mother in most great
affliction of spirit hath sent me to you.

HAMLET
You are welcome.

GUILDENSTERN
Nay, good my lord, this courtesy is not

retirement – *withdrawal*; marvellous – *marvellously*
distempered – *out of temper*

choler – *anger*   Q2 – with choler F – rather with choler

signify – *tell*   Q2 – the F – his
purgation – *cleansing of the body* (physical/spiritual)   Q2 – more choler
                                                                 F – far more choler

frame – *coherent order*; start – *recoil*; affair – *business*

tame – *calm*; pronounce – *speak your message*

of the right breed. If it shall please you to make me a   310
wholesome answer, I will do your mother's
commandment. If not, your pardon and my return
shall be the end of business.

HAMLET
Sir, I cannot.

ROSENCRANTZ
What, my lord?   315

HAMLET
Make you a wholesome answer. My wit's
diseased. But, sir, such answer as I can make you shall
command. Or rather, as you say, my mother. Therefore
no more. But to the matter – my mother, you say?

ROSENCRANTZ
Then thus she says. Your behaviour hath   320
struck her into amazement and admiration.

HAMLET
O wonderful son that can so astonish a mother!
But is there no sequel at the heels of this mother's
admiration? [Impart.]

ROSENCRANTZ
She desires to speak with you in her   325
closet ere you go to bed.

HAMLET
We shall obey, were she ten times our mother.
Have you any further trade with us?

breed – *kind/breeding*
wholesome – *healthy/sane*
pardon – *permission to leave*

Q2 – business F – my business

SP – Q2 – ʀᴏsᴇɴᴄʀᴀɴᴛᴢ F – ɢᴜɪʟᴅᴇɴsᴛᴇʀɴ

Q2 – answer F – answers
my mother – *(shall command)*   Q2 – as you say F – you say

admiration – *wonder*

no sequel at the heels – *nothing following*
Impart – *Tell*   Q2 – Impart – not in F

closet – *private chamber;* ere – *before*

were she – *if she was*
trade – *business*

ROSENCRANTZ
My lord, you once did love me.

HAMLET
And do still, by these pickers and stealers.   330

ROSENCRANTZ
Good my lord, what is your cause of
distemper? You do surely bar the door upon your own
liberty if you deny your griefs to your friend.

HAMLET
Sir, I lack advancement.

ROSENCRANTZ
How can that be, when you have the   335
voice of the King himself for your succession in
Denmark?

HAMLET
Ay, sir, but while the grass grows – the proverb
is something musty.

Enter the Players with recorders.

O, the recorders! Let me see one. To withdraw with   340
you, why do you go about to recover the wind of me, as
if you would drive me into a toil?

GUILDENSTERN
O my lord, if my duty be too bold, my
love is too unmannerly.

pickers and stealers – *hands*   Q2 – And F – So I

distemper – *bad temper*   Q2 – surely F – freely; Q2 – upon F – of
liberty – *freedom from mental anguish*; deny – *refuse to tell*

advancement – *promotion*

while the grass grows – *Prov.* (, . . . *the horse starves'*)   Q2 – Ay, sir F – Ay
musty – *stale*

          SD – In F, only one person enters here with a single recorder

withdraw – *speak privately*   Q2 – recorders F – recorder; Q2 – see one F – see
recover the wind of me – *get on the windward side of me* (hunting metaphor – a way
toil – *trap*   of driving an animal into a trap)

if . . . bold – *if I am too forward in my behaviour*
my . . . unmannerly – *it is because my love makes me forget my manners*

HAMLET

I do not well understand that. Will you play   345
upon this pipe?

GUILDENSTERN

My lord, I cannot.

HAMLET

I pray you.

GUILDENSTERN

Believe me, I cannot.

HAMLET

I do beseech you.   350

GUILDENSTERN

I know no touch of it, my lord.

HAMLET

It is as easy as lying. Govern these ventages with
your fingers and thumb, give it breath with your
mouth, and it will discourse most eloquent music.
Look you, these are the stops.   355

GUILDENSTERN

But these cannot I command to any
utterance of harmony. I have not the skill.

HAMLET

Why, look you now how unworthy a thing you
make of me: you would play upon me! You would seem
to know my stops, you would pluck out the heart of my   360
mystery, you would sound me from my lowest note to

that – *(i.e. your love)*
pipe – *recorder*

no touch of it – *do not know how to play it*

Govern – *technical term for cover*; ventages – *holes*

stops – *holes*

Q2 – It is F – 'Tis
Q2 – fingers F – finger
Q2 – eloquent F – elegant

cannot I – *I cannot*
utterance of harmony – *harmonious sound*

unworthy – *worthless*

mystery – *secret/skill*; sound me – *play on me/probe me*

Q2 – to my F – to the
top of my

205

my compass. And there is much music, excellent voice,
in this little organ. Yet cannot you make it speak.
'Sblood! Do you think I am easier to be played on than
a pipe? Call me what instrument you will, though   365
you can fret me you cannot play upon me.

Enter POLONIUS.

God bless you, sir.

POLONIUS
My lord, the Queen would speak with you,
and presently.

HAMLET
Do you see yonder cloud that's almost in shape   370
of a camel?

POLONIUS
By th' mass and 'tis like a camel indeed.

HAMLET
Methinks it is like a weasel.

POLONIUS
It is backed like a weasel.

HAMLET
Or like a whale?   375

POLONIUS
Very like a whale.

compass – *limit*

this little organ – *this recorder*

'Sblood – *God's blood (oath)*   Q2 – 'Sblood F – Why; Qq – think F – think that

fret me – *play on my frets* (ridges on a stringed instrument)/*anger me*

presently – *immediately*

                                                              Q2/Q1 – yonder F – that
                                                                  Qq – of F – like

By th'mass – *By the mass* (oath)   Q2 – 'tis F – it's

Methinks – *I think*

It is backed – *It has a back*

HAMLET
Then I will come to my mother, by and by.
[*aside*] They fool me to the top of my bent. – I will
come by and by. – Leave me, friends. – I will. Say so.
'By and by' is easily said.   380

[Exeunt all but Hamlet.]

'Tis now the very witching time of night
When churchyards yawn and hell itself breaks out
Contagion to this world. Now could I drink hot blood
And do such bitter business as the day
Would quake to look on. Soft, now to my mother.   385
O heart, lose not thy nature. Let not ever
The soul of Nero enter this firm bosom –
Let me be cruel, not unnatural:
I will speak daggers to her but use none.
My tongue and soul in this be hypocrites.   390
How in my words somever she be shent
To give them seals never my soul consent.   *Exit.*

3.3 *Enter KING, ROSENCRANTZ and GUILDENSTERN.*

KING
I like him not, nor stands it safe with us
To let his madness range. Therefore prepare you.
I your commission will forthwith dispatch
And he to England shall along with you.
The terms of our estate may not endure   5
Hazard so near us as doth hourly grow
Out of his brows.

GUILDENSTERN   We will ourselves provide.

by and by – *immediately*

fool me – *make me play the fool*; to the top of my bent – *to my limit*

SP – In F, POLONIUS speaks 'I will say so'. In Q2, Hamlet seems to direct these words to Polonius

witching time of night – *time of night for witchcraft*   Hamlet moves into VERSE

yawn – *open wide*; breaks out – *lets loose*   Q2 – breaks F – breathes

Contagion – *Poison*

bitter – *unpleasant*   F – bitter business as the Q2 – business as the bitter

Soft – *Be quiet*

nature – *natural feelings*

Nero – *Roman emperor who had his mother murdered*

cru-el (equiv. 2 syl.); un-**nat**-u-**ral** (equiv. 4 syl.)

My ... hypocrites – *May I speak and seem as though I intend violence* (although I don't)

How ... shent – *However much I scold her with my words*

To ... consent – *Do not let me act on them*

him – *his behaviour*; stands it safe with us – *it is not safe for us*

range – *roam freely*

dispatch – *make ready*

terms of our estate – *responsibilities as king*

Q5 – near us F – dangerous

brows – *looks/madness*   Q2 – brows F – lunacies

ourselves provide – *prepare ourselves*

Most holy and religious fear it is
To keep those many many bodies safe
That live and feed upon your majesty.   10

ROSENCRANTZ
The single and peculiar life is bound
With all the strength and armour of the mind
To keep itself from noyance; but much more
That spirit upon whose weal depends and rests
The lives of many. The cess of majesty   15
Dies not alone, but like a gulf doth draw
What's near it with it. It is a massy wheel
Fix'd on the summit of the highest mount
To whose huge spokes ten thousand lesser things
Are mortis'd and adjoin'd, which when it falls   20
Each small annexment, petty consequence,
Attends the boisterous ruin. Never alone
Did the king sigh but with a general groan.

KING
Arm you, I pray you, to this speedy voyage
For we will fetters put about this fear   25
Which now goes too free-footed.

ROSENCRANTZ   We will haste us.

Exeunt Rosencrantz and Guildenstern.

Enter POLONIUS.

POLONIUS
My lord, he's going to his mother's closet.
Behind the arras I'll convey myself
To hear the process. I'll warrant she'll tax him home

fear – *responsibility/concern*

live and feed – *live by feeding* (hendiadys – see Introduction)

single and peculiar – *individual and private*; bound – *obliged*   pe-**cu**-liar (equiv. 3 syl.)

noyance – *harm*
That spirit – *(i.e. the king)*; weal – *welfare*   spirit (equiv. 1 syl.)
cess – *decease*   -ny. The **cess** (anapest); Q2 – cess F – cease
gulf – *whirlpool*
massy – *massive*   F – it. It is Q2 – it, or it is; 'it. It **is**' or 'is a **mass-**' – anapest

mortis'd – *fastened securely*
annexment – *hanger-on*; petty consequence – *trivial thing*
Attends – *Accompanies*; **boi**-sterous (equiv. 2 syl.) – *turbulent*   Never (equiv. 1 syl.)
general – *collective*

Arm you – *make yourselves ready*
fetters – *chains*; fear – *danger*   Q2 – about F – upon

SP – Q2 – ROSENCRANTZ F – BOTH

arras – *curtain/wall-hanging*
process – *proceedings*; warrant – *guarantee*;   -cess. I'll **war**-; -rant she'll **tax**
tax him home – *reprove him for his behaviour*   (both anapests)

And, as you said – and wisely was it said –   30
'Tis meet that some more audience than a mother
(Since nature makes them partial) should o'er-hear
The speech of vantage. Fare you well, my liege,
I'll call upon you ere you go to bed
And tell you what I know.

KING   Thanks, dear my lord.   35

Exit Polonius.

O, my offence is rank: it smells to heaven;
It hath the primal eldest curse upon't –
A brother's murder. Pray can I not:
Though inclination be as sharp as will,
My stronger guilt defeats my strong intent   40
And like a man to double business bound
I stand in pause where I shall first begin
And both neglect. What if this cursèd hand
Were thicker than itself with brother's blood?
Is there not rain enough in the sweet heavens   45
To wash it white as snow? Whereto serves mercy
But to confront the visage of offence?
And what's in prayer but this twofold force
– To be forestallèd ere we come to fall
Or pardon'd, being down? Then I'll look up: 50
My fault is past. But O, what form of prayer
Can serve my turn: 'Forgive me my foul murder'?
That cannot be, since I am still possess'd
Of those effects for which I did the murder,
My crown, mine own ambition and my Queen.   55
May one be pardon'd and retain th'offence?
In the corrupted currents of this world
Offence's gilded hand may shove by justice,

meet – *appropriate*; more – *other*   **au**-dience (equiv. 2 syl.)

of vantage – *in addition/from a vantage point*

rank – *foul*
primal eldest curse – *God's curse on Cain for killing Abel*
Metre – line is short by 1 syl. (possibly at mid-line caesura – see 'A Note on Metre')
inclination ... will – *my desire is as strong my determination*

double business bound – *sworn to undertake two tasks*

Whereto – *What function*
But to – *if not to*; confront the visage of offence – *confront sin face to face*
what's in – *what is the use of*; twofold – *double*   **pray**-er (equiv. 2 syl.)
forestallèd – *prevented*; ere – *before*
pardon'd – *forgiven*; being – *once we are*

turn – *purpose*

effects – *benefits*
mine own ambition – *the fulfilment of my ambition*
th'offence – *the profits*
currents – *practices*
gilded – *bearing gold*; shove by – *throw aside*

And oft 'tis seen the wicked prize itself
Buys out the law; but 'tis not so above: 60
There is no shuffling, there the action lies
In his true nature, and we ourselves compell'd
Even to the teeth and forehead of our faults
To give in evidence. What then? What rests?
Try what repentance can – what can it not? –   65
Yet what can it, when one cannot repent?
O wretched state, O bosom black as death,
O limèd soul that struggling to be free
Art more engag'd. Help, angels, make assay.
Bow, stubborn knees, and heart with strings of steel   70
Be soft as sinews of the new-born babe.
All may be well.

Enter HAMLET.

HAMLET
Now might I do it. But now he is a-praying.
And now I'll do it [*Draws sword.*] – and so he goes to
      heaven,
And so am I reveng'd! That would be scann'd: 75
A villain kills my father, and for that
I, his sole son, do this same villain send
To heaven.
Why, this is hire and salary, not revenge.
He took my father grossly full of bread   80
With all his crimes broad blown, as flush as May,
And how his audit stands who knows, save heaven,
But in our circumstance and course of thought
'Tis heavy with him. And am I then reveng'd
To take him in the purging of his soul   85
When he is fit and season'd for his passage?
No.   [*Sheathes sword.*]

Buys out – *bribes*; above – *in heaven*

There – *i.e. in heaven*; shuffling – *deceit*; the action lies – *the sin is laid bare*

we … evidence – *we're forced to give evidence of our worst faults* -ture, and **we** (anapest)

teeth and forehead – *forward parts* (hendiadys – see Introduction)   Even (equiv. 1 syl.)

rests – *remains*

can – *can do*

limèd – *trapped* (like a bird)

engag'd – *entangled*; assay – *effort*

sinews – *tendons*

Metre – line is short by 6 syl.

it. But **now** (anapest); Q2 – do it. But F – do it pat; F – he Q2 – 'a;

Q2 – a-praying F – praying

it – and **so** (anapest – see 'A Note on Metre'); F – he Q2 – 'a

would be scann'd – *needs to be examined*

Metre – line is short by 7 syl. in Q2 (linked with line above in F)

hire and salary – *reward*   Q2 – Why F – Oh; F – hire and salary Q2 – base and silly

took – *killed*; grossly – *sinfully* (Claudius or Old Hamlet)   F/Q1 – He Q2 – 'A

broad blown – *in full bloom*; flush – *vigorous*   Q2 – flush F – fresh

his – *i.e. Old Hamlet*; audit – *account* (to heaven); save – *excepting*

circumstance and course of thought – *situation and way of thinking*

'Tis heavy with him – *His sins weigh heavily*   him. And **am** (anapest)

him – *i.e. Claudius*; in the purging … soul – *whilst he is purging his soul of its sins*

season'd – *prepared*; passage – *journey into the next world*

Metre – line is short by 9 syl. in Q2 (linked with line above in F)

Up sword, and know thou a more horrid hent
When he is drunk, asleep or in his rage,
Or in th'incestuous pleasure of his bed,   90
At game a-swearing, or about some act
That has no relish of salvation in't.
Then trip him that his heels may kick at heaven
And that his soul may be as damn'd and black
As hell whereto it goes. My mother stays;   95
This physic but prolongs thy sickly days.   *Exit.*

KING
My words fly up, my thoughts remain below.
Words without thoughts never to heaven go.   *Exit.*

3.4 *Enter* QUEEN *and* POLONIUS.

POLONIUS
He will come straight. Look you lay home to him.
Tell him his pranks have been too broad to bear with,
And that your grace hath screened and stood between
Much heat and him. I'll silence me even here.
Pray you be round.

[HAMLET (*within*) Mother, mother, mother]

QUEEN   I'll warrant you, fear me not.   5
Withdraw, I hear him coming.

[Polonius hides behind the arras.]

Enter HAMLET.

HAMLET
Now, mother, what's the matter?

hent – *time*

Punct. Q2 – drunk, asleep F – drunk asleep

th'in-**ces**-tous (equiv. 3 syl.)

At . . . swearing – *swearing as he gambles*   Q2 – game a-swearing F – gaming, swearing
relish – *trace*
may . . . heaven – *spurn heaven*

physic – *medicine* (the King's prayers or Hamlet's postponement of his murder)

A – *He*; straight – *straight away*; lay . . . him – *speak strictly to him*   F – He Q2 – 'A
pranks – *actions*; broad – *excessive*; bear with – *tolerate*

heat – *(i.e. Claudius' anger)*   even (equiv. 1 syl.); Q2 – even F – e'en
round – *severe*   Q2 – round F – round with him.

Metre – Ambiguous metrical connection – possibly indicting an overlap in
dialogue (see Series Introduction)   The line 'Mother, mother, mother' is only in F.
warrant – *assure*   warrant (equiv. 1 syl.)

Metre – line is short by 3 syl.

Hamlet's line is short by 3 syl. or in PROSE.

QUEEN
  Hamlet, thou hast thy father much offended.

HAMLET
  Mother, you have my father much offended.

QUEEN
  Come, come, you answer with an idle tongue.   10

HAMLET
  Go, go, you question with a wicked tongue.

QUEEN
  Why, how now, Hamlet!

HAMLET   What's the matter now?

QUEEN
  Have you forgot me?

HAMLET   No, by the rood, not so.
  You are the Queen, your husband's brother's wife,
  And, would it were not so, you are my mother.   15

QUEEN
  Nay then, I'll set those to you that can speak.

HAMLET
  Come, come, and sit you down. You shall not budge.
  You go not till I set you up a glass
  Where you may see the inmost part of you.

thy father – *i.e. Claudius* (his stepfather)

my father – *i.e. Old Hamlet*

idle – *foolish/senseless*

Q2 – a wicked F – an idle

forgot me – *forgotten that I am your mother*

rood – *Christian cross*   by the **rood** (anapest – see 'A Note on Metre')

Q2 – And F – But; Q2 – it F – you

set ... speak – *get those who can speak more forcefully to you*

budge – *move*
glass – *mirror*
Where – *In which*

QUEEN
>What wilt thou do? Thou wilt not murder me –   20
>Help, ho!

POLONIUS *[behind the arras]*
>What ho! Help!

HAMLET
>How now! A rat! Dead for a ducat, dead!

>*[Kills Polonius.]*

POLONIUS
>O, I am slain!

QUEEN   O me, what hast thou done?

HAMLET
>Nay, I know not. Is it the King?

QUEEN
>O, what a rash and bloody deed is this!   25

HAMLET
>A bloody deed – almost as bad, good mother,
>As kill a king and marry with his brother.

QUEEN
>As kill a king?

HAMLET   Ay, lady, it was my word.

>*[Uncovers the body of Polonius.]*

Metre – shared line is short by 5 syl. Q2 – What ho! Help!

F – What hoa help, help, help

Dead for a ducat – *I'll bet a ducat* (gold coin) *he'll soon be dead/I'll kill him for a ducat*

Hamlet's line is short by 2 syl. or in PROSE.

As kill – *As to kill*

-dy it **was** (anapest – see 'A Note on Metre'); Q2 – it was F – 'twas

– Thou wretched, rash, intruding fool, farewell:
I took thee for thy better. Take thy fortune;   30
Thou find'st to be too busy is some danger.
– Leave wringing of your hands. Peace, sit you down
And let me wring your heart. For so I shall
If it be made of penetrable stuff,
If damnèd custom have not braz'd it so   35
That it be proof and bulwark against sense.

QUEEN
What have I done that thou dar'st wag thy tongue
In noise so rude against me?

HAMLET   Such an act
That blurs the grace and blush of modesty,
Calls virtue hypocrite, takes off the rose   40
From the fair forehead of an innocent love
And sets a blister there, makes marriage vows
As false as dicers' oaths – O, such a deed
As from the body of contraction plucks
The very soul, and sweet religion makes   45
A rhapsody of words. Heaven's face does glow
O'er this solidity and compound mass
With heated visage as against the doom,
Is thought-sick at the act.

QUEEN   Ay me, what act
That roars so loud and thunders in the index?   50

HAMLET
Look here upon this picture, and on this,
The counterfeit presentment of two brothers:
See what a grace was seated on this brow,
Hyperion's curls, the front of Jove himself,
An eye like Mars to threaten and command,   55

thy better – *i.e. the King*; Take thy fortune – *Accept thy fate*
busy – *interfering/prying*

braz'd – *hardened* (like brass)
proof and bulwark – *armoured and fortified* (hendiadys)   Q2 – be F – is

wag thy tongue ... against – *scold me so violently*

an act – *i.e. the Queen's remarriage*
grace and blush – *innocent grace* (hendiadys – see Introduction)
Calls ... hypocrite – *makes any claim to virtue seem hypocritical*; the rose – *signifying idealized love*   **inn**-ocent (equiv. 2 syl.)
a blister – *reference to branding of prostitutes*   Q2 – sets F – makes
dicers' – *gamblers'*
body of contraction – *marriage contract*

rhapsody – *muddled collection*; Heaven's (equiv. 1 syl.); face – *the sky* Q2 – does F – doth
solidity and compound mass – *the earth*
heated – *angry*; visage – *face*; as ... doom – *as if it were doomsday* Q2 – heated F – tristful
thought-sick at – *sick at the thought of*

in the index – *at the start*

counterfeit presentment – *painted representation*
                    Q2 – this F/Q1 – his
Hyperion – (see Myth); front – *forehead*; Jove – (see Myth)
eye – *glare*; Mars – (see Myth)   Q2 – and F – or

A station like the herald Mercury
New-lighted on a heaven-kissing hill,
A combination and a form indeed
Where every god did seem to set his seal
To give the world assurance of a man;   60
This was your husband. Look you now what follows:
Here is your husband like a mildew'd ear
Blasting his wholesome brother. Have you eyes?
Could you on this fair mountain leave to feed
And batten on this moor? Ha, have you eyes?   65
You cannot call it love, for at your age
The heyday in the blood is tame, it's humble
And waits upon the judgement, and what judgement
Would step from this to this? [Sense, sure, you have –
Else could you not have motion. But sure, that sense   70
Is apoplex'd, for madness would not err
Nor sense to ecstasy was ne'er so thrall'd
But it reserv'd some quantity of choice
To serve in such a difference.] What devil was't
That thus hath cozen'd you at hoodman-blind?   75
[Eyes without feeling, feeling without sight,
Ears without hands or eyes, smelling sans all,
Or but a sickly part of one true sense
Could not so mope.] O shame, where is thy blush?
Rebellious hell,   80
If thou canst mutine in a matron's bones,
To flaming youth let virtue be as wax
And melt in her own fire; proclaim no shame
When the compulsive ardour gives the charge,
Since frost itself as actively doth burn   85
And reason panders will.

QUEEN   O Hamlet, speak no more.
Thou turn'st my very eyes into my soul

station – *stance*; Mercury – (see Myth)

New-lighted – *newly landed*; heaven-kissing – *high*

combination – *(of physical attributes)*

seal – *mark of approval*

ear – *(of corn)*

Blasting – *blighting with mould*   Q2 – brother F – breath

leave – *cease*

batten – *feed greedily*; moor – *waste-ground* (with play on 'blackamoor' – an

inhabitant of North Africa)

heyday in the blood – *sexual excitement of youth*

waits upon – *is ruled by*

                     Lines 69 ('Sense, sure') to 74 ('difference') are not in F

Else . . . motion – *Otherwise you wouldn't be moving*   -tion. But **sure** (anapest)

apoplex'd – *paralysed*; madness . . . err – *even a mad person wouldn't make this mistake*

to . . . thrall'd – *was never so enthralled to frenzy*

To . . . difference – *enable it to differentiate*   -fference. What **dev**- (anapest)

cozen'd – *cheated*; hoodman-blind – *the game of blind man's buff*

                     Lines 76 to 79 ('mope') are not in F

sans – *without*

Metre – line is 6 syl. short in Q2. In F 'O shame . . . hell' make up a single line

mutine – *mutiny*; matron – *mature woman*

flaming – *lustful*; virtue – *chastity*

compulsive . . . charge – *compelling sexual passion gives the signal to attack*

frost – *age*;   frost . . . burn – Prov.

panders – *acts as a go-between*; will – *sexual desire*   Q2 – And F – As; F –

                                   panders Q2 – pardons

          Irregular shared line – can be scanned with quartus paeon/as hexameter

          Q2 – my very eyes F – mine eyes; Q2 – my soul F – my very soul

And there I see such black and grievèd spots
As will leave there their tinct.

HAMLET   Nay, but to live
In the rank sweat of an enseamèd bed   90
Stew'd in corruption, honeying and making love
Over the nasty sty –

QUEEN   O speak to me no more!
These words like daggers enter in my ears.
No more, sweet Hamlet.

HAMLET   A murderer and a villain,
A slave that is not twentieth part the tythe   95
Of your precedent lord, a vice of kings,
A cutpurse of the empire and the rule,
That from a shelf the precious diadem stole
And put it in his pocket, –

QUEEN   No more!

HAMLET   – a king of shreds and patches –

Enter GHOST.

Save me and hover o'er me with your wings,   100
You heavenly guards! What would your gracious figure?

QUEEN
Alas, he's mad!

HAMLET
Do you not come your tardy son to chide
That, laps'd in time and passion, lets go by

grievèd – *grievous*

Q2 – grievèd F – grainèd

tinct – *stain*

Q2 – leave there F – not leave

rank – *offensive*; enseamèd – *stained with grease/semen*

Stew'd – *Soaked*; honeying – *exchanging endearments*   -eying and **mak**- (anapest)

Irregular shared line (12 syl.) – can be scanned with quartus paeon/as hexameter

(see 'A Note on Metre')

Q2 – my F – mine

-let./A **mur**- (anapest – see 'A Note on Metre')

murd-erer (equiv. 2 syl.)

tythe – *tenth part*   **twen**-tieth (equiv. 2 syl.); F – tythe Q2 – kith

precedent lord – *previous husband*; vice – *epitome of evil*

cutpurse – *pickpocket*; rule – *kingdom*

diadem – *crown*   **dia**-dem (equiv. 2 syl.)

Metre – Ambiguous metrical connection – possibly indicating an overlap in

dialogue (see Series Introduction)

shreds and patches – *patchwork* (like a fool)

SD – The Q1 stage direction indicates that the ghost appears 'in his night gown'

o'er (equiv. 1 syl.)

heavenly guards – *angels*   **heav**-enly (equiv. 2 syl.); Q2 – your F – you

Metre – line is short by 6 syl.

tardy – *late*; chide – *tell off*

laps'd in time – *having wasted time*

Th'important acting of your dread command?   105
O say!

GHOST   Do not forget! This visitation
Is but to whet thy almost blunted purpose.
But look, amazement on thy mother sits!
O step between her and her fighting soul.
Conceit in weakest bodies strongest works.   110
Speak to her, Hamlet.

HAMLET   How is it with you, lady?

QUEEN   Alas, how is't with you,
That you do bend your eye on vacancy
And with th'incorporal air do hold discourse?
Forth at your eyes your spirits wildly peep,
And as the sleeping soldiers in th'alarm   115
Your bedded hair like life in excrements
Start up and stand on end. O gentle son,
Upon the heat and flame of thy distemper
Sprinkle cool patience. Whereon do you look?

HAMLET
On him, on him! Look you how pale he glares,   120
His form and cause conjoin'd preaching to stones
Would make them capable. [*to Ghost*] Do not look upon me
Lest with this piteous action you convert
My stern effects! Then what I have to do
Will want true colour, tears perchance for blood.   125

QUEEN
To whom do you speak this?

important – *urgent*

whet – *sharpen*
amazement . . . sits – *your mother is amazed*
fighting – *conflicted*
Conceit – *Imagination*

Metre – Ambiguous metrical connection (see Series Introduction)

bend – *focus*; vacancy – *an empty space*
incorporal (th'in-**cor**-poral) – *insubstantial*; hold discourse – *have a conversation*
spirits – *bodily fluids*
in th'alarm – *when the call to arms given*
bedded – *rooted*; like life in excrements – *as if it had a life of its own*
                                        Q2/F – Start up and stand Q3 – Starts up and stands
distemper – *ill humour*

form . . . conjoin'd – *appearance and reason combined*
capable – *(of some sort of response)*   **cap**-able (equiv. 2 syl.)
piteous – *pitiful*   **pit**-eous (equiv. 2 syl.)
convert . . . effects – *distract me from my stern deeds*
want – *lack*; colour – *motivation/quality*; perchance for – *rather than*

                                        Q2 – whom F – who

HAMLET   Do you see nothing there?

QUEEN
Nothing at all, yet all that is I see.

HAMLET
Nor did you nothing hear?

QUEEN   No, nothing but ourselves.

HAMLET
Why, look you there! Look how it steals away –
My father in his habit as he lived.   130
Look where he goes even now out at the portal! *Exit Ghost.*

QUEEN
This is the very coinage of your brain.
This bodiless creation ecstasy
Is very cunning in.

HAMLET
[Ecstasy?]   135
My pulse as yours doth temperately keep time
And makes as healthful music. It is not madness
That I have utter'd. Bring me to the test
And I the matter will reword, which madness
Would gambol from. Mother, for love of grace   140
Lay not that flattering unction to your soul
That not your trespass but my madness speaks.
It will but skin and film the ulcerous place
Whiles rank corruption mining all within
Infects unseen. Confess yourself to heaven,   145
Repent what's past, avoid what is to come,
And do not spread the compost on the weeds

Irregular shared line – can be scanned with quartus paeon/as hexameter
(see 'A Note on Metre')

Irregular shared line – can be scanned with quartus paeon/hexameter
(see 'A Note on Metre')

habit – *clothes*; as – *as when/as if*
portal – *doorway*   even (equiv.1 syl.)

coinage – *invention*
This . . . in – *madness is skilful at creating fantasies/illusions*
                                                    Metre – line is short by 4 syl.

                                                    This short line is only in F
as – *like*; temperately . . . time – *keep a moderate time*   **tem**-perate-**ly** (equiv. 3 syl.)
                                                    -sic. It **is** (anapest – see 'A Note on Metre')
Bring . . . test – *Test me*
reword – *repeat*
gambol from – *be incapable of doing*
Lay . . . soul – *Don't comfort yourself*   Q2 – that F – a; **flatt**-ering (equiv 2 syl.)
trespass – *sin*
skin and film – *cover up*   **ul**-cerous (equiv. 2 syl.)
mining – *corroding*   Q2 – Whiles F – Whilst

To make them ranker. Forgive me this my virtue,
For in the fatness of these pursy times
Virtue itself of Vice must pardon beg.   150
Yea, curb and woo for leave to do him good.

QUEEN
O Hamlet, thou hast cleft my heart in twain.

HAMLET
O throw away the worser part of it
And live the purer with the other half.
Goodnight, but go not to my uncle's bed;   155
Assume a virtue if you have it not.
[That monster Custom, who all sense doth eat
Of habits devil, is angel yet in this,
That to the use of actions fair and good
He likewise gives a frock or livery   160
That aptly is put on.] Refrain tonight
And that shall lend a kind of easiness
To the next abstinence, [the next more easy.
For use almost can change the stamp of nature
And either shame the devil or throw him out   165
With wondrous potency.] Once more goodnight,
And when you are desirous to be blessed
I'll blessing beg of you. For this same lord
I do repent, but heaven hath pleased it so
To punish me with this, and this with me,   170
That I must be their scourge and minister.
I will bestow him and will answer well
The death I gave him. So again goodnight.
I must be cruel only to be kind.
Thus bad begins and worse remains behind.   175
[One word more, good lady!]

ranker – *more vigorous*; virtue – *virtuous words*   Q2 – ranker F – rank; -ker. For-**give**
pursy – *swollen*   (anapest)

curb – *bow*; leave – *permission*

cleft ... twain – *split my heart in two* (Prov.)

Q2 – my F – mine

who ... devil – *who destroys all sensitivity to wickedness*   Ll. 157–61 – not in F
                                                                                                 devil (equiv. 1 syl.)
use – *habit*
frock – *coat*; livery – *uniform*
aptly – *readily*

abstinence – *refraining from sex*   Lines 163 (the next) to 166 (potency) are not in F
use – *habit*; stamp of – *character bestowed by*   use ... nature – Prov.
                                    Hudson – either shame Q2 – either; devil (equiv. 1 syl.)
wondrous – *remarkable*; potency – *power*
are desirous – *desire*
I'll ... you – *i.e. as befits a son of his mother*; this ... lord – *Polonius*
                                                                                          heaven (equiv. 1 syl.)
To ... me – *Hamlet will be punished for the crime of punishing Polonius*
scourge and minister – *punishing minister* (hendiadys – see Introduction)
bestow – *dispose of*; answer well – *pay for*

cru-el (equiv. 2 syl.)
remains behind – *will follow*   bad ... behind – Prov.; F – Thus Q2 – This
                                Metre – this shared line is headless (see 'A Note on Metre');
                                                Hamlet's last line is not in F

QUEEN   What shall I do?

HAMLET
  Not this, by no means, that I bid you do –
  Let the bloat King tempt you again to bed,
  Pinch wanton on your cheek, call you his mouse
  And let him for a pair of reechy kisses,   180
  Or paddling in your neck with his damn'd fingers,
  Make you to ravel all this matter out
  That I essentially am not in madness
  But mad in craft. 'Twere good you let him know,
  For who that's but a queen – fair, sober, wise –   185
  Would from a paddock, from a bat, a gib,
  Such dear concernings hide? Who would do so?
  No, in despite of sense and secrecy
  Unpeg the basket on the house's top,
  Let the birds fly and like the famous ape   190
  To try conclusions in the basket creep
  And break your own neck down.

QUEEN
  Be thou assur'd, if words be made of breath
  And breath of life, I have no life to breathe
  What thou hast said to me.   195

HAMLET
  I must to England – you know that.

QUEEN
  Alack, I had forgot; 'tis so concluded on.

[HAMLET
  There's letters sealed and my two schoolfellows –
  Whom I will trust as I will adders fanged –

Can be scanned with '-dy! What **shall** or 'shall I **do**' as anapests

Not . . . do – *(This whole speech is sarcastic)*
bloat – *bloated/fat*
Pinch wanton – *Give you sexual pinches/pinch you rudely*
reechy – *dirty*

ravel . . . out – *reveal all this*

in craft – *through cunning/pretence*

paddock – *toad*; gib – *tom-cat* (all three are witches' familiars)
dear concernings – *important matters*
despite – *contempt*
Unpeg – *unfasten*
the famous ape – *(clearly some sort of fable)*
try conclusions – *experiment*
And . . . down – *(presumably by falling, attempting to imitate the birds in flight)*

Metre – line is short by 4 syl.

Metre – line is short by 2 syl.

Metre – irregular line (12 syl.) Ambiguous lineation (Alack may form a full pentameter with the previous line)

Lines 198–206 are not in F

They bear the mandate, they must sweep my way 200
And marshal me to knavery. Let it work.
For 'tis the sport to have the enginer
Hoist with his own petard, and't shall go hard
But I will delve one yard below their mines
And blow them at the moon. O, 'tis most sweet 205
When in one line two crafts directly meet.]
This man shall set me packing;
I'll lug the guts into the neighbour room.
Mother, goodnight indeed. This councillor
Is now most still, most secret and most grave, 210
Who was in life a foolish prating knave.
Come, sir, to draw toward an end with you.
Goodnight, mother.

Exit [Hamlet tugging in Polonius].

4.1 *Enter* KING *with* ROSENCRANTZ *and* GUILDENSTERN.

KING
There's matter in these sighs, these profound heaves.
You must translate; 'tis fit we understand them.
Where is your son?

QUEEN
[Bestow this place on us a little while.]

[Exeunt Rosencrantz and Guildenstern.]

Ah, mine own lord, what have I seen tonight! 5

KING
What, Gertrude? How does Hamlet?

bear ... mandate – *have the orders*; sweep my way – *prepare the way for me*

marshal ... knavery – *drive me to trickery/villainy*; it – *their plan*; work – *unfold*

enginer – *maker of military equipment* (Pron. **en**-gin-**er** or **en**-gin-**eer**)

Hoist ... petard – *blown up by his own explosives*; go hard – *be bad luck*

But – *If I don't*; delve – *dig*; mines – *tunnels of attack*

in ... meet – *two plots collide*

set me packing – *get me sent away/make me start plotting*   Metre – line is short

by 3 syl.

grave – *dignified* (with play on dead)

prating – *prattling*

draw ... you – *finish my business with you/drag you to your grave*

This scene division may be misleading (see SI pp. xv–xvi)

SD – ROSENCRANTZ and GUILDENSTERN do not

enter with the KING in F.

Q2 – matter F – matters; Punct. Rowe – heaves. Q2 – heaves, F – heaves

translate – *explain*

Metre – line is short by 6 syl.

Bestow ... us – *Give this place to us*   This line is not in F.

Q2 – mine own F – my good

QUEEN

Mad as the sea and wind when both contend
Which is the mightier. In his lawless fit,
Behind the arras hearing something stir,
Whips out his rapier, cries 'A rat, a rat!'   10
And in this brainish apprehension kills
The unseen good old man.

KING   O heavy deed!
It had been so with us had we been there.
His liberty is full of threats to all,
To you yourself, to us, to everyone.   15
Alas, how shall this bloody deed be answer'd?
It will be laid to us whose providence
Should have kept short, restrain'd and out of haunt
This mad young man. But so much was our love,
We would not understand what was most fit,   20
But like the owner of a foul disease,
To keep it from divulging, let it feed
Even on the pith of life. Where is he gone?

QUEEN

To draw apart the body he hath killed,
O'er whom – his very madness like some ore   25
Among a mineral of metals base
Shows itself pure – he weeps for what is done.

KING

O Gertrude, come away.
The sun no sooner shall the mountains touch
But we will ship him hence, and this vile deed   30
We must with all our majesty and skill
Both countenance and excuse. Ho, Guildenstern!

contend – *argue about*
lawless – *out of control*
arras – *curtain*

brainish apprehension – *deluded understanding*

Mad as the sea – Prov.; Q2/Q1 – sea F – seas
migh-tier (equiv. 2 syl.)

ra-pier (equiv. 2 syl.)
Q2 – this F/Q1 – his

heavy – *sorrowful*
us – *me* (royal 'we')

answer'd – *accounted for/responded to*
laid to us – *blamed on me*; providence – *foresight*
short – *on a short leash*; out of haunt – *away from company*

divulging – *being apparent*
pith – *essence*

Q2 – let F – lets
Even (equiv. 1 syl.)

apart – *away*
ore – *precious metal*
mineral – *mine*

F – he Q2 – 'a

Metre – line is short by 4 syl.
The sun … touch – *As soon as dawn breaks*

majesty and skill – *royal skill* (hendiadys – see Introduction)
countenance – *confront*

coun-tenance (equiv. 2 syl.)

Enter ROSENCRANTZ and GUILDENSTERN.

Friends both, go join you with some further aid:
Hamlet in madness hath Polonius slain
And from his mother's closet hath he dragged him.   35
Go seek him out, speak fair and bring the body
Into the chapel. I pray you haste in this.

[Exeunt Rosencrantz and Guildenstern.]

Come, Gertrude, we'll call up our wisest friends
And let them know both what we mean to do
And what's untimely done. [ ]   40
[Whose whisper o'er the world's diameter,
As level as the cannon to his blank,
Transports his poisoned shot, may miss our name
And hit the woundless air.] O come away,
My soul is full of discord and dismay.   *Exeunt.*   45

4.2 *Enter* HAMLET.

HAMLET
Safely stowed!

GENTLEMAN (*within*)   [Hamlet, Lord Hamlet.]
[But soft,] what noise? Who calls
on Hamlet? O, here they come!

Enter ROSENCRANTZ, GUILDENSTERN [and others.]

ROSENCRANTZ
What have you done, my lord, with the   5
dead body?

This SD comes after line 31 in Q2 – making 'Ho' a greeting rather than a summons

join . . . aid – *get some additional men to help you*

speak fair – *address him politely*

-pel. I **pray** (anapest – see 'A Note on Metre')

wisest friends – *councillors*

Q2 – And F – To

what's untimely done – *Polonius's untimely death*

Metre – line is short by 4 syl.

o'er . . . diameter – *throughout the world*;

Lines 41–4 (. . . air) are not in F

level – *direct*; blank – *target*

miss our name – *avoid damaging my reputation*

woundless – *invulnerable*

stowed – *hidden away*

This scene is in PROSE

Line 2 is only in F

But soft – not in F

SD – the 'others' are implied by Claudius's previous orders

HAMLET
Compounded it with dust, whereto 'tis kin.

ROSENCRANTZ
Tell us where 'tis, that we may take it
thence and bear it to the chapel.

HAMLET
Do not believe it.   10

ROSENCRANTZ
Believe what?

HAMLET
That I can keep your council and not mine own.
Besides, to be demanded of a sponge! What replication
should be made by the son of a king?

ROSENCRANTZ
Take you me for a sponge, my lord?   15

HAMLET
Ay, sir – that soaks up the King's countenance,
his rewards, his authorities. But such officers do the
King best service in the end: he keeps them like an ape
in the corner of his jaw, first mouthed to be last
swallowed. When he needs what you have gleaned, it is   20
but squeezing you and, sponge, you shall be dry again!

ROSENCRANTZ
I understand you not, my lord.

HAMLET
I am glad of it. A knavish speech sleeps in a foolish ear.

Compounded – *Combined*; whereto 'tis kin – *Bib.*

F – Compounded
Q – Compound

thence – *from there*

council – *secret*
demanded of – *questioned by*; replication – *response*

Take you me – *Do you take me*

countenance – *favour*
authorities – *power*
like an ape – *like an ape does* (food)
mouthed – *taken into his mouth*
gleaned – *gathered*; it is but – *he does it by*

knavish – *wicked*; sleeps in – *is wasted on*

ROSENCRANTZ

My lord, you must tell us where the body   25
is, and go with us to the King.

HAMLET

The body is with the King, but the King is not
with the body. The King is a thing.

GUILDENSTERN

A thing, my lord?

HAMLET

Of nothing. Bring me to him.   30

Exeunt.

4.3   *Enter* KING *and two or three.*

KING

I have sent to seek him and to find the body.
How dangerous is it that this man goes loose!
Yet must not we put the strong law on him:
He's loved of the distracted multitude,
Who like not in their judgement but their eyes,   5
And where 'tis so th'offender's scourge is weigh'd
But never the offence. To bear all smooth and even
This sudden sending him away must seem
Deliberate pause; diseases desperate grown
By desperate appliance are reliev'd,   10
Or not at all.

The ... body – *Complex riddle, possibly playing on the notion of the king's two bodies*
Punct. Q2 – thing. F – thing – (suggesting interruption)

Q2 – to him. F – to him, hide Fox, and all after.

SD – In F the King enters alone (making the speech a soliloquy)

I have **sent** (anapest – see 'A Note on Metre')
loose – *free*   **dan**-gerous (equiv. 2 syl.)
must not we – *we must not*; put ... him – *punish him heavily*
of – *by*; distracted – *confused/foolish*; multitude – *populace*
not ... eyes – *by appearance rather than judgement*
scourge – *punishment*; weigh'd – *taken seriously*
bear ... even – *manage everything smoothly and evenly*   never; offence
                                                                       (both equiv. 1 syl.)

Deliberate pause – *the result of careful consideration*   **des**-perate (equiv. 2 syl.)
diseases ... reliev'd – *desperate diseases must have*   **des**-per-**ate** (equiv. 3 syl.)
desperate remedies – (Prov.)

Enter ROSENCRANTZ *[and* GUILDENSTERN*] and all the rest.*

How now, what hath befallen?

ROSENCRANTZ
Where the dead body is bestow'd, my lord,
We cannot get from him.

KING   But where is he?

ROSENCRANTZ
Without, my lord, guarded, to know your pleasure.

KING
Bring him before us.

ROSENCRANTZ   Ho! Bring in the lord!   15

[Enter HAMLET *and Attendants.]*

KING
Now, Hamlet, where's Polonius?

HAMLET
At supper.

KING
At supper! Where?

HAMLET
Not where he eats but where he is eaten. A
certain convocation of politic worms are e'en at him.   20
Your worm is your only emperor for diet. We fat all
creatures else to fat us, and we fat ourselves for maggots.

SD – F entrance is only for ROSENCRANTZ

befallen – *happened*

bestow'd – *hidden*

Without – *Outside*

Q2 – Ho! F – Hoa, Guildenstern?

SD – Q2 – *They enter* F – *Enter Hamlet and Guildenstern*

The scene moves into PROSE.

F/Q1 – he is Q2 – 'a is

convocation – *political assembly*; politic – *shrewd*; e'en – *even now*   politic – not in F

fat – *fatten*

Q2 – ourselves F – our self

Your fat king and your lean beggar is but variable
service, two dishes to one table. That's the end.

[KING
    Alas, alas.   25

HAMLET
    A man may fish with the worm that hath eat of
    a king and eat of the fish that hath fed of that worm.]

KING
    What dost thou mean by this?

HAMLET
    Nothing but to show you how a king may go a
    progress through the guts of a beggar.   30

KING
    Where is Polonius?

HAMLET
    In heaven. Send thither to see. If your
    messenger find him not there, seek him i'th' other place
    yourself. But if indeed you find him not within this
    month you shall nose him as you go up the stairs into   35
    the lobby.

KING
    [*to some Attendants*] Go, seek him there!

HAMLET
    He will stay till you come.

[Exeunt Attendants.]

is – *are*; variable service – *interchangeable dishes*
to one table – *at one meal*

Lines 25 to 27 are not in F.

eat – *eaten*

progress – *official royal journey*

i'th other place – *in Hell*
                    Q2 – if indeed F – indeed, if; Q2 – not within this F – not this
nose – *smell*
lobby – *corridor/ante-room*

F – He will Q2 – 'A will; Q2/Q1 – you F – ye

KING

    Hamlet, this deed for thine especial safety –
    Which we do tender, as we dearly grieve   40
    For that which thou hast done – must send thee hence.
    With fiery quickness therefore prepare thyself:
    The bark is ready and the wind at help,
    Th'associates tend and everything is bent
    For England.

HAMLET   For England?

KING   Ay, Hamlet.

HAMLET   Good.   45

KING

    So is it if thou knewst our purposes.

HAMLET

    I see a cherub that sees them. But come, for England.
    Farewell, dear mother.

KING   Thy loving father, Hamlet.

HAMLET

    My mother. Father and mother is man and wife.
    Man and wife is one flesh. So – my mother.   50
    Come, for England!   *Exit.*

KING   Follow him at foot.
    Tempt him with speed aboard.
    Delay it not – I'll have him hence tonight.
    Away, for everything is sealed and done
    That else leans on th'affair. Pray you make haste.   55

The scene moves into VERSE.

tender – *hold dear*; dearly – *heavily*

F – With fiery quickness therefore; Q2 – Therefore; -fore pre-**pare** (anapest)

bark – *ship*; at help – *favourable*

tend – *await*; bent – *prepared*   Th'a-**sso**-ciates (equiv. 3 syl.)

cherub – *overseeing angel*   -rub that **sees**; them. But **come**
                                               (both anapests)

                                -ther. Thy **lov**- (anapest – see 'A Note on Metre')

                -ther and **moth**; -er is **man** (both anapests – see 'A Note on Metre')

Man … flesh – *Bib.*   Metre – line is headless; Q2 – So F/Q1 – And so
                    Metre – shared line is headless (see 'A Note on Metre')

at foot – *closely*   Ambiguous lineation – 'Follow … aboard' is a single line in F

Tempt – *Encourage*   Metre – line is 4 syl. short in Q2

else – *otherwise*; leans on – *relates to*   th'a-**ffair** (equiv. 2 syl.)

[Exeunt all but the King.]

And England, if my love thou hold'st at aught
As my great power thereof may give thee sense,
Since yet thy cicatrice looks raw and red
After the Danish sword, and thy free awe
Pays homage to us, thou mayst not coldly set   60
Our sovereign process, which imports at full
By letters congruing to that effect
The present death of Hamlet. Do it, England!
For like the hectic in my blood he rages
And thou must cure me. Till I know 'tis done,   65
Howe'er my haps my joys were ne'er begun.   *Exit.*

4.4   *Enter* FORTINBRAS *[and a Captain] with his army over
the stage.*

FORTINBRAS
Go, Captain, from me greet the Danish King:
Tell him that by his licence Fortinbras
Craves the conveyance of a promis'd march
Over his kingdom. You know the rendezvous.
If that his majesty would aught with us   5
We shall express our duty in his eye,
And let him know so.

CAPTAIN
I will do't, my lord.

FORTINBRAS
Go softly on.   *[Exeunt all but Captain.]*

Enter HAMLET, ROSENCRANTZ, *[*GUILDENSTERN*] and others.*

aught – *any value*

thereof . . . sense – *may give you a sense of the value of my love*   power (equiv. 1 syl.)

cicatrice – *scar*

After . . . sword – *After a war with Denmark*; free awe – *voluntary submission*

coldly set – *ignore*   us, thou **mayst** (anapest – see 'A Note on Metre')

sovereign (**sov**-ereign) process – *royal order*; imports – *conveys instructions*

congruing – *agreeing*   Q2 – congruing F – conjuring

present – *immediate*

hectic – *fever*

Howe'er my haps – *Whatever my fortunes*   F – were ne'er begun Q2 –
                                                      will ne'er begin

licence – *permission*

Craves – *Wishes*; conveyance of – *granting of*   Q2/Q1 – Craves F – Claims

rendezvous – *arranged meeting place*   -dom. You **know** (anapest)

would aught with us – *wants to see us*

duty – *respects*; eye – *presence*

           There is an ambiguous metrical connection between lines 7 and 14.

softly – *quietly/carefully*

[HAMLET
Good sir, whose powers are these?   10

CAPTAIN
They are of Norway, sir.

HAMLET
How purposed, sir, I pray you?

CAPTAIN
Against some part of Poland.

HAMLET
Who commands them, sir?

CAPTAIN
The nephew to old Norway, Fortinbras.   15

HAMLET
Goes it against the main of Poland, sir,
Or for some frontier?

CAPTAIN
Truly to speak, and with no addition,
We go to gain a little patch of ground
That hath in it no profit but the name.   20
To pay five ducats – five – I would not farm it,
Nor will it yield to Norway or the Pole
A ranker rate should it be sold in fee.

HAMLET
Why then the Polack never will defend it.

powers – *armed forces*

Lines 10–67 are not in F or Q1.

it – *the army*; main – *mainland*

Metre – line is short by 5 syl.

addition – *exaggeration*

and with **no** (anapset – see 'A Note on Metre');
a-**ddi**-ti-**on** (equiv. 4 syl.)

name – *fame of achieving it*
farm it – *rent it as a farm*
yield to – *gain for*; the Pole – *the King of Poland*
ranker – *higher*; in fee – *outright*

the Polack – *the King of Poland*

CAPTAIN

Yes, it is already garrison'd.   25

HAMLET

Two thousand souls and twenty thousand ducats
Will not debate the question of this straw.
This is th'impostume of much wealth and peace
That inward breaks and shows no cause without
Why the man dies. I humbly thank you, sir.   30

CAPTAIN

God buy you, sir.   *[Exit.]*

ROSENCRANTZ   Will't please you go, my lord?

HAMLET

I'll be with you straight. Go a little before.

[Rosencrantz, Guildenstern and the others move away.]

How all occasions do inform against me
And spur my dull revenge. What is a man
If his chief good and market of his time   35
Be but to sleep and feed? A beast – no more.
Sure he that made us with such large discourse,
Looking before and after, gave us not
That capability and godlike reason
To fust in us unused. Now whether it be   40
Bestial oblivion or some craven scruple
Of thinking too precisely on th'event
(A thought which quarter'd hath but one part wisdom
And ever three parts coward) I do not know
Why yet I live to say this thing's to do,   45
Sith I have cause and will and strength and means

garrison'd – *defended by the army*   Metre – line is headless
                                                                (see 'A Note on Metre')

Will not debate – *Will not be enough to contest*; straw – *thing of no importance* (Prov.)
th'impostume – *abscess*
breaks – *bursts*

God by you – *Goodbye* (God be with you)

straight – *straightaway*; before – *ahead*   Metre – Irregular line (11 syl.)/PROSE

occasions – *circumstances*; inform against – *accuse*
dull – *slow/sluggish*
chief good and market – *best use* (hendiadys – see Introduction)

discourse – *powers of reasoning*
Looking . . . after – *able to remember the past and think about the future*
capability and godlike reason – *godlike capacity for reason* (hendiadys – see Introduction)
fust – *decay*   whether (equiv. 1 syl.)
Bestial oblivion (**Bes**-tial o-**bli**-vion) – *animal-like obliviousness*; craven scruple
Of – *caused by*; precisely – *exactly*; event – *outcome*   – *cowardly doubt*
quarter'd – *when divided into quarters*

                                                                        coward (equiv. 1 syl.)

to do – *still left to do*
Sith – *Since*

To do't. Examples gross as earth exhort me –
Witness this army of such mass and charge,
Led by a delicate and tender prince
Whose spirit with divine ambition puff'd   50
Makes mouths at the invisible event
Exposing what is mortal and unsure
To all that fortune, death and danger dare
Even for an eggshell. Rightly to be great
Is not to stir without great argument   55
But greatly to find quarrel in a straw
When honour's at the stake. How stand I then
That have a father kill'd, a mother stain'd,
Excitements of my reason and my blood,
And let all sleep; while to my shame I see   60
The imminent death of twenty thousand men
That for a fantasy and trick of fame
Go to their graves like beds, fight for a plot
Whereon the numbers cannot try the cause,
Which is not tomb enough and continent   65
To hide the slain? O, from this time forth
My thoughts be bloody or be nothing worth.]   *Exeunt.*

4.5 *Enter HORATIO, QUEEN and a Gentleman.*

QUEEN
  I will not speak with her.

GENTLEMAN
  She is importunate – indeed, distract.
  Her mood will needs be pitied.

QUEEN   What would she have?

gross – *large*; exhort – *admonish*   do't (equiv. 1 syl.)

mass – *size*; charge – *cost*

a … prince – *Fortinbras*

puff'd – *inflated*

Makes mouths at – *laughs at*; invisible – *unknowable*

dare – *threaten*

eggshell – *worthless thing*   Even (equiv. 1 syl.)

not … argument – *(it is not clear whether Hamlet is saying that the great man will not stir unless he has good cause, or the reverse)*

at the stake – *at stake*

kill'd – *who has been kill'd*; stain'd – *who has been dishonour'd*

Excitements – *motives to spur*

                                                          imm-inent (equiv. 2 syl.)

fantasy and trick – *fantastical illusion*; fame – *honour*

Go … beds (*i.e. easily*); plot – *piece of land*

Whereon … cause – *on which there is not enough room for so many men to fight*

tomb enough and continent – *a large enough piece of land for a tomb* (hendiadys)

hide – *bury*; forth – *forwards*   Metre – short by 1 syl. possibly at caesura

nothing worth – *worth nothing*

                                        SD – The Gentleman is not present in F.

                                        Metre – line is short by 4 syl.

                        SP – In F the Gentleman's lines are all assigned to Horatio.

importunate – *persistent*; distract – *mad*

will needs be – *must be*   'tied./What **would**' or 'would she **have**' (anapest)

What … have? – *What does she want?*

GENTLEMAN
  She speaks much of her father, says she hears
  There's tricks i'th' world, and hems and beats her heart,   5
  Spurns enviously at straws, speaks things in doubt
  That carry but half sense. Her speech is nothing,
  Yet the unshapèd use of it doth move
  The hearers to collection. They yawn at it
  And botch the words up fit to their own thoughts   10
  Which, as her winks and nods and gestures yield them,
  Indeed would make one think there might be thought,
  Though nothing sure, yet much unhappily.

HORATIO
  'Twere good she were spoken with, for she may strew
  Dangerous conjectures in ill-breeding minds.   15
  Let her come in.

                [Exit Gentleman.]

                Enter OPHELIA.

QUEEN [*aside*]
  To my sick soul, as sin's true nature is,
  Each toy seems prologue to some great amiss,
  So full of artless jealousy is guilt
  It spills itself in fearing to be spilt.   20

OPHELIA
  Where is the beauteous majesty of Denmark?

QUEEN
  How now, Ophelia?

tricks – *plots*; hems – *coughs/makes noises*   i'th' (equiv. 1 syl.)

Spurns . . . straws – *strikes spitefully at nothing*; in doubt – *incomprehensible*

nothing – *nonsense*   **en**-vious-**ly** (equiv. 3 syl.)

unshapèd use – *incoherence*

collection – *understanding*; yawn – *gape* -tion. They **yawn** (anapest); Q2 – yawn F – aim

botch – *patch*; up – *together to*

Which – (*i.e. Her words*); yield – *add meaning to*

unhappily – *awry*

strew – *scatter/sew*   she were **spo**- (anapest – see 'A Note on Metre')

conjectures – *suspicions*; ill-breeding – *evil spreading*   Dan-**gerous** (equiv. 2 syl.)

        Metre – line is short by 6 syl.

SD – Q1 – *Enter Ophelia playing on a lute, and her hair down singing*
(see Introduction – Q1 SD's)

sick – *sinful*   These rhyming lines may be considered quotable sayings.

toy – *trivial thing*; prologue – *to precede*; amiss – *disaster*

artless jealousy – *unskilled suspicion*

spills – *betrays*; spilt – *betrayed*

Ophelia may be referring to the Queen or King here. Ophelia speaks
PROSE in this scene.

How now – *What does this mean*   Metre – line is short by 5 syl./PROSE

OPHELIA (*Sings.*)
> *How should I your true love know*
> *From another one?*
> *By his cockle hat and staff*   25
> *And his sandal shoon.*

QUEEN
Alas, sweet lady, what imports this song?

OPHELIA
Say you? Nay, pray you, mark.

Sings.

> *He is dead and gone, lady,*
> *He is dead and gone.*   30
> *At his head a grass-green turf,*
> *At his heels a stone.*
[O ho!]

QUEEN
Nay, but Ophelia –

OPHELIA
Pray you mark.   35

[Sings.]

White his shroud as the mountain snow –

Enter KING.

QUEEN
Alas, look here, my lord.

cockle hat – *hat with a cockleshell*

shoon – *shoes*; cockle ... shoon – (*typical attire of a pilgrim*)

what ... song? – *what does this song mean?*

Say you? – *What did you say?*; mark – *listen*

O ho! – *(a sigh)*   This line is not in Q1/F.

SD – The King's entrance is earlier in F – after 'At his heels a stone'

OPHELIA (*Sings.*)
>   *Larded with sweet flowers*
>   *Which bewept to the ground did not go*
>   *With true-love showers.*   40

KING
How do you, pretty lady?

OPHELIA
Well, God dild you. They say the owl was a
baker's daughter. Lord, we know what we are but know
not what we may be. God be at your table.

KING
Conceit upon her father –   45

OPHELIA
Pray, let's have no words of this, but when they
ask you what it means, say you this:

Sings.

>   *Tomorrow is Saint Valentine's Day*
>   *All in the morning betime,*
>   *And I a maid at your window*   50
>   *To be your valentine.*
>   *Then up he rose and donned his clothes*
>   *And dupped the chamber door –*
>   *Let in the maid that out a maid*
>   *Never departed more.*   55

KING
Pretty Ophelia –

Larded – *Covered*   F/Q1 – Larded Q2 – Larded all
                                                 Q2 – ground F/Q1 – grave
showers – *(of tears)*

                                                 Q2 – do you F – do ye

God dild you – *God yield you* (reward you)   F – God Q2 – good
owl . . . daughter – *reference to the tale of a baker's daughter turned into an owl by*
Jesus when she refused him bread

Conceit upon – *Thinking about*

                                                 Q2/Q1 – Pray F – Pray you

The song is based on the myth that the first person one sees on St Valentine's Day
will be one's lover.

betime – *early*

valentine – *sweetheart*
rose – *(possibly with sexual connotations)*; donned – *put on*
dupped – *opened*
that . . . more – *that left no longer a virgin*

OPHELIA

Indeed, without an oath I'll make an end on't.

[Sings.]

> *By Gis and by Saint Charity,*
> *Alack and fie for shame,*
> *Young men will do't if they come to't:*   60
> *By Cock they are to blame.*

> *Quoth she, 'Before you tumbled me*
> *You promised me to wed.'*
> *[He answers:]*
> *'So would I ha' done by yonder sun*   65
> *An thou hadst not come to my bed.'*

KING

How long hath she been thus?

OPHELIA

I hope all will be well. We must be patient. But
I cannot choose but weep to think they would lay him
i'th' cold ground. My brother shall know of it. And so   70
I thank you for your good counsel. Come, my coach!
Goodnight, ladies, goodnight. Sweet ladies, goodnight,
goodnight.   *[Exit.]*

KING

Follow her close. Give her good watch, I pray you.

[Exit Horatio.]

O, this is the poison of deep grief. It springs   75
All from her father's death, [and now behold –]

Q2 – Indeed F – Indeed la?

Gis – (Pron. Jis) – *Jesus*

do't – *have sex*; come to't – *get the opportunity*
Cock – *corruption of God* (with play on penis)

tumbled – *had sex with*

Q2 – He answers (not in F/Q1)

An – *If*

Q2 – would F – should

close – *closely*

is the **poi**- (anapest – see 'A Note on Metre')
Q2 – 'and now behold' – not in F

O Gertrude, Gertrude,
When sorrows come they come not single spies
But in battalions: first, her father slain;
Next, your son gone, and he most violent author   80
Of his own just remove; the people muddied,
Thick and unwholesome in their thoughts and whispers
For good Polonius' death, and we have done but greenly
In hugger-mugger to inter him; poor Ophelia
Divided from herself and her fair judgement,   85
Without the which we are pictures or mere beasts;
Last, and as much containing as all these,
Her brother is in secret come from France,
Feeds on this wonder, keeps himself in clouds
And wants not buzzers to infect his ear   90
With pestilent speeches of his father's death –
Wherein necessity, of matter beggar'd,
Will nothing stick our person to arraign
In ear and ear. O my dear Gertrude, this,
Like to a murdering-piece in many places   95
Gives me superfluous death.

A noise within.

Enter a Messenger.

Attend!
Where is my Switzers? Let them guard the door.
What is the matter?

MESSENGER   Save yourself, my lord.
The ocean overpeering of his list
Eats not the flats with more impiteous haste   100
Than young Laertes in a riotous head
O'erbears your officers. The rabble call him lord

Metre – line is 5 syl. short in Q2, but forms a full line with 'All . . . death' in F.

single spies – *lone spies sent ahead of the army*

battalions – *large armies*   batt-**a**-lions (equiv. 3 syl.)

author – *instigator*

just remove – *deserved removal*; muddied – *stirred up*

F – in their thoughts Q2 – in thoughts

greenly – *foolishly*   Metre – lines 83 and 84 are metrically irregular

hugger-mugger – *secrecy*; inter – *bury*

pictures . . . beasts – *(both lacking in reason)*   we are **pic**- (anapest)

as much containing – *of as much significance*

Feeds – *gains fuel for revenge*; in clouds – *uncertain*   Q2 – Feeds F – Keeps

wants not – *does not lack*; buzzers – *gossips*

pestilent – *infectious*   **pes**-tilent (equiv. 2 syl.)

of matter beggar'd – *driven by lack of substance*

Will nothing stick – *Will in no way refrain from*; arraign – *accuse*

ear and ear – *one listener after another*

murdering-piece – *small canon which fired multiple shot*   **mur**-dering (equiv. 2 syl.)

Gives . . . death – *Kills me many times over*   su-**per**-fluous (equiv. 3 syl.)

Metre – 2 syl. short in Q2. Q2 – Attend! F – QUEEN – Alack, what noise is this?

is – *are*; Switzers – *Swiss guards*   Q2 – is F – are

overpeering – *looking over*; list – *shore*

Eats not – *doesn't overflow*; flats – *low land*; im-**pi**-teous – *pitiless*

head – *insurrection*   **rio**-tous (equiv. 2 syl.)

                        Irregular line – can be scanned with quartus paeon/as hexameter

And, as the world were now but to begin,
Antiquity forgot, custom not known,
The ratifiers and props of every word,   105
They cry, 'Choose we: Laertes shall be king!' –
Caps, hands and tongue, applaud it to the clouds –
'Laertes shall be king! Laertes king!'

QUEEN
How cheerfully on the false trail they cry.

A noise within

O, this is counter, you false Danish dogs!   110

KING
The doors are broke.

Enter LAERTES with Followers.

LAERTES
Where is this king? Sirs, stand you all without.

FOLLOWERS
No, let's come in.

LAERTES   I pray you give me leave.

FOLLOWERS   We will, we will.

LAERTES
I thank you, keep the door.

[Exeunt Followers and Messenger.]

as . . . begin – *as if the world were starting again*
Antiquity – *Ancient tradition*; custom – *customs*
The . . . word – *the things that confirm and support every word*   **ra**-ti-**fiers** (equiv. 3 syl.)

Caps – *(thrown into the air)*

false trail – *(like hunting dogs)*

counter – *following the wrong scent*; false – *disloyal*

broke – *broken open*   Metre – line is short by 6 syl.

SD – This stage direction comes after 'Danish dogs' in Q2 and F.

without – *outside*   Q2 – this F – the; Punct. Q2 – king? Sirs, F – King, sirs?

Metre – Ambiguous metrical connection (see Series Introduction)

give me leave – *leave me alone* (with the King)

keep – *guard*

                                O thou vile King,
Give me my father.

QUEEN   Calmly, good Laertes.   115

LAERTES
That drop of blood that's calm proclaims me bastard,
Cries 'Cuckold!' to my father, brands the harlot
Even here between the chaste unsmirchèd brow
Of my true mother.

KING   What is the cause, Laertes,
That thy rebellion looks so giant-like?   120
Let him go, Gertrude, do not fear our person.
There's such divinity doth hedge a king
That treason can but peep to what it would,
Acts little of his will. Tell me, Laertes,
Why thou art thus incens'd. Let him go, Gertrude. 125
Speak, man.

LAERTES   Where is my father?

KING   Dead.

QUEEN
But not by him.

KING   Let him demand his fill.

LAERTES
How came he dead? I'll not be juggl'd with.
To hell allegiance, vows to the blackest devil,
Conscience and grace to the profoundest pit.   130
I dare damnation. To this point I stand –

Q2 – that's calm F – that calms

'Cuckold' – *man with an unfaithful wife*; harlot – *prostitute*
between – *in the middle of*; unsmirchèd – *unstained*　　　　Even (equiv. 1 syl.)

is the **cause** (anapest – see 'A Note on Metre')
giant-like – *large/like the war of the Titans*　　　　re-**bell**-ion (equiv. 3 syl.)
fear – *fear for*
hedge – *protect* (reference to the divine right of kings)
can ... would – *can only glimpse what it wishes to do*
Acts ... will – *can perform little of its intention*

Metre – this shared line short by 2 syl.

juggl'd with – *deceived*
allegiance – *(to one's King)*　　　　to the **black**- (anapest – see 'A Note on Metre')
pit – *(of hell)*
To this point I stand – *I am firm in this resolve*

That both the worlds I give to negligence.
Let come what comes, only I'll be reveng'd
Most throughly for my father.

KING   Who shall stay you?

LAERTES   My will, not all the world's.
And for my means I'll husband them so well   135
They shall go far with little.

KING   Good Laertes,
If you desire to know the certainty
Of your dear father, is't writ in your revenge
That swoopstake you will draw both friend and foe,
Winner and loser?

LAERTES   None but his enemies.

KING   Will you know them, then? 140

LAERTES
To his good friends thus wide I'll ope my arms
And like the kind life-rendering pelican
Repast them with my blood.

KING   Why, now you speak
Like a good child and a true gentleman.
That I am guiltless of your father's death   145
And am most sensibly in grief for it
It shall as level to your judgement 'pear
As day does to your eye.

A noise within.

both the worlds – *this world and the next*; give to negligence – *disregard*

throughly – *thoroughly*   Metre – Ambiguous metrical connection
                                                                  (see Series Introduction)

stay – *prevent*

My … world's – *I'll have my will in spite of that of the world*   Q2 – world's F – world
means – *resources*; husband – *manage*

certainty – *truth*
is't – *is it*; writ in – *required by*   -er, is't **writ** (anapest – see 'A Note on Metre')
swoopstake – *as in a sweepstake*; draw – *gather*
                    Metre – Ambiguous metrical connection (see Series Introduction)

ope – *open*

Repast – *feed*; life-rendering … blood – *the pelican was believed to*   **ren**-dering
feed its young on its own blood   (equiv. 2 syl.)

sensibly – *feelingly*   Q2 – sensibly F – sensible
level – *easily*; 'pear – *appear*   Q2 – 'pear F – pierce

Enter OPHELIA.

LAERTES   Let her come in.
How now, what noise is that?
O heat, dry up my brains, tears seven times salt   150
Burn out the sense and virtue of mine eye.
By heaven, thy madness shall be paid with weight
Till our scale turn the beam. O rose of May,
Dear maid, kind sister, sweet Ophelia,
O heavens, is't possible a young maid's wits   155
Should be as mortal as a poor man's life?
[Nature is fine in love, and where 'tis fine
It sends some precious instance of itself
After the thing it loves.]

OPHELIA (*Sings.*)
They bore him bare-faced on the bier   160
[Hey non nony, nony, hey nony]
And in his grave rained many a tear.
Fare you well, my dove.

LAERTES
Hadst thou thy wits and didst persuade revenge
It could not move thus.   165

OPHELIA
You must sing 'a-down a-down', an you call him
'a-down-a'. O how the wheel becomes it. It is the false
steward that stole his master's daughter.

LAERTES
This nothing's more than matter.

Ambiguous Lineation – Let . . . that? would form a regular line

sense and virtue – *sensory virtue* (ability to see) (hendiadys – see Introduction)
paid with weight – *heavily revenged*   Q2 – with F – by
turn the beam – *tips* (in our favour)   Q2 – turn F – turns

                                                    Q2 – a poor F – an old
Nature – *Human nature*; fine in – *refined by*   Lines 157–9 are only in F.
instance – *part*

                                                    Metre – line is short by 4 syl.

bare-faced – *without/with open coffin*; bier – *stretcher on which a corpse is carried*
                                                    This line is only in F.
                                    Q2 – in F – on; Q2 – rained F – rains

Hadst thou thy wits – *If you were sane*

                                                    Metre – line is short by 5 syl.

'a-down a-down' – *a well known song refrain*; an – *if*   The scene moves into PROSE.
wheel – *refrain*; It is the false . . . daughter – *a reference to an unidentified story*

nothing's more than matter – *apparent nonsense is more meaningful than sensible speech*

OPHELIA

    There's rosemary: that's for remembrance.   170
    Pray you, love, remember. And there is pansies: that's
    for thoughts.

LAERTES

    A document in madness – thoughts and remembrance
    fitted!

OPHELIA

    There's fennel for you, and columbines.   175
    There's rue for you, and here's some for me. We may
    call it herb of grace o'Sundays. You may wear your rue
    with a difference. There's a daisy. I would give you
    some violets, but they withered all when my father
    died. They say he made a good end.   180

Sings.

    For bonny sweet Robin is all my joy.

LAERTES

    Thought and afflictions, passion, hell itself
    She turns to favour and to prettiness.

OPHELIA (*Sings.*)

    And will he not come again?
    And will he not come again?   185
    No, no, he is dead,
    Go to thy deathbed.
    He never will come again.

    His beard was as white as snow,
    Flaxen was his poll.   190

rosemary – *(presumably given to Laertes)*

Q2 – Pray you F – Pray

document – *lesson*
fitted – *put together correctly*

fennel – *symbolising flattery*; columbines – *symbolising infidelity* (presumably offered
to the Queen); rue – *symbolising repentence* (presumably to the King or Queen)
herb of grace – *another name for rue*; o' – *on* Q2 – herb of grace F – herb-grace;
daisy – *symbolising deception or love* Q2 – You may F – Oh you must
violets – *symbolising fidelity/chastity* (presumably directed to the Queen)

F – he Q2 – 'a

Thought – *melancholy*; passion – *suffering* Q2 –afflictions F – affliction
favour – *attractiveness*

F/Q1 – he Q2 –'a
F/Q1 – he Q2 –'a

Q2 – was as F/Q1 – as
flaxen – *white*; poll – *head* Q2 – Flaxen F/Q1 – All flaxen

He is gone, he is gone,
And we cast away moan.
God a' mercy on his soul.
And of all Christians' souls. God buy you.   *[Exit.]*

LAERTES
Do you see this, O God?   195

KING
Laertes, I must commune with your grief
Or you deny me right. Go but apart,
Make choice of whom your wisest friends you will,
And they shall hear and judge 'twixt you and me.
If by direct or by collateral hand   200
They find us touch'd, we will our kingdom give –
Our crown, our life, and all that we call ours –
To you in satisfaction. But, if not,
Be you content to lend your patience to us
And we shall jointly labour with your soul   205
To give it due content.

LAERTES   Let this be so.
His means of death, his obscure funeral –
No trophy, sword nor hatchment o'er his bones,
No noble rite, nor formal ostentation –
Cry to be heard as 'twere from heaven to earth   210
That I must call't in question.

KING   So you shall,
And where th'offence is let the great axe fall.
I pray you go with me.   *Exeunt.*

cast away moan – *waste our lamentations*

God a' mercy – *God have mercy*   Q2/Q1 – God a' mercy F – Gramercy

God buy you – *Goodbye*   Q2 – Christians' souls. God buy you F – Christian
                                                                        soules I pray God buy ye

                                                        Q2 – O God F – you Gods

commune with – *take part in/converse with*

Go but apart – *Let's go somewhere private*

whom – *whichever of*

'twixt – *between*

collateral – *indirect*   co-**llat**-eral (equiv. 3 syl.)

touch'd – *implicated* (in Polonius' death)

To you – *We will give to you*

                                                        Q2 – funeral F – burial

trophy – *memorial*; hatchment – *tablet bearing the coat of arms of the deceased*

ostentation – *ceremony*

                                                                heaven (equiv. 1 syl.)

call't in question – *demand an explanation*

great axe – *(method of execution)*

                                                        Metre – this line is short by 4 syl.

4.6 *Enter* HORATIO *and* [*a* Gentleman].

HORATIO

What are they that would speak with me?

GENTLEMAN

Sea-faring men, sir. They say they have
letters for you.

HORATIO

Let them come in.   [*Exit Gentleman.*]
I do not know from what part of the world I should be   5
greeted if not from Lord Hamlet.

Enter Sailors.

SAILOR

God bless you, sir.

HORATIO

Let Him bless thee too.

SAILOR

He shall, sir, an please Him. There's a letter for
you, sir – it came from th'ambassador that was bound   10
for England – if your name be Horatio, as I am let to
know it is.

HORATIO

[*Reads.*] Horatio, when thou shalt have overlooked
this, give these fellows some means to the King: they have
letters for him. Ere we were two days old at sea, a pirate of   15
very warlike appointment gave us chase. Finding ourselves
too slow of sail, we put on a compelled valour and in the

Q1 has a different scene – between Gertrude and Horatio (see Introduction).

What are they – *What sort of men are they*   This scene starts in PROSE.

                                                Q2 – Sea-faring F – Sailors

                                                SD – Q2 – Sailors F – Sailor

an – *if it*   F – He Q2 – 'A; Q2 – an F – an't
                              Q2 – came F – comes; Q2 – th'ambassador F – th'ambassadors
let – *led*

overlooked – *read*
means – *means of access*
were two days old – *had spent two days*
appointment – *equipment*
compelled – *necessary*; valour – *bravery*   Q2 – valour and F – valour.

grapple I boarded them. On the instant they got clear of our
ship, so I alone became their prisoner. They have dealt with
me like thieves of mercy, but they knew what they did: I   20
am to do a turn for them. Let the King have the letters I
have sent, and repair thou to me with as much speed as thou
wouldest fly death. I have words to speak in thine ear will
make thee dumb. Yet are they much too light for the bore
of the matter. These good fellows will bring thee where I   25
am. Rosencrantz and Guildenstern hold their course for
England. Of them I have much to tell thee. Farewell. He
that thou knowest thine. Hamlet.
Come. I will give you way for these your letters.
And do't the speedier that you may direct me   30
To him from whom you brought them.   *Exeunt.*

4.7 *Enter* KING *and* LAERTES.

KING
    Now must your conscience my acquittance seal
    And you must put me in your heart for friend
    Sith you have heard and with a knowing ear
    That he which hath your noble father slain
    Pursu'd my life.

LAERTES   It well appears. But tell me   5
    Why you proceeded not against these feats
    So criminal and so capital in nature
    As by your safety, wisdom, all things else,
    You mainly were stirred up.

KING
    O, for two special reasons   10
    Which may to you perhaps seem much unsinew'd

grapple – *seizing of the ship*; them – *their ship*

thieves of mercy – *merciful thieves*

a turn – *a favour in return*   Q2 – turn F – good turn

repair – *come*   Q2 – speed F – haste

                                                                               Q2 – thine F – your

much . . . matter – *inadequate to convey the importance of the matter*

                                              Punct. Q2 – thine. Hamlet. F – thine Hamlet.

way – *access* (to the King)   The scene moves into VERSE for the last three lines.

Ask R

my acquittance seal – *confirm my innocence*

for – *as a*

Sith – *Since*; knowing – *understanding*

Pursu'd my life – *Tried to kill me*

proceeded not – *didn't take legal proceedings*; feats – *deeds*   Q2 – proceed

capital – *punishable by death*   **crim**-inal (equiv. 2 syl.)

As . . . up – *Since your safety, wisdom and everything else incited you to take action*

                                              Metre – line is short by 4 syl.

                                              Metre – line is short by 3 syl.

unsinew'd – *weak*

But yet to me they're strong. The Queen his mother
Lives almost by his looks and for myself,
My virtue or my plague, be it either which,
She is so conjunct to my life and soul   15
That as the star moves not but in his sphere
I could not but by her. The other motive
Why to a public count I might not go
Is the great love the general gender bear him,
Who, dipping all his faults in their affection,   20
Would like the spring that turneth wood to stone,
Convert his gyves to graces, so that my arrows,
Too slightly timber'd for so loud a wind,
Would have reverted to my bow again
And not where I have aim'd them.   25

LAERTES
And so have I a noble father lost,
A sister driven into desperate terms
Whose worth, if praises may go back again,
Stood challenger on mount of all the age
For her perfections. But my revenge will come.   30

KING
Break not your sleeps for that; you must not think
That we are made of stuff so flat and dull
That we can let our beard be shook with danger
And think it pastime. You shortly shall hear more.
I loved your father and we love ourself,   35
And that, I hope, will teach you to imagine –

Enter a Messenger with letters.

MESSENGER
These to your majesty, this to the Queen.

Q2 – But F – And

be it either which – *whichever it may be*   be it **ei**- (anapest – see 'A Note on Metre')
conjunct – *coupled*   Q2 – She is F – She's; Oxf – conjunct F – conjunctive
sphere – *(stars and planets were thought to move within their own transparent spheres)*
I . . . her – *I could not live without her*
count – *account*
general gender – *common people*

that . . . stone – *with a high level of lime could calcify wood*   F – Would Q2 – Work
gyves (Pron. jives) – *shackles/crimes*
Too . . . timber'd – *too light*; loud – *strong*
reverted – *returned*
   F – And Q2 – But; Q2 – have aim'd F – had arm'd. Metre – line is short by 3 syl.

terms – *circumstances*   **des**-perate (equiv. 2 syl.)
may . . . again – *may remember her as she was*   Q2 – Whose worth F – Who was
on mount – *on high*
                              -tions. But **my** (anapest – see 'A Note on Metre')

Break . . . that – *Don't lose any sleep over that*
flat – *inactive*; dull – *slow*
let . . . danger – *be insulted*
pastime – *agreeable*   -time. You **short**- (anapest – see 'A Note on Metre')

KING
From Hamlet! Who brought them?

MESSENGER
Sailors, my lord, they say. I saw them not.
They were given me by Claudio. He received them   40
[Of him that brought them.]

KING   Laertes, you shall hear them.
Leave us.

[Exit Messenger.]

[*Reads.*] *High and mighty. You shall know I am set naked*
on your kingdom. Tomorrow shall I beg leave to see your
kingly eyes. When I shall (first asking you pardon)   45
thereunto recount the occasion of my sudden return.
What should this mean? Are all the rest come back,
Or is it some abuse, and no such thing?

LAERTES
Know you the hand?

KING   'Tis Hamlet's character. 'Naked',
And in a postscript here he says 'alone'.   50
Can you advise me?

LAERTES
I am lost in it, my lord, but let him come.
It warms the very sickness in my heart
That I live and tell him to his teeth
'Thus diddest thou.'

KING   If it be so, Laertes –   55

Metre – line is short by 4 syl.

They were **giv**- (anapest – see 'A Note on Metre'); **Clau**-dio (equiv. 2 syl.)
Claudio – *it is not clear who this is. Some productions substitute Horatio.*   Not in F.

them./La-**er** (anapest – see 'A Note on Metre')
Metre – line is short by 8 syl. in Q2 (linked to previous line in F)

naked – *destitute*

pardon – *forgiveness*   Q2 – you F – your
occasion – *circumstances*   Q2 – the occasion F – th'occasions; Q2 – sudden return.
                                        F – sudden, and more strange return. Hamlet.
abuse – *trick*   Q2 – abuse, and F – abuse? Or

character – *handwriting*   **charac**-ter (equiv. 2 syl.)

F – advise Q2 – devise; Metre – line is short by 5 syl.

lost in – *confused by*   I am **lost** (anapest – see 'A Note on Metre'); Q2 – I am F – I'm
warms – *treats*
Metre – line is headless in Q2 (see 'A Note on Metre'); Q2 – I F – I shall
F – diddest Q2 – dids't Dover Wilson – diest

As how should it be so, how otherwise? –
Will you be rulèd by me?

LAERTES   [Ay, my lord,]
So you will not o'errule me to a peace.

KING
To thine own peace. If he be now return'd
As checking at his voyage, and that he means   60
No more to undertake it, I will work him
To an exploit, now ripe in my device,
Under the which he shall not choose but fall.
And for his death no wind of blame shall breathe
But even his mother shall uncharge the practice   65
And call it accident.

LAERTES   [My lord, I will be rul'd
The rather if you could devise it so
That I might be the organ.

KING   It falls right.
You have been talked of since your travel much,
And that in Hamlet's hearing, for a quality   70
Wherein they say you shine. Your sum of parts
Did not together pluck such envy from him
As did that one, and that in my regard
Of the unworthiest siege.

LAERTES
What part is that, my lord?   75

KING
A very ribbon in the cap of youth.
Yet needful too, for youth no less becomes

Q2 – Ay ... will F – If so you'll

So – *So long as*; o'errule – *overrule*

To ... peace – *To your own satisfaction*

As checking at – *As a result of giving up*; that – *if*

exploit – *favourable outcome*; ripe ... device – *freshly devised*

shall not choose but – *must*

uncharge the practice – *acquit the plot from blame* even (equiv. 1 syl.)

Links to form regular pentameter line with 'Some two months hence' (line 80) in F

Irregular shared line in Q2 – can be scanned with quartus paeon/as hexameter

The rather – *all the more quickly* Lines 66 (My lord) to 80 (graveness) are not in F.

organ – *instrument* (of revenge)

It falls right – *That fits well*

sum of parts – *whole list of attributes*

regard – *opinion*

siege – *importance* un-**wor**-thiest (equiv. 3 syl.); Metre – line is short by 4 syl.

Metre – line is short by 4 syl.

very ribbon – *crowning decoration*

becomes – *suits*

The light and careless livery that it wears
Than settl'd age his sables and his weeds
Importing health and graveness.] Two months since   80
Here was a gentleman of Normandy –
I have seen myself, and served against, the French
And they can well on horseback, but this gallant
Had witchcraft in't; he grew unto his seat
And to such wondrous doing brought his horse   85
As had he been incorps'd and demi-natur'd
With the brave beast. So far he topp'd my thought
That I in forgery of shapes and tricks
Come short of what he did.

LAERTES

A Norman was't?   90

KING

A Norman.

LAERTES

Upon my life, Lamord!

KING

The very same.

LAERTES

I know him well. He is the brooch, indeed,
And gem of all the nation.   95

KING

He made confession of you
And gave you such a masterly report
For art and exercise in your defence,
And for your rapier most especially,

light and careless livery – *frivolous uniform/the art of fencing*   **liv**-ery (equiv. 2 syl.)

sables – *furs*; weeds – *clothes*

Importing – *Indicating a concern for*; since – *ago*   Q2 – Two months since

                                                                        F – Some two months hence

served – *fought*   I have **seen** (anapest – see 'A Note on Metre'); Q2 – I have   F – I've

they – *Normans*; can well – *are skilled*; gallant (Pron. **gall**-ant) – *daring young man*

grew unto – *became one with*   Q2 – unto   F – into

doing – *performance*

As – *As if*; incorps'd – *of one body*; demi-natur'd – *half of the same nature*   F – he had

brave – *splendid*; topp'd my thought – *exceeded my expectations*   Q2 – topp'd   F – past

shapes and tricks – *imaginary tricks* (hendiadys – see Introduction)

Lines 89–93 have an ambiguous metrical connection (See Series Introduction)

                                        Q2 – Lamord   F – Lamound

brooch – *jewel*

                    Q2 – the   F – our; Metre – line is short by 3 syl.

made ... you – *testified to your skill*   Metre – line is short by 3 syl.

art and exercise – *skilful practice* (hendiadys); your defence – *self-defence*

                            ra-pier (equiv. 2 syl.); F – especially   Q2 – especial

That he cried out 'twould be a sight indeed   100
If one could match you. [Th'escrimers of their nation
He swore had neither motion, guard nor eye
If you oppos'd them.] Sir, this report of his
Did Hamlet so envenom with his envy
That he could nothing do but wish and beg   105
Your sudden coming o'er to play with you.
Now out of this –

LAERTES   What out of this, my lord?

KING
Laertes, was your father dear to you?
Or are you like the painting of a sorrow,
A face without a heart?

LAERTES   Why ask you this?   110

KING
Not that I think you did not love your father
But that I know love is begun by time
And that I see in passages of proof
Time qualifies the spark and fire of it.
[There lives within the very flame of love   115
A kind of wick or snuff that will abate it,
And nothing is at a like goodness still,
For goodness growing to a pleurisy
Dies in his own too much. That we would do
We should do when we would, for this 'would' changes   120
And hath abatements and delays as many
As there are tongues, are hands, are accidents,
And then this 'should' is like a spendthrift's sigh
That hurts by easing.] But to the quick of th'ulcer –
Hamlet comes back. What would you undertake   125

one – *anyone*; Th'escrimers – *The skilled fencers*   you. Th'es-**crim** (anapest)

had – *would have*; eye – *visual perception*   Ll. 101 (pt.) to 103 (pt.) are not in F.

            this re-**port** (anapest); Punct. Q2 – Sir, this report F – Sir. This report

envenom – *embitter*

nothing do – *do nothing*

sudden – *immediate*; coming o'er – *returning from France*   Q2 – you F – him

What. . . lord – *(Either Laertes interrupts in frustration*   Q2 – What F – Why
or the king breaks off)

begun by time – *generated by particular circumstances*

passages of proof – *experiences which prove this*

qualifies – *modifies*

                    Lines 115–24 are not in F.

snuff – *part of the candle wick that burns down*

at a like – *at the same level of*

pleurisy – *excess*

would do – *wish to do*   That we would . . . when we would – Prov.

abatements – *reductions*

hands – *actions*

spendthrift's sigh – *sigh of a man who has spent all his money*

by easing – *at the same time as easing pain*; quick – *centre*   to the **quick** (anapest)

To show yourself in deed your father's son
More than in words?

LAERTES   To cut his throat i'th' church.

KING
No place indeed should murder sanctuarize.
Revenge should have no bounds. But, good Laertes,
Will you do this? Keep close within your chamber;   130
Hamlet return'd shall know you are come home;
We'll put on those shall praise your excellence
And set a double varnish on the fame
The Frenchman gave you, bring you in fine together
And wager on your heads. He being remiss,   135
Most generous and free from all contriving,
Will not peruse the foils, so that with ease,
Or with a little shuffling, you may choose
A sword unbated and in a pass of practice
Requite him for your father.

LAERTES   I will do't.   140
And for that purpose I'll anoint my sword.
I bought an unction of a mountebank
So mortal that, but dip a knife in it,
Where it draws blood no cataplasm so rare,
Collected from all simples that have virtue   145
Under the moon, can save the thing from death
That is but scratch'd withal. I'll touch my point
With this contagion, that if I gall him slightly
It may be death.

KING   Let's further think of this,
Weigh what convenience both of time and means   150
May fit us to our shape. If this should fail

in deed – *through actions*   Malone – in deed your father's son Q2 – indeed your
                                                                    father's son F – your father's son indeed

                                                                    i'th' (equiv. 1 syl.)

sanctuarize – *give protection*

close – *concealed*

put on those – *arrange some people*

in fine – *finally*   Can be scanned with 'you, bring **you**' or 'you in **fine**' as an anapest
wager on your heads – *bet on you both*; remiss – *negligent*   being (equiv. 1 syl.)
generous – *noble-minded/lacking suspicion*; contriving – *deception*
peruse – *examine*

unbated – *not blunted*; pass of practice – *treacherous, calculated thrust* Can be scanned
Requite him – *Have revenge on him*   with '-ted and **in**' or 'in a **pass**' as an anapest
                                                                    – see 'A Note on Metre'

unction – *ointment*; mountebank – *itinerant charlatan selling medicine*
mortal – *deadly*   Q2 – that, but dip F – I but dipt
cataplasm – *medicinal poultice*; rare – *excellent*   **cat**-a-**plasm** (equiv. 3 syl.)
simples – *medicinal herbs*
Under the moon – *anywhere/gathered by moonlight*
withal – *with it*; touch my point – *anoint the end of my sword*
contagion – *poison*; gall – *scratch*   -gion, that **if** (anapest – see 'A Note on Metre')

convenience – *suitable correspondence*   con-**ve**-nience (equiv. 3 syl.)
fit us to our shape – *suit our plan/suit the roles we are to play*

And that our drift look through our bad performance
'Twere better not essay'd. Therefore this project
Should have a back or second that might hold
If this did blast in proof. Soft, let me see: 155
We'll make a solemn wager on your cunnings –
I ha't!
When in your motion you are hot and dry
(As make your bouts more violent to that end)
And that he calls for drink, I'll have prepar'd him   160
A chalice for the nonce, whereon but sipping,
If he by chance escape your venom'd stuck,
Our purpose may hold there. But stay, what noise?

Enter QUEEN.

QUEEN
One woe doth tread upon another's heel,
So fast they follow. Your sister's drown'd, Laertes.   165

LAERTES
Drown'd! O, where?

QUEEN
There is a willow grows askant the brook
That shows his hoary leaves in the glassy stream.
Therewith fantastic garlands did she make
Of crowflowers, nettles, daisies and long purples,   170
That liberal shepherds give a grosser name
But our cold maids do dead men's fingers call them.
There on the pendent boughs her crownet weeds
Clambering to hang, an envious sliver broke,
When down her weedy trophies and herself   175
Fell in the weeping brook. Her clothes spread wide
And mermaid-like awhile they bore her up,

drift look through – *scheme becomes visible*

essay'd – *attempted*

back – *backup*; second – *second string*; hold – *work*

blast in proof – *go wrong in the execution*   Q2 – did F – should

cunnings – *skills*

ha't – *have it*   Metre – line is short by 8 syl. (extra-metrical exclamation)

motion – *movement*; dry – *thirsty*

As – *As you should*; bouts – *rounds of fencing*; end – *purpose*   Q2 – that F – the

F – prepar'd Q2 – preferr'd

chalice – *drinking goblet*; nonce – *occasion*

stuck – *thrust*

Q2 – But stay, what noise? F – How now sweet Queen.

Q2 – they F – they'll; -llow. Your **sis**- (anapest – see 'A Note on Metre')

Drown'd! – *(This may be considered an exclamation*   Metre – line is short by 7 syl.
or question – see Introduction*)*

askant – *across*   Q2 – askant the F – aslant a

hoary – *grey-white*   Q2 – hoary F – hoar; in the **glass**- (anapest)

Therewith – *With the willow*   Q2 – Therewith F – There with; Q2 – make F – come

crowflowers – *buttercups*; long purples – *orchid* (with tubers resembling testicles)

liberal – *free-speaking*; grosser – *more vulgar*   **li**-beral (equiv. 2 syl.)

cold – *chaste*

pendent – *overhanging*; crownet weeds– *coronet of weeds*   Q2 – crownet F – coronet

envious – *malicious*; sliver – *(of branch)*   **Clam**-bering; **en**-vious (both equiv. 2 syl.)

weedy trophies – *wildflower garlands*   Q2 – her F – the

Which time she chanted snatches of old lauds
As one incapable of her own distress,
Or like a creature native and endued   180
Unto that element. But long it could not be
Till that her garments, heavy with their drink,
Pulled the poor wretch from her melodious lay
To muddy death.

LAERTES   Alas, then she is drown'd.

QUEEN   Drowned, drowned.

LAERTES
Too much of water hast thou, poor Ophelia,   185
And therefore I forbid my tears. But yet
It is our trick – nature her custom holds
Let shame say what it will. [*Weeps.*] When these are gone
The woman will be out. Adieu, my lord,
I have a speech of fire that fain would blaze   190
But that this folly drowns it.   *Exit.*

KING   Let's follow, Gertrude.
How much I had to do to calm his rage!
Now fear I this will give it start again.
Therefore let's follow.   *Exeunt.*

5.1 *Enter two Clowns [a Gravedigger and a Second Man].*

GRAVEDIGGER
Is she to be buried in Christian burial,
when she wilfully seeks her own salvation?

Which time – *During which time*; lauds – *hymns*   Q2 – lauds F/Q1 – tunes

incapable – *uncomprehending*; distress – *calamity*   in-**cap**-able (equiv. 3 syl.)

endued – *adapted*

that element – *(water)*   **ele**-ment (equiv. 2 syl.); -ment. But **long** (anapest)

lay – *song*   me-**lo**-dious (equiv. 3 syl.)

Metre – Ambiguous metrical connection (see Series Introduction);
Q2/Q1 – she is drown'd F – is she drown'd?
Drowned can be pronounced either with an accented èd or without

our trick – *our natural impulse*

these – *my tears*

woman – *womanish* (weak) *part of me*; Adieu – *Farewell*

fain would – *is eager to*

folly – *foolish behaviour* (weeping)   Q2 – drowns F – doubts;

it./Let's **foll**- (anapest – see 'A Note on Metre')

give it – *make it*

Metre – line is short by 5 syl.

Clowns – Rustics

This scene begins in PROSE.

salvation – *heavenly salvation or a malapropism for damnation*   Q2 – when she
F – that

2 MAN

I tell thee she is. Therefore make her grave
straight. The crowner hath sat on her and finds it
Christian burial.   5

GRAVEDIGGER

How can that be unless she drowned
herself in her own defence?

2 MAN

Why, 'tis found so.

GRAVEDIGGER

It must be *se offendendo.* It cannot be else.
For here lies the point: if I drown myself wittingly, it   10
argues an act, and an act hath three branches – it is to
act, to do, to perform. Argal, she drowned herself
wittingly.

2 MAN

Nay, but hear you, goodman delver.

GRAVEDIGGER

Give me leave. Here lies the water – good.   15
Here stands the man – good. If the man go to this water
and drown himself, it is, willy-nilly, he goes. Mark you
that. But if the water come to him and drown him, he
drowns not himself. Argal, he that is not guilty of his
own death shortens not his own life.   20

2 MAN

But is this law?

Q2 – Therefore F – and therefore

straight – *straightaway*; crowner – *coroner*; sat – *held an inquest*; finds it – *finds in favour of*

The Gravedigger implies that Ophelia committed suicide (differently from Gertrude)

in her own defence – *a common mitigation for murder*

se offendendo – *malapropism for se defendendo* (in self-defence)
wittingly – *knowingly*
three . . . perform – *(reference to a contemporary legal case)*   Q2 – to act F – an act
Argal – *malapromism for ergo* (therefore)   Q2 – to do F – to do and

goodman – *title for person below the rank of gentleman*; delver – *digger*

willy-nilly – *whether he is willing or not*; Mark – *Remember*
                                                      Punct. Q2 – that. F – that?

Q2 and F – Punct. death, shortens (may indicate phrasing – see Introduction)

GRAVEDIGGER

Ay, marry is't. Crowner's 'quest law.

2 MAN

Will you ha' the truth on't? If this had not been a
gentlewoman she should have been buried out
of Christian burial.   25

GRAVEDIGGER

Why, there thou sayst, and the more pity
that great folk should have countenance in this world to
drown or hang themselves more than their even–
Christen. Come, my spade. There is no ancient
gentlemen but gardeners, ditchers and grave-makers.   30
They hold up Adam's profession.

2 MAN

Was he a gentleman?

GRAVEDIGGER

He was the first that ever bore arms.

[2 MAN

Why he had none.

GRAVEDIGGER

What, ar't a Heathen? how dost thou understand the   35
Scripture? The Scripture says Adam digged; could he
dig without arms?]
I'll put another question to thee. If thou answerest me
not to the purpose, confess thy self.

2 MAN

Go to.   40

Crowner's 'quest – *Coroner's inquest*

on't – *of it*

there thou sayest – *you make a good point*
countenance – *authority*
even-Christen – *fellow Christians*
no ancient – *no such venerable*
ditchers – *ditch-makers*
hold up – *keep up*; Adam's profession – *Adam looked after the Garden of Eden* (Bib.)

Was . . . gentleman – Prov.

bore arms – *had a coat of arms/pun on had arms* (as the first man)   F – He Q2 – 'A

Lines 34–7 are only in F.

to the purpose – *correctly*; confess thyself – *(the saying is 'confess thyself and be hanged')*

Go to – *Be quiet*

GRAVEDIGGER

What is he that builds stronger than
either the mason, the shipwright or the carpenter?

2 MAN

The gallows-maker, for that outlives a thousand
tenants.

GRAVEDIGGER

I like thy wit well, in good faith. The   45
gallows does well. But how does it well? It does well to
those that do ill. Now, thou dost ill to say the gallows is
built stronger than the church. Argal, the gallows may
do well to thee. To't again, come.

2 MAN

Who builds stronger than a mason, a shipwright or   50
a carpenter?

GRAVEDIGGER

Ay, tell me that and unyoke.

2 MAN

Marry, now I can tell.

GRAVEDIGGER

To't!

2 MAN

Mass, I cannot tell.   55

GRAVEDIGGER

Cudgel thy brains no more about it, for
your dull ass will not mend his pace with beating. And
when you are asked this question next, say a grave-

mason – *stonemason*

that – *(the gallows)*   Q2 – that F – that frame
tenants – *(those that are hanged)*

gallows does well – *gallows is a good example*; does it well – *does it serve well*

may . . . thee – *(by hanging you)*
To't again – *Try again*

unyoke – *give up*

Marry – *By the Virgin Mary* (oath)

To't – *Go on*

Mass – *By the Mass* (oath)

Cudgel . . . it – *Don't beat your brains over it* (Prov.)
dull – *stupid*; mend – *improve*   dull . . . beating – Prov.

maker. The houses he makes lasts till doomsday. Go get
thee in and fetch me a stoup of liquor.   60

[Exit Second Man.]

Sings

In youth when I did love, did love,
Methought it was very sweet
To contract-a the time for-a my behove,
O, methought there-a was nothing-a meet!

Enter HAMLET and HORATIO.

HAMLET
Has this fellow no feeling of his business, that he   65
sings in grave-making.

HORATIO
Custom hath made it in him a property of
easiness.

HAMLET
'Tis e'en so. The hand of little employment
hath the daintier sense.   70

GRAVEDIGGER
(*Sings.*)
But age with his stealing steps
Hath clawed me in his clutch
And hath shipped me into the land
As if I had never been such.

[Throws up a skull.]

Q2/Q1 – houses F – houses that; Q2/F – lasts Q1 – last

stoup – *jug*   Q2 – thee in and; F – thee to Yaughan

-a – *(an extra-metrical sound)*; contract – *pass*; for my behove – *for my own pleasure*
meet – *more fitting*

SD – In F, Hamlet and Horatio enter 'far off' after line 51.

F – that he Q2 – 'A

in – *whilst*   Q2 – in F – at

a property of easiness – *something he can do with indifference*

'Tis e'en so – *It is true*; The . . . sense – *The hand that does little work is more sensitive*
(Prov.)

Q2 – clawed F – caught

shipped me into the land – *transported me into the earth/my grave*
been such – *been a young man*

HAMLET

That skull had a tongue in it and could sing   75
once. How the knave jowls it to the ground, as if 'twere
Cain's jawbone, that did the first murder. This might be
the pate of a politician which this ass now o'erreaches –
one that would circumvent God, might it not?

HORATIO

It might, my lord.   80

HAMLET

Or of a courtier which could say, 'Good
morrow, sweet lord, how dost thou, sweet lord?' This
might be my Lord Such-a-One, that praised my Lord
Such-a-One's horse when he meant to beg it, might it
not?   85

HORATIO

Ay, my lord.

HAMLET

Why, e'en so. And now my Lady Worm's –
chapless and knocked about the mazard with a
sexton's spade. Here's fine revolution an we had the
trick to see't. Did these bones cost no more the   90
breeding but to play at loggets with them? Mine ache to
think on't.

GRAVEDIGGER (*Sings.*)
    A pickaxe and a spade, a spade,
    For and a shrouding-sheet,
    O, a pit of clay for to be made   95
    For such a guest is meet.

jowls – *hurls*   Q2 – 'twere F – it were
Cain – *who killed his brother Abel using an ass's jawbone* (Bib.)   Q2 – This F – It
pate – *head*; o'erreaches – *outwits*   Q2 – now o'erreaches F – o're offices
circumvent – *outwit*   Q2 – would F – could

Q2 – thou, sweet lord F – thou, good lord

beg – *beg for*   F/Q1 – he meant Q2 – 'a went

Lady Worm – *Lady who is food for worms/an ironic title*
chapless – *jawless*; mazard – *head*
sexton – *grave-digger*; revolution – *reversal of the social hierarchy*; an – *if*   Q2 – an F – if
trick – *skill*; Did. . . breeding – *Did these people's bones cost so little to bring up*
loggets – *skittles*   Q2 – them F – 'em

For and – *and moreover*; shrouding-sheet – *sheet in which a corpse was wrapped*

meet – *fitting*

[Throws up another skull.]

HAMLET
There's another! Why, may not that be the skull
of a lawyer? Where be his quiddities now – his quillets,
his cases, his tenures and his tricks? Why does he suffer
this mad knave now to knock him about the sconce with   100
a dirty shovel and will not tell him of his action of
battery? Hum! This fellow might be in's time a great
buyer of land, with his statutes, his recognizances, his
fines, his double vouchers, his recoveries [Is this the
fine of his fines and the recovery of his recoveries,] to   105
have his fine pate full of fine dirt! Will vouchers vouch
him no more of his purchases and doubles than the
length and breadth of a pair of indentures? The very
conveyances of his lands will scarcely lie in this box,
and must th'inheritor himself have no more, ha?   110

HORATIO
Not a jot more, my lord.

HAMLET
Is not parchment made of sheepskins?

HORATIO
Ay, my lord, and of calves' skins too.

HAMLET
They are sheep and calves which seek out
assurance in that. I will speak to this fellow. Whose   115
grave's this, sirrah?

GRAVEDIGGER
Mine, sir,

Q2 – may F – might

quiddities – *scholarly arguments*; quillets – *quibbling arguments* Q – quiddities

tenures – *property documents*; tricks – *legal tricks* F – quiddits

sconce – *head* Q2 – mad F – rude

action of battery – *lawsuit for physical assault*

statutes – *securities for mortgages*; recognizances – *legal documents acknowledging a debt*

double-vouchers – *practice of securing two guarantors*; recoveries – *suits for obtaining*

possession; fine – *conclusion* Lines 104 (pt.). 105 (pt.) – not in Q2

pate – *head*; vouch – *guarantee* Q2 – vouchers F – his vouchers

doubles – *double-vouchers* (see above) Q2 – doubles F – double ones too

pair of indentures – *two copies of a legal agreement on the same sheet of paper*;

conveyances of – *deeds relating to transfer of*; box – *coffin* Q2 – scarcely F – hardly

inheritor – *owner* Q2 – th'inheritor F – the inheritor

parchment – *material used for legal documents*

Q2 – calves' skins F – calf skins

sheep and calves – *fools* Q2 – which F – that

assurance – *legal evidence*

sirrah – *sir* Q2 – sirrah F – sir

[Sings.]

O, a pit of clay for to be made –
[For such a guest is meet.]

HAMLET
I think it be thine, indeed, for thou liest in't.   120

GRAVEDIGGER
You lie out on't, sir, and therefore 'tis not
yours. For my part I do not lie in't, yet it is mine.

HAMLET
Thou dost lie in't, to be in't and say it is thine.
'Tis for the dead, not for the quick. Therefore thou
liest.   125

GRAVEDIGGER
'Tis a quick lie, sir, 'twill away again from
me to you.

HAMLET
What man dost thou dig it for?

GRAVEDIGGER
For no man, sir.

HAMLET
What woman, then?   130

GRAVEDIGGER
For none, neither.

HAMLET
Who is to be buried in't?

Line 119 is only in F.

Q2 – 'tis F – it is
lie – *tell untruths/dwell*   Q2 – yet F – and yet

lie – *tell an untruth*   Q2 – it is F – 'tis
quick – *living*

quick – *quick-witted/speedy*

GRAVEDIGGER
    One that was a woman, sir, but rest her
    soul she's dead.

HAMLET
    [*to Horatio*] How absolute the knave is! We must   135
    speak by the card or equivocation will undo us. By the
    Lord, Horatio, this three years I have took note of it,
    the age is grown so picked that the toe of the peasant
    comes so near the heel of the courtier he galls his
    kibe.– How long hast thou been grave-maker?   140

GRAVEDIGGER
    Of the days i'th' year I came to't that day
    that our last King Hamlet overcame Fortinbras.

HAMLET
    How long is that since?

GRAVEDIGGER
    Cannot you tell that? Every fool can tell
    that! It was that very day that young Hamlet was born   145
    – he that is mad and sent into England.

HAMLET
    Ay, marry. Why was he sent into England?

GRAVEDIGGER
    Why, because he was mad. He shall recover
    his wits there. Or if he do not, 'tis no great matter there.

HAMLET
    Why?   150

absolute – *precise*
by the card – *by the book/precisely;* equivocation – *verbal ambiguity*

Q2 – this F – these; Q2 – took F – taken

picked – *refined*
galls his kibe – *rubs the sore on his heel*

Q2/Q1 – heel F – heels
Q2 – been F – been a

Q2 – Of F – Of all

Q2 – that very day F – the very day
Q2 – is F – was

F – he ... He Q2 – 'a ...'A
F – he Q2 – 'a; Q2 – 'tis F – it's

GRAVEDIGGER
'Twill not be seen in him there. There the
men are as mad as he.

HAMLET
How came he mad?

GRAVEDIGGER
Very strangely, they say.

HAMLET
How, strangely?   155

GRAVEDIGGER
Faith, e'en with losing his wits.

HAMLET
Upon what ground?

GRAVEDIGGER
Why, here in Denmark. I have been
sexton here, man and boy, thirty years.

HAMLET
How long will a man lie i'th' earth ere he rot?   160

GRAVEDIGGER
Faith, if he be not rotten before he die (as
we have many pocky corpses that will scarce hold the
laying in) he will last you some eight year – or nine year
– a tanner will last you nine year.

HAMLET
Why he more than another?   165

seen – *noticed*   Q2 – him there. There F – him, there

Upon ... ground – *For what reason?* – taken by the gravedigger to mean 'Where?'

thirty years – *(this gives the indication of Hamlet's age* – see Introduction*)*

                              Q2 – Faith F/Q1 – I'faith; F/Q1 – he ... he Q2 – 'a ... 'a
pocky – *marked with the pox*;   Q2 – corpses F – corses nowadays
hold ... in – *stay unrotten during burial*   F/Q1 – he Q2 – 'a
tanner – *one who tans animal hides* (to make them into leather)

GRAVEDIGGER
Why, sir, his hide is so tanned with his
trade that he will keep out water a great while. And your
water is a sore decayer of your whoreson dead body.
Here's a skull now hath lain i'th' earth three and
twenty years.   170

HAMLET
Whose was it?

GRAVEDIGGER
A whoreson mad fellow's it was. Whose
do you think it was?

HAMLET
Nay, I know not.

GRAVEDIGGER
A pestilence on him for a mad rogue. 'A   175
poured a flagon of Rhenish on my head once! This
same skull, sir, was, sir, Yorick's skull, the King's jester.

HAMLET
This?

GRAVEDIGGER
E'en that.

HAMLET
Alas, poor Yorick. I knew him, Horatio. A   180
fellow of infinite jest, of most excellent fancy. He hath
borne me on his back a thousand times, and now how
abhorred in my imagination it is. My gorge rises at it.
Here hung those lips that I have kissed I know not how

hide – *skin*

F – he Q2 – 'a

whoreson – *son of a whore*

Q2 – now F – now: this skull; F – has lain Q2 – hath lien you

F – three and twenty Q2 – 23 Q1 – this dozen (see Introduction)

'A – *He*

Rhenish – *wine from the Rhine area of Germany*

Q2 – This same skull, sir, was, sir

F – This same skull, sir, this same skull sir was

Q2 – Alas F – Let me see. Alas

fancy – *invention*

F – borne Q2 bore; Q2 – now (not in F)

abhorred – *horrible*; My gorge rises – *I feel sick*   Q2 – abhorred ... is

F – abhorred my imagination is

oft. Where be your jibes now – your gambols, your   185
songs, your flashes of merriment, that were wont to set
the table on a roar? Not one now to mock your own
grinning, quite chapfallen. Now get you to my lady's
chamber and tell her, let her paint an inch thick, to this
favour she must come. Make her laugh at that. Prithee,   190
Horatio, tell me one thing.

HORATIO
What's that, my lord?

HAMLET
Dost thou think Alexander looked o'this
fashion i'th' earth?

HORATIO
E'en so.   195

HAMLET
And smelt so? Pah!

HORATIO
E'en so, my lord.

HAMLET
To what base uses we may return, Horatio!
Why may not imagination trace the noble dust of
Alexander till he find it stopping a bung-hole?   200

HORATIO
'Twere to consider too curiously to consider so.

HAMLET
No, faith, not a jot. But to follow him thither

jibes – *taunts*; gambols – *playful tricks*
wont to set – *accustomed to setting*
on a roar – *roaring* (presumably with laughter)
chapfallen – *crestfallen/lacking lower jaw*

Q2 – Not F – No
Q2 – grinning F – leering
F – chamber Q2 – table

favour – *appearance*

Alexander – *Alexander the Great*

bung-hole – *mouth of a bottle*

F – he Q2 – 'a

curiously – *closely/ingeniously*

with modesty enough and likelihood to lead it:
Alexander died, Alexander was buried, Alexander
returneth to dust, the dust is earth, of earth we make   205
loam, and why of that loam whereto he was converted
might they not stop a beer-barrel?
    Imperious Caesar, dead and turn'd to clay,
    Might stop a hole to keep the wind away.
    O, that that earth which kept the world in awe   210
    Should patch a wall t'expel the water's flaw.

Enter KING, QUEEN, LAERTES and [other Lords, with a Priest
after] the corpse.

But soft, but soft awhile, here comes the King,
The Queen, the courtiers. Who is this they follow?
And with such maimèd rites? This doth betoken
The corpse they follow did with desperate hand   215
Fordo its own life. 'Twas of some estate.
Couch we awhile and mark.

[Hamlet and Horatio stand aside.]

LAERTES   What ceremony else?

HAMLET *[aside to Horatio]*
    That is Laertes – a very noble youth, mark.

LAERTES
    What ceremony else?

PRIEST
    Her obsequies have been as far enlarg'd   220
    As we have warranty. Her death was doubtful;
    And but that great command o'ersways the order
    She should in ground unsanctified have lodg'd

modesty – *moderation*

> Q2 – Alexander died F – as thus. Alexander died
> Q2 – to F – into

loam – *clay used to make plaster*

> METRE – These four lines are a rhyme in iambic pentameter;
> Im-**per**-ious (equiv. 3 syl.); Q2 – Imperious F – Imperial

that earth – *Caesar's body*

flaw – *flow*   Q2 – water's F – winter's

> Hamlet begins speaking blank VERSE (see Introduction).

soft – *be quiet*   Q2 – soft awhile F – soft, aside

> **cour**-tiers (equiv. 2 syl.); Q2 – this F – that

maimèd – *truncated*; betoken – *signify*

Fordo – *Destroy*; estate – *social status*   Q3 – its Q2/F – it

Couch – *Hide*

else – *further*   **cere**-mony (equiv. 2 syl.)

> -tes a **ver**- (anapest – see 'A Note on Metre')

> METRE – line is short by 4 syl.

obsequies – *funeral rites*; enlarg'd – *expanded*

warranty – *authorisation*; doubtful – *suspicious*

great ... order – *the commands of the powerful prevail over the proper process*

unsanctified – *unholy*   F – have Q2 – been

Till the last trumpet: for charitable prayers,
Flints and pebbles should be thrown on her.   225
Yet here she is allowed her virgin crants,
Her maiden strewments, and the bringing home
Of bell and burial.

LAERTES   Must there no more be done?

PRIEST   No more be done.
We should profane the service of the dead
To sing a requiem and such rest to her   230
As to peace-parted souls.

LAERTES   Lay her i'th' earth,
And from her fair and unpolluted flesh
May violets spring. I tell thee, churlish priest,
A ministering angel shall my sister be
When thou liest howling.

HAMLET [*aside to Horatio*]
                    What, the fair Ophelia?

QUEEN   Sweets to the sweet. Farewell.   235
I hoped thou shouldst have been my Hamlet's wife:
I thought thy bride-bed to have deck'd, sweet maid,
And not have strew'd thy grave.

LAERTES   O, treble woe
Fall ten times double on that cursèd head
Whose wicked deed thy most ingenious sense   240
Depriv'd thee of. Hold off the earth awhile,
Till I have caught her once more in mine arms.

[Leaps in the grave.]

the last trumpet – *Doomsday*; for – *instead of*   -pet for **char**- (anapest)

                    Metre – line is headless in Q2; Q2 – Flints F – Shards, flints

virgin crants – *garlands signifying virginity*   Q2 – crants F – rites

strewments – *flowers strewn on the grave/coffin*; bringing home/Of – *bringing her to the grave with*; bell and burial – *religious burial* (hendiadys)

         Metre – Ambiguous metrical connection (see Series Introduction)

profane – *desecrate*

requiem (**re**-quiem) – *funeral song*; such rest – *pray for the same rest*   Q2 – a F – sage

peace-parted – *those who departed peacefully/naturally*

                         i'th' (equiv. 1 syl.)

violets – *flowers associated with chastity*

                     min-istering (equiv. 2 syl.)

howling – *(in hell)*   Metre – Ambiguous metrical connection (see Series Introduction)

Sweets – *(probably some flowers)*

                     Q2 – have F – t'have

                     Q2 – double F – treble

ingenious sense – *intelligent mind*   in-**gen**-ious (equiv. 3 syl.)

Hold off the earth – *Stop filling the grave with earth*

Now pile your dust upon the quick and dead
Till of this flat a mountain you have made
T'o'ertop old Pelion or the skyish head   245
Of blue Olympus.

HAMLET
[*Comes forward.*] What is he whose grief
Bears such an emphasis, whose phrase of sorrow
Conjures the wandering stars and makes them stand
Like wonder-wounded hearers? This is I,
Hamlet the Dane.

LAERTES *[leaps out and grapples with him.]*
          The devil take thy soul!

HAMLET   Thou pray'st not well.   250
I prithee take thy fingers from my throat,
For, though I am not splenative and rash,
Yet have I in me something dangerous
Which let thy wisdom fear. Hold off thy hand.

KING
Pluck them asunder.   255

QUEEN Hamlet! Hamlet!

LORDS Gentlemen!

HORATIO Good my lord, be quiet.

HAMLET
Why, I will fight with him upon this theme
Until my eyelids will no longer wag.   260

quick – *living*
flat – *level ground*
Pelion (pron. **Peh**-leeon) – *Greek mountain*   T'o'er-**top** (equiv. 2 syl.)
Olympus (pron. A-**lim**-puss) – *Greek mountain, home of the gods*

Bears such as emphasis – *Is so forcefully expressed*
Conjures – *Casts a spell on*; wandering stars – *planets*   **wan**-dering (equiv. 2 syl.)
wonder-wounded – *struck with wonder*
                    Metre – Ambiguous metrical connection (see Series Introduction)

    SD – In Q1, Hamlet leaps into the grave with Laertes – see Introduction – Q1 SDs

splenative – *hot tempered*   Q2/Q1 – For F – Sir; Q2 – splenative rash
                            Q2 – in me something F/Q1 – something in me
                    Q2/Q1 – wisdom F – witness; Q2/Q1 – Hold off F – Away

            Metre – Ambiguous metrical connection (see Series Introduction)

                    SP – This line is given to A GENTLEMAN in F.

theme – *subject*
wag – *open and shut*

QUEEN

    O my son, what theme?

HAMLET

    I loved Ophelia – forty thousand brothers
    Could not with all their quantity of love
    Make up my sum. What wilt thou do for her?

KING

    O, he is mad, Laertes.   265

QUEEN

    For love of God, forbear him.

HAMLET

    'Swounds, show me what thou'lt do.
    Woul't weep, woul't fight, woul't fast, woul't tear thyself,
    Woul't drink up eisel, eat a crocodile?
    I'll do't. Dost thou come here to whine,   270
    To outface me with leaping in her grave?
    Be buried quick with her, and so will I.
    And if thou prate of mountains let them throw
    Millions of acres on us till our ground,
    Singeing his pate against the burning zone,   275
    Make Ossa like a wart. Nay, an thou'lt mouth,
    I'll rant as well as thou.

QUEEN   This is mere madness,
    And thus awhile the fit will work on him.
    Anon, as patient as the female dove
    When that her golden couplets are disclos'd,   280
    His silence will sit drooping.

HAMLET   Hear you, sir,

Metre – line is short by 5 syl.

Metre – line is short by 3 syl.

forbear – *bear with*   Metre – line is short by 3 syl.

'Swounds – *By God's wounds*; 'lt – *wilt*   Metre – line is short by 4 syl.

Woul't – *Wouldst thou*; tear – *injure*   Q2 – 'Swounds F – Come

eisel – *vinegar*; crocodile – *tough-skinned supposed to shed hypocritical tears*

         F – Dost thou come Q2 – Dost come; Metre – line is short by 2 syl. in F

outface – *outdo*

quick – *alive*

prate – *boast*

our ground – *the earth on top of us*

pate – *head*; burning zone – *the sun*

Ossa – *Greek mountain*; wart – *i.e. small*; an – *if*; mouth – *shout*

mere – *complete*

Anon – *Soon*

golden couplets – *baby birds (*covered with yellow down*)*; disclos'd – *hatched*

His . . . drooping – *He will be silent and downcast*

What is the reason that you use me thus?
I loved you ever – but it is no matter.
Let Hercules himself do what he may,
The cat will mew and dog will have his day.   *Exit.*   285

KING

I pray thee, good Horatio, wait upon him.
[*aside to Laertes*] Strengthen your patience in our last
     night's speech,
We'll put the matter to the present push.
– Good Gertrude, set some watch over your son.
This grave shall have a living monument.   290
An hour of quiet shortly shall we see;
Till then in patience our proceeding be.   *Exeunt.*

5.2 *Enter HAMLET and HORATIO.*

HAMLET

So much for this, sir. Now shall you see the other:
You do remember all the circumstance?

HORATIO

Remember it, my lord?

HAMLET

Sir, in my heart there was a kind of fighting
That would not let me sleep. Methought I lay   5
Worse than the mutines in the bilboes. Rashly –
And prais'd be rashness for it – let us know
Our indiscretion sometime serves us well
When our deep plots do fall – and that should learn us
There's a divinity that shapes our ends,   10
Rough-hew them how we will.

use – *treat*

Hercules – (see Myth); may – *can* (i.e. to stop me)
dog ... day – Prov. – *my day will come*

wait upon – *keep a close eye on*   Q2 – thee F – you
in – *by remembering*

present push – *test immediately*

living monument – *lasting memorial* (possibly through Hamlet's murder)
       F – shortly Q2 – thereby
in ... be – *let's proceed with patience*

       This scene begins in mid conversation.
see – *hear*, other – *other matter*   shall you **see** (anapest); Q2 – shall you F – let me
circumstance – *details*

       Metre – line is short by 4 syl.

Methought – *I thought*
mutines – *mutineers*; bilboes – *iron shackles*; Rashly – *Impulsively*
know – *acknowledge*
indiscretion – *unpremeditated action*   Q2 – sometime F – sometimes
fall – *fail*; learn – *teach*   Q2 – deep F dear; Q2 – learn F – teach
divinity – *divine purpose*; ends – *intentions*
Rough-hew – *roughly carve*

HORATIO   That is most certain.

HAMLET   Up from my cabin,
My sea-gown scarf'd about me, in the dark
Groped I to find out them, had my desire,
Finger'd their packet, and in fine withdrew
To mine own room again, making so bold,   15
My fears forgetting manners, to unfold
Their grand commission; where I found, Horatio,
A royal knavery, an exact command
(Larded with many several sorts of reasons
Importing Denmark's health, and England's too)   20
With – ho! – such bugs and goblins in my life,
That on the supervise, no leisure bated
– No, not to stay the grinding of the axe! –
My head should be struck off.

HORATIO   Is't possible?

HAMLET
Here's the commission; read it at more leisure.   25
But wilt thou hear now how I did proceed?

HORATIO
I beseech you.

HAMLET
Being thus benetted round with villains,
Ere I could make a prologue to my brains
They had begun the play. I sat me down,   30
Devis'd a new commission, wrote it fair –
I once did hold it as our statists do
A baseness to write fair and labour'd much
How to forget that learning, but, sir, now

Metre – Ambiguous metrical connection – possibly indicting an overlap in dialogue (see Series Introduction)

sea-gown – *sailor's coat*; scarf'd – *wrapped*

Finger'd – *stole*; in fine – *finally*
room – *cabin*
unfold – *discover*

Q2 – unfold F – unseal

knavery – *trickery*
Larded – *elaborated*; several – *different*
Importing – *concerning*
bugs . . . life – *horrors to be feared if I were allowed to live*
supervise – *reading*; leisure bated – *time wasted*
stay – *await*; grinding – *sharpening*

Q2 – A F – Oh; **kna**-very (equiv. 2 syl.)
Q2 – reasons F – reason

Q2 – now F – me

beseech – *beg*

Metre – line is short by 6 syl.

benetted round – *surrounded*
make a prologue – *outline a plan* (theatre metaphor)

Metre – line is headless (see 'A Note on Metre')

fair – *in neat handwriting*
statists – *statesmen*
A baseness – *beneath me*

335

It did me yeoman's service – wilt thou know   35
Th'effect of what I wrote?

HORATIO   Ay, good my lord.

HAMLET

An earnest conjuration from the King,
As England was his faithful tributary,
As love between them like the palm might flourish,
As peace should still her wheaten garland wear   40
And stand a comma 'tween their amities,
And many such like 'as', sir, of great charge,
That on the view and knowing of these contents,
Without debatement further more or less,
He should those bearers put to sudden death,   45
Not shriving time allow'd.

HORATIO   How was this seal'd?

HAMLET

Why even in that was heaven ordinant:
I had my father's signet in my purse –
Which was the model of that Danish seal –
Folded the writ up in the form of th'other,   50
Subscrib'd it, gave't th'impression, placed it safely,
The changeling never known. Now the next day
Was our sea-fight, and what to this was sequent
Thou knowest already.

HORATIO

So Guildenstern and Rosencrantz go to't.   55

HAMLET

[Why man, they did make love to this employment]

yeoman – *loyal attendant*

effect – *nature*   Q2– Th'effect F – The effects

conjuration – *request*

tributary – *country paying a tribute following war*   **tri**-bu-**tary** (equiv. 3 syl.)

palm – *palm tree*   Q2 – like F – as; Q2 – might F – should

still – *always*; wheaten garland – *(emblem of peace)*

comma – *the slightest break*; amities – *friendship*

'as' – *phrases beginning with 'as'*; charge – *weight*   Q2 – 'as' sir F – Assis Rowe – As's

                                         Q2 – knowing F – know; knowing (equiv. 1 syl.)

debatement further – *further debate*

sudden – *immediate*   Q2 – those F – the

shriving time – *time for confession*

ordinant – *guiding*   even (equiv. 1 syl.); Q2 – ordinant F – ordinate

signet – *signet ring* (seal)

model – *exact copy*

writ – *letter*   Q2 – the form of th'other F – form of the other

Subscrib'd – *Signed*; th'impression – *the wax seal*

changeling – *substitution* (usually used of a fairy child substituted for a human one)

to this was sequent – *followed this*

                              knowest (equiv. 1 syl.); Metre – line is short by 5 syl.

go to't – *go to their deaths*

                                         Line 56 is only in F.

They are not near my conscience. Their defeat
Does by their own insinuation grow.
'Tis dangerous when the baser nature comes
Between the pass and fell incensèd points   60
Of mighty opposites.

HORATIO   Why, what a king is this!

HAMLET
Does it not, think thee, stand me now upon?
He that hath killed my King and whor'd my mother,
Popp'd in between th'election and my hopes,
Thrown out his angle for my proper life   65
And with such cozenage. Is't not perfect conscience?
[To quit him with this arm? And is't not to be damned
To let this canker of our nature come
In further evil?

HORATIO
It must be shortly known to him from England   70
What is the issue of the business there.

HAMLET
It will be short. The interim's mine,
And a man's life's no more than to say one.
But I am very sorry, good Horatio,
That to Laertes I forgot myself,   75
For by the image of my cause I see
The portraiture of his. I'll count his favours;
But sure the bravery of his grief did put me
Into a towering passion.

HORATIO   Peace, who comes here?]

defeat – *destruction*

insinuation – *ingratiating behaviour*   Q2 – Does F – Doth

baser – *inferior*   **dan**-gerous (equiv. 2 syl.)

pass and fell incensèd points – *thrusting points* (hendiadys – see Introduction)

    Irregular shared line – can be scanned with quartus paeon/as hexameter (see 'A

                                        Note on Metre')

Does . . . upon – *Is it not . . . incumbent on me*   Q2 – think F – think'st

Popp'd . . . hopes – *Come between me and my place as king*

angle – *fishhook*; proper – *own*

cozenage – *trickery*; perfect conscience – *morally justifiable*   **coz**-enage (equiv. 2 syl.)

quit – *repay*   Lines 67–79 are only in F. And is't **not**; to be **dam** (both anapests)

canker – *ulcer*; our nature – *human nature*; come/In – *commit*

issue – *outcome*

                                Metre – line is short by 1 syl.

no more than to say one – *no longer than it takes to say one.*

forgot myself – *behaved badly*

by . . . his – *in my situation, I recognise his*

count his favours – *note his good characteristics*

bravery – *extravagance*   **brave**-ry (equiv. 2 syl.)

              -ssion. Peace, **who** (anapest – see 'A Note on Metre')

Enter [OSRIC,] a courtier.

OSRIC
Your lordship is right welcome back to Denmark.   80

HAMLET
I humbly thank you, sir. [*aside to Horatio*] Dost
know this water-fly?

HORATIO [*aside*]
No, my good lord.

HAMLET [*aside*]
Thy state is the more gracious, for 'tis a
vice to know him. He hath much land, and fertile. Let   85
a beast be lord of beasts and his crib shall stand at the
king's mess. 'Tis a chough but, as I say, spacious in the
possession of dirt.

OSRIC
Sweet lord, if your lordship were at leisure I
should impart a thing to you from his majesty.   90

HAMLET
I will receive it, sir, with all diligence of spirit.
Your bonnet to his right use: 'tis for the head.

OSRIC
I thank your lordship, it is very hot.

HAMLET
No, believe me, 'tis very cold; the wind is
northerly.   95

The scene moves from VERSE to PROSE.

water-fly – *buzzing insect*

state – *condition*; gracious – *blessed*
Let . . . beasts – *Even if an animal is the master of other animals*
crib – *food trough*
mess – *table*; chough – *crow* (one who chatters); spacious . . . dirt – *possessing lots of land*

Q2 – lordship F – friendship

a thing – *something*

diligence of spirit – *earnest endeavour*   Q2 – it, sir with F – it with
Your – (*i.e. Put your*); bonnet – *hat*   Q2 – Your F – Put your

Q2 – it is F – 'tis

OSRIC

It is indifferent cold, my lord, indeed.

HAMLET

[But yet] methinks it is very sultry and hot, or
my complexion –

OSRIC

Exceedingly, my lord, it is very sultry, as 'twere – I
cannot tell how. My lord, his majesty bade me signify   100
to you that he has laid a great wager on your head.
Sir, this is the matter –

HAMLET

I beseech you remember.

OSRIC

Nay, good my lord, for my ease, in good faith. Sir,
[here is newly come to court Laertes – believe me, an   105
absolute gentleman, full of most excellent differences,
of very soft society and great showing. Indeed, to speak
sellingly of him, he is the card or calendar of gentry, for
you shall find in him the continent of what part a
gentleman would see.   110

HAMLET

Sir, his definement suffers no perdition in you,
though I know to divide him inventorially would dazzle
th'arithmetic of memory, and yet but yaw neither, in
respect of his quick sail; but in the verity of extolment
I take him to be a soul of great article and his infusion   115
of such dearth and rareness as, to make true diction of
him, his semblable is his mirror, and who else would
trace him, his umbrage, nothing more.

indifferent – *rather*

But yet (not in F); Q2 – hot, or my complexion – F – hot for my complexion
complexion – *constitution*

as 'twere – *as if it were*
bade – *asked*   Q2 – how. My F – how but my
                                                                    F – he Q2 – 'a

I … remember – *(i.e. Please remember to put your hat on)*

ease – *comfort*   Q2 – good my lord F – in good faith; Q2 – my ease F – mine ease
                                    Lines 105 ('here is newly') to 133 ('Well sir?') are not in F.
absolute – *perfect*; differences – *distinctive qualities*
soft society – *pleasing company*; showing – *appearance*
sellingly – *like a salesman*; card … gentry – *model of gentility*   Q2 – sellingly
continent – *embodiment*; what part – *whatever quality*   Q3 – feelingly
would – *might wish to*

definement – *description*; perdition – *loss* (Hamlet parodies Osric's style of speech)
divide … inventorially – *list his attributes*   Arden 3 – dazzle Q2 – dazzy Q3 – dizzy
dazzle … memory – *tax one's memory*; but … sail – *not come close to describing his
virtues* – (sailing metaphor); the verity of extolment – *praising him truthfully*
article – *importance/quality*; infusion – *natural character*
dearth – *splendour*; to … diction – *to speak truly*
semblable – *only likeness*
trace – *come close to*; umbrage – *shadow*

OSRIC

    Your lordship speaks most infallibly of him.

HAMLET

    The concernancy, sir – why do we wrap the   120
    gentleman in our more rawer breath?

OSRIC

    Sir?

HORATIO

    Is't not possible to understand in another
    tongue? You will do't, sir, really.

HAMLET

    What imports the nomination of this   125
    gentleman?

OSRIC

    Of Laertes.

HORATIO

    His purse is empty already – all's golden words
    are spent.

HAMLET

    Of him, sir.   130

OSRIC

    I know you are not ignorant –

HAMLET

    I would you did, sir. Yet, in faith, if you did, it
    would not much approve me. Well, sir?]

infallibly – *truthfully*

The concernancy – *How does this concern us*
in ... breath – *in our inferior words*

Is't ... tongue? – *Can't he understand his own tongue?* (style of language)
do't – *manage it*

imports – *signifies*; nomination – *mention*

This line (127) is possibly a question.

His ... spent – *He has nothing left to say*

would – *wish*
approve – *commend*

OSRIC

You are not ignorant of what excellence Laertes is.

[HAMLET

I dare not confess that, lest I should compare with him 135
in excellence. But to know a man well were to
know himself.

OSRIC

I mean, sir, for his weapon. But in the imputation
laid on him by them in his meed he's unfellow'd.]

HAMLET

What's his weapon? 140

OSRIC

Rapier and dagger.

HAMLET

That's two of his weapons. But well.

OSRIC

The King, sir, hath wagered with him six Barbary
horses, against the which he has impawned, as I take it,
six French rapiers and poniards, with their assigns, as 145
girdle, hanger and so. Three of the carriages, in faith,
are very dear to fancy, very responsive to the hilts, most
delicate carriages and of very liberal conceit.

HAMLET

What call you the carriages?

[HORATIO

I knew you must be edified by the margin ere 150
you had done.]

Q2 – You F – Sir, you; Q2 – is F – is at his weapon

Lines 135 ('I dare not') to 139 ('unfellowed') are not in F.

lest . . . excellence – *in case I should claim to match it* (Prov.)

But . . . himself – *to know a man truly one must know oneself* (Prov.)

imputation – *attribution*

in his meed – *who know his merit*; unfellow'd – *unmatched*

wagered with – *bet on*; Barbary – *Arabian*   Q2 – hath wagered F – has waged

impawned – *wagered*; take – *understand*   Q2 – has impawned F – imponed

poniards – *daggers*; assigns – *accessories*

girdle – *sword belt*; hanger – *straps*   Q2 – hangers F – hangers; Q2 – and F – or

dear to fancy – *fancy in design*; responsive to – *matching*; hilts – *handles*

liberal conceit – *elaborate design*

edified . . . margin – *informed by a marginal note*   Lines 150–1, 'I knew' to 'done',
                                                          are not in F.

OSRIC

The carriages, sir, are the hangers.

HAMLET

The phrase would be more germane to the
matter if we could carry a cannon by our sides. I would
it might be 'hangers' till then. But on. Six Barbary   155
horses against six French swords, their assigns and
three liberal-conceited carriages – that's the French bet
against the Danish. Why, is this all you call it?

OSRIC

The King, sir, hath laid, sir, that in a dozen passes
between yourself and him he shall not exceed you three 160
hits. He hath laid on twelve for nine, and it would come
to immediate trial if your lordship would vouchsafe the
answer.

HAMLET

How if I answer no?

OSRIC

I mean, my lord, the opposition of your person in   165
trial.

HAMLET

Sir, I will walk here in the hall. If it please his
majesty, it is the breathing time of day with me. Let the
foils be brought, the gentleman willing and the King
hold his purpose – I will win for him an I can; if not, I 170
will gain nothing but my shame and the odd hits.

OSRIC

Shall I deliver you so?

hangers – *the straps on which the weapons hang*

germane – *relevant*
a cannon – *(i.e. needing a gun carriage)*
on – *continue*
against – *wagered against*; assigns – *accessories*
liberal-conceited – *elaborately designed*
is . . . it? – *is this what you said?* Q2 – all F – imponed as

laid – *wagered*; passes – *rounds* (of fencing) Q2 – hath laid, sir F – hath laid
he . . . nine – *(a notoriously difficult wager to decipher* Q2 – yourself F – you
but the King is backing Hamlet) Q2 – it F – that
vouchsafe the answer – *accept the challenge*

the opposition of your person – *presenting yourself as an opponent*

breathing . . . me – *time of day for exercise* Q2 – it is F – 'tis

an – *if* Q2 – an F – if
  Q2 – I will F – I'll

deliver you so – *deliver this as your response* Q2 – deliver F – redeliver; Q2 – so F
  – e'en so

HAMLET

To this effect, sir, after what flourish your
nature will.

OSRIC

I commend my duty to your lordship.   175

HAMLET

Yours. He does well to commend it himself.

[Exit Osric.]

There are no tongues else for's turn.

HORATIO

This lapwing runs away with the shell on his
head.

HAMLET

He did comply with his dug before he sucked it.   180
Thus has he, and many more of the same breed that I
know the drossy age dotes on, only got the tune of the
time and, out of an habit of encounter, a kind of
yeasty collection, which carries them through and
through the most profane and winnowed opinions; and   185
do but blow them to their trial – the bubbles are out.

Enter a Lord.

[LORD

My lord, his majesty commended him to you by
young Osric, who brings back to him that you attend
him in the hall. He sends to know if your pleasure hold
to play with Laertes, or that you will take longer time.   190

after what flourish – *in whatever elaborate manner*

commend – *dedicate*

commend – *recommend*   F – He Q2 – 'A

There . . . turn – *No one else will do it* (Prov.)

runs . . . head – (*as the newly hatched chicks of the lapwing were thought to do* – Prov.)
– *a reference to Osric's hat/youth*

                                           F – He ... he Q2 – 'A ...'a;
He . . . dug – *He paid compliments to his mother's nipple*   F – comply Q2 – so, sir;
                                  Q2 – has F – had; Q2 – breed F – bevy
the drossy age – *worthless times*; the . . . time – *the superficial fashions of speech*
out . . . encounter – *from frequent social encounters*   Q2 – out of an F – outward
yeasty collection – *trivial repertoire of words and habits*; carries them – *allows them to get*
profane – *vulgar*; winnowed – *selective*   Q2 – profane F – fond
do . . . trial – *If you test them by just blowing on them*;   Q2 – trial F – trials
are out – *will burst*
                                    SD – The Lord does not enter in F.

commended him – *greeted you*   Lines 187–98 are not in F.

play – *fence*; that – *if*

HAMLET

I am constant to my purposes. They follow the
King's pleasure. If his fitness speaks, mine is ready.
Now or whensoever, provided I be so able as now.

LORD

The King and Queen and all are coming down.

HAMLET

In happy time.   195

LORD

The Queen desires you to use some gentle
entertainment to Laertes before you fall to play.

HAMLET

She well instructs me.   [*Exit Lord.*]]

HORATIO

You will lose, my lord.

HAMLET

I do not think so. Since he went into France I   200
have been in continual practice. I shall win at the odds.
Thou wouldst not think how ill all's here about my
heart – but it is no matter.

HORATIO

Nay, good my lord –

HAMLET

It is but foolery, but it is such a kind of   205
gaingiving as would perhaps trouble a woman.

his fitness speaks – *it is convenient to him*

use ... entertainment – *show some courtesy*

Q2 – lose F – lose this wager

at the odds – *given the nature of the odds*

Q2 – Thou F – But thou

gaingiving – *misgiving*

HORATIO

If your mind dislike anything, obey it. I will
forestall their repair hither and say you are not fit.

HAMLET

Not a whit. We defy augury. There is special
providence in the fall of a sparrow. If it be now, 'tis not to 210
come. If it be not to come, it will be now. If it be not
now, yet it will come. The readiness is all, since no man
of aught he leaves knows, what is't to leave betimes.
[Let be.]

*A table prepared. Trumpets, Drums and Officers with
cushions, foils and daggers. [Enter] KING, QUEEN,
LAERTES, [OSRIC] and all the state.*

KING

Come, Hamlet, come and take this hand from me. 215

[Puts Laertes' hand into Hamlet's.]

HAMLET

Give me your pardon, sir. I have done you wrong,
But pardon't as you are a gentleman.
This presence knows, and you must needs have heard,
How I am punished with a sore distraction.
What I have done 220
That might your nature, honour and exception
Roughly awake, I here proclaim was madness.
Was't Hamlet wrong'd Laertes? Never Hamlet.
If Hamlet from himself be ta'en away
And when he's not himself does wrong Laertes, 225
Then Hamlet does it not; Hamlet denies it.
Who does it then? His madness. If't be so,

repair – *coming*

a whit – *at all*; augury – *prophecy*; special providence –   Q2 – There is F/Q1 – There's a
God's intervention; fall of a sparrow – (Bib. – Matthew 10.29); F/Q1 – be now Q2 – be
it – *my time of death*
readiness – *readiness for death*;
of . . . knows – *knows anything*   Q2 – of . . . knows F – has aught of what he leaves
of what he leaves behind; betimes – *early*   This line is not in F.

this hand – *i.e. Laertes' hand*   The scene moves into VERSE.

                                        I have **done** (anapest); Q2 – I have F – I've
                                                    pardon't (equiv. 1 syl.)
presence – *assembly*   The lineation of lines 218–20 is ambiguous.
sore distraction – *serious insanity*
                This short line is the result of editorial relineation (see Introduction).
exception – *disapproval*
awake – *arouse*

Hamlet is of the faction that is wronged –
His madness is poor Hamlet's enemy.
[Sir, in this Audience]   230
Let my disclaiming from a purpos'd evil
Free me so far in your most generous thoughts
That I have shot my arrow o'er the house
And hurt my brother.

LAERTES   I am satisfied in nature,
Whose motive in this case should stir me most   235
To my revenge. But in my terms of honour
I stand aloof and will no reconcilement
Till by some elder masters of known honour
I have a voice and precedent of peace
To keep my name ungor'd. But till that time   240
I do receive your offer'd love like love
And will not wrong it.

HAMLET   I embrace it freely
And will this brothers' wager frankly play.
Give us the foils. [Come on.]

LAERTES   Come, one for me.

HAMLET
I'll be your foil, Laertes. In mine ignorance   245
Your skill shall like a star i'th' darkest night
Stick fiery off indeed.

LAERTES   You mock me, sir.

HAMLET   No, by this hand.

faction – *party*

This line is only in F.

disclaiming from – *denial of;* purpos'd – *intended*

gen-erous (equiv. 2 syl.)

That I have – *To think that I have*   Q2 – my F/Q1 – mine

And hurt my – *(i.e. unintentionally)*   Q2 – brother F – mother

nature – *my natural feelings*   Irregular – (can be scanned with quartus paeon)

Whose motive – *The motive of which*

in … honour – *where my sense of honour is concerned*

aloof – *at a distance;* will – *wish for*

elder masters – *experienced men*

voice and precedent – *opinion that will serve as precedent* (hendiadys)

name ungor'd – *reputation free from injury*   F – till Q2 – all

Q2 – I F – I do

frankly – *freely*

F – Come on (not in Q2)

foil – *background setting* (for a jewel) (pun on sword)   **ig**-norance (equiv. 2 syl.)

i'th (equiv. 1 syl.)

Stick – *Sparkle*   Metre – Ambiguous metrical connection

(see Series Introduction)

KING

    Give them the foils, young Osric. Cousin Hamlet,
    You know the wager.

HAMLET   Very well, my lord.
    Your grace has laid the odds o'th' weaker side.   250

KING

    I do not fear it. I have seen you both
    But since he is better we have therefore odds.

LAERTES

    This is too heavy, let me see another.

HAMLET

    This likes me well. These foils have all a length?

OSRIC

    Ay, my good lord.   255

KING

    Set me the stoups of wine upon that table.
    If Hamlet give the first or second hit
    Or quit in answer of the third exchange
    Let all the battlements their ordnance fire.
    The King shall drink to Hamlet's better breath   260
    And in the cup an union shall he throw
    Richer than that which four successive kings
    In Denmark's crown have worn. Give me the cups,
    And let the kettle to the trumpet speak,
    The trumpet to the cannoneer without,   265
    The cannons to the heavens, the heaven to earth.

Trumpets the while

laid the odds – *bet*   Q2 – has F – hath; o'th' (equiv. 1 syl.)

odds – *arranged a handicap*   he is **bet**- (anapest – see 'A Note on Metre');
                                                                                    Q2 – better F – better'd

likes – *pleases*; have all a length – *are all the same length*

                              Metre – this line is short by 6 syl. in Q2 (F lineates differently)

Set me – *Put*; stoups – *cups*

quit . . . exchange – *repay Laertes by winning the third bout*
ordnance – *cannons*   **ord**-nance (equiv. 2 syl.)
breath – *performance*
union – *pearl*

kettle – *kettledrum*   Q2 – trumpet F – trumpets
cannoneer – *cannon firer*; without – *outside*
                                            heavens (equiv. 1 syl.); heaven (equiv. 1 syl.)

Now the King drinks to Hamlet. Come, begin.
And you, the judges, bear a wary eye.

HAMLET
Come on, sir.

LAERTES
Come, my lord.   270

[They play.]

HAMLET
One!

LAERTES
No!

HAMLET
Judgement?

OSRIC
A hit, a very palpable hit.

Drum, trumpets and shot

LAERTES
Well, again.   275

KING
Stay, give me drink. Hamlet, this pearl is thine:
Here's to thy health. Give him the cup.

HAMLET
I'll play this bout first. Set it by awhile. *[They play.]*

bear . . . eye – *watch carefully*

Metre – a series of seven short lines

Q2 – Come, my lord. F – Come on sir.

palpable – *definite*

Stay – *stop*

Metre – this line is short by 2 syl.

Come, another hit! – What say you?

LAERTES   I do confess't.

KING
Our son shall win.

QUEEN   He's fat and scant of breath.   280
Here, Hamlet, take my napkin, rub thy brows –
The Queen carouses to thy fortune, Hamlet.

HAMLET
Good madam.

KING
Gertrude, do not drink.

QUEEN
I will, my lord. I pray you pardon me.   285

KING [*aside*]
It is the poison'd cup! It is too late.

HAMLET
I dare not drink yet, madam. By and by.

QUEEN
Come, let me wipe thy face.

LAERTES [*aside to King*]
                My lord, I'll hit him now.

KING [*aside to Laertes*]
                            I do not think't.

Come an-**oth**-; you?/I **do** (both anapests – see 'A Note on Metre')

Q2 – I do confess't. F – A touch, a touch, I do confess.

fat – *sweaty/out of condition*
napkin – *handkerchief*
carouses – *raises a toast*

Metre – line is short by 7 syl.

Metre – line is short by 5 syl.

By and by – *In a bit*

Metre – Ambiguous metrical connection (see Series Introduction)

LAERTES [*aside*]
　　And yet it is almost against my conscience.

HAMLET
　　Come for the third, Laertes, you do but dally.　　　　　290
　　I pray you pass with your best violence.
　　I am sure you make a wanton of me.

LAERTES
　　Say you so? Come on.

[They play.]

OSRIC
　　Nothing neither way.

LAERTES
　　Have at you now!　　　　　295

[In scuffling they change rapiers.]

KING
　　Part them – they are incens'd.

HAMLET
　　Nay, come again.

[Queen falls.]

OSRIC
　　Look to the Queen there, ho!

Q2 – And . . . conscience F – And yet 'tis almost 'gainst my **con**-sci-**ence**

(equiv. 3 syl.)

dally – *play idly*   -tes you **do** (anapest); Q2 – do but F – but

pass – *thrust*   **vi**-o-**lence** (equiv. 3 syl.)

wanton – *spoilt child*   Metre – line is headless (see 'A Note on Metre'); Q2 – sure

F – affear'd

Metre – The next 6 lines have an ambiguous metrical connection (see Series

Introduction)

Nothing neither way – *No advantage on either side*

Have at you – *(exclamation indicating an imminent attack)*

SD – In Q1, the stage directions reads *They catch one another's rapiers,*
and both are wounded, Laertes falls down, the Queen falls down and dies
(see Q1 Stage Directions in Introduction).

HORATIO
They bleed on both sides. How is it, my lord?

OSRIC
How is't, Laertes?   300

LAERTES
Why, as a woodcock to mine own springe, Osric:
I am justly kill'd with mine own treachery.

HAMLET
How does the Queen?

KING   She swoons to see them bleed.

QUEEN
No, no, the drink, the drink, O my dear Hamlet,
The drink, the drink – I am poisoned.   [*Dies.*]   305

HAMLET
O villainy, ho! Let the door be lock'd.
Treachery! Seek it out.   [*Exit Osric.*]

LAERTES
It is here, Hamlet. Hamlet thou art slain.
No medicine in the world can do thee good:
In thee there is not half an hour's life;   310
The treacherous instrument is in thy hand
Unbated and envenom'd. The foul practice
Hath turn'd itself on me. Lo, here I lie,
Never to rise again. Thy mother's poison'd –
I can no more – the King, the King's to blame.   315

Metre – line is short by 1 syl. (possibly at mid-line caesura)

Metre – line is short by 5 syl.

woodcock – *a bird notoriously easy to catch* (Prov.); springe – *trap*

I am **just**- (anapest – see 'A Note on Metre')

I am **poi**- (anapest – see 'A Note on Metre'); Metre – line is short by 3 syl.

Metre – line is short by 4 syl.

F – It … slain Q2 – It is here, Hamlet, thou art slain

med-icine (equiv. 2 syl.)

ho-ur's (equiv. 2 syl.); Q2 – hour's F/Q1 – hour of

treach-erous (2 syl.)

Unbated – *not blunted*; envenom'd – *dipped in poison*; practice – *plot*

HAMLET

The point envenom'd too? Then venom to thy work!

[Hurts the King.]

LORDS

Treason, treason!

KING

O, yet defend me, friends, I am but hurt.

HAMLET

Here, thou incestuous, murdrous, damnèd Dane!
Drink of this potion. Is the union here?   320
Follow my mother.

[King dies.]

LAERTES   He is justly serv'd.
It is a poison temper'd by himself.
Exchange forgiveness with me, noble Hamlet,
Mine and my father's death come not upon thee,
Nor thine on me.   *[Dies.]*   325

HAMLET

Heaven make thee free of it. I follow thee.
I am dead, Horatio. Wretched Queen, adieu.
You that look pale and tremble at this chance,
That are but mutes or audience to this act,
Had I but time (as this fell sergeant Death   330
Is strict in his arrest) – O, I could tell you –
But let it be. Horatio, I am dead.

Irregular line – can be scanned with quartus paeon/as hexameter

Metre – line is short by 6 syl.

F – murdrous (not in Q2)

union – *pearl*   Q2 – of F – off; Q2 – the F/Q1 – thy

temper'd – *prepared*

come not upon thee – *should not be blamed on you* (at the Last judgement)

Metre – line is short by 6 syl.

free – *absolved*   Heaven (equiv. 1 syl.)

Wretched – *Unhappy*   I am **dead** (anapest – see 'A Note on Metre')

chance – *mischance/event*

mutes – *silent actors*; act – *event*   **au**-dience (equiv. 2 syl.)

fell – *cruel*

Thou livest: report me and my cause aright
To the unsatisfied.

HORATIO   Never believe it.
I am more an antique Roman than a Dane: 335
Here's yet some liquor left.

HAMLET   As thou'rt a man
Give me the cup. Let go! By heaven I'll ha't!
O God, Horatio, what a wounded name,
Things standing thus unknown, shall I leave behind me!
If thou didst ever hold me in thy heart   340
Absent thee from felicity awhile
And in this harsh world draw thy breath in pain
To tell my story.

A march afar off [and a sound of shooting]

What warlike noise is this?

Enter OSRIC.

OSRIC
Young Fortinbras with conquest come from Poland
To th'ambassadors of England gives   345
This warlike volley.

HAMLET   O, I die, Horatio.
The potent poison quite o'ercrows my spirit,
I cannot live to hear the news from England,
But I do prophesy th'election lights
On Fortinbras: he has my dying voice.   350
So tell him with th'occurrents more and less
Which have solicited. – The rest is silence.   [*Dies.*]

cause – *actions*; aright – *accurately*   livest (equiv. 1 syl.); Q2 – cause aright
unsatisfied – *those who wish to know*   F – causes right

antique Roman – *ancient Roman* (who viewed suicide   I am **more**
as an honourable death)   (anapest – see 'A Note on Metre)

                                                 thou'rt (equiv. 1 syl.)
ha't – *have it*   Q2 – ha't F – have't
name – *reputation*   Q2 – God F – good
                                   shall I **leave** (anapest – see 'A Note on Metre')

hold me in thy heart – *love me*
felicity – *happiness* (i.e. heaven)

                      -ry. What **war**- (anapest – see 'A Note on Metre')

                      Metre – line is headless (see 'A Note on Metre')
volley – *military salute*

o'ercrows – *triumphs over*

th'election – *(of the next King of Denmark)*
voice – *vote*
with – *along with*; th'occurents – *the events*
solicited – *prompted this*   Q2 – silence. F – silence. O, o, o, o.

HORATIO

    Now cracks a noble heart. Goodnight, sweet Prince,
    And flights of angels sing thee to thy rest.
    Why does the drum come hither?   355

Enter FORTINBRAS with [his train and] the Ambassadors.

FORTINBRAS   Where is this sight?

HORATIO   What is it you would see?
    If aught of woe or wonder, cease your search.

FORTINBRAS

    This quarry cries on havoc. O proud Death,
    What feast is toward in thine eternal cell
    That thou so many princes at a shot
    So bloodily hast struck?

AMBASSADOR   The sight is dismal   360
    And our affairs from England come too late.
    The ears are senseless that should give us hearing
    To tell him his commandment is fulfill'd
    That Rosencrantz and Guildenstern are dead.
    Where should we have our thanks?

HORATIO   Not from his mouth, 365
    Had it th'ability of life to thank you;
    He never gave commandment for their death.
    But, since so jump upon this bloody question
    You from the Polack wars and you from England
    Are here arriv'd, give order that these bodies   370
    High on a stage be placèd to the view,
    And let me speak to th'yet unknowing world
    How these things came about. So shall you hear

Metre – Ambiguous metrical connection (see Series Introduction)

would – *wish to*   Q2 – you F – ye
aught – *anything*

quarry – *pile of dead bodies*; cries on havoc – *proclaims a massacre* Q2 – This F – His
toward – *imminent*   toward (equiv. 1 syl.)
a shot – *a single time*

The ears – *(of Claudius)*

Where – *From whom*

jump upon – *immediately after*; question – *affair*

stage – *platform*; view – *general view*
                 to th' **yet** – anapest (see 'A Note on Metre')

Of carnal, bloody and unnatural acts,
Of accidental judgements, casual slaughters,   375
Of deaths put on by cunning, and forc'd cause,
And in this upshot purposes mistook
Fallen on th'inventors' heads. All this can I
Truly deliver.

FORTINBRAS   Let us haste to hear it
And call the noblest to the audience.   380
For me, with sorrow I embrace my fortune.
I have some rights of memory in this kingdom
Which now to claim my vantage doth invite me.

HORATIO
Of that I shall have also cause to speak
And from his mouth whose voice will draw no more.   385
But let this same be presently perform'd
Even while men's minds are wild, lest more mischance
On plots and errors happen.

FORTINBRAS   Let four captains
Bear Hamlet like a soldier to the stage,
For he was likely, had he been put on,   390
To have proved most royal. And for his passage
The soldiers' music and the rite of war
Speak loudly for him.
Take up the bodies. Such a sight as this
Becomes the field but here shows much amiss.   395
Go, bid the soldiers shoot.   *Exeunt.*

FINIS

carnal – *sexual*

judgements – *punishments*; casual – *chance*

put on – *instigated*; forc'd – *false*   F – forc'd Q2 – for no

upshot – *conclusion*

                                                   Fallen (equiv. 1 syl.)

deliver – *report*

For – *As for*; fortune – *good luck*

of memory – *unforgotten*   **mem**-ory (equiv. 2 syl.)

vantage – *advantage/good fortune*

whose voice will draw – *who will draw breath*   Q2 – no F – on

this same – *(what Horatio requested earlier* – lines 370–1*)*; presently – *immediately*

wild – *agitated*   Even (equiv. 1 syl.); Q2 – while F – whiles

On – *On top of*

stage – *platform*

put on – *tested* (as king)

passage – *journey into death*   To have **prove**- – anapest; Q2 – royal F – royally

soldiers' music – *drums*; rite of war – *gunfire*   Q2 – rite F – rites

                                           Metre – line is short by 5 syl.

                                                   Q2 – bodies F/Q1 – body

Becomes the field – *Is appropriate to a battlefield*; shows much amiss – *is out of place*

                                           Metre – line is short by 4 syl.